ASPECTS OF TOURISM: 79

Quantitative Methods in Tourism

A Handbook

2nd edition

Rodolfo Baggio and Jane Klobas

CHANNEL VIEW PUBLICATIONS
Bristol • Blue Ridge Summit

DOI 10.21832/BAGGIO6195

Library of Congress Cataloging in Publication Data
A catalog record for this book is available from the Library of Congress.
Names: Baggio, Rodolfo, author. | Klobas, Jane E., author.
Title: Quantitative Methods in Tourism: A Handbook/Rodolfo Baggio and Jane Klobas.
Description: Second edition. | Bristol, UK; Blue Ridge Summit, PA, USA:
    Channel View Publications, [2017] | Series: Aspects of Tourism: 79 |
    Includes bibliographical references and index.
Identifiers: LCCN 2017006686| ISBN 9781845416195 (hbk: alk. paper) | ISBN
    9781845416188 (pbk: alk. paper) | ISBN 9781845416225 (kindle)
Subjects: LCSH: Tourism. | Tourism–Statistics.
Classification: LCC G155.A1 B316 2017 | DDC 910.01/5195–dc23 LC record available at
    https://lccn.loc.gov/2017006686

British Library Cataloguing in Publication Data
A catalogue entry for this book is available from the British Library.

ISBN-13: 978-1-84541-619-5 (hbk)
ISBN-13: 978-1-84541-618-8 (pbk)

Channel View Publications
UK: St Nicholas House, 31-34 High Street, Bristol BS1 2AW, UK.
USA: NBN, Blue Ridge Summit, PA, USA.

Website: www.channelviewpublications.com
Twitter: Channel_View
Facebook: https://www.facebook.com/channelviewpublications
Blog: www.channelviewpublications.wordpress.com

The policy of Multilingual Matters/Channel View Publications is to use papers that
are natural, renewable and recyclable products, made from wood grown in sustainable
forests. In the manufacturing process of our books, and to further support our policy,
preference is given to printers that have FSC and PEFC Chain of Custody certification.
The FSC and/or PEFC logos will appear on those books where full certification has been
granted to the printer concerned.

Typeset by Deanta Global Publishing Services Limited.
Printed and bound in the UK by Short Run Press Ltd.
Printed and bound in the US by Edwards Brothers Malloy, Inc.

Contents

Contributors xi

Foreword xiii

Introduction to the Second Edition xv

Introduction xvii

Part 1: The Analysis of Data **1**

1 The Nature of Data in Tourism 3

 Data: A Taxonomy 3

  Primary data 4

  Secondary data 5

  Combining primary and secondary data 6

 Data Harmonisation, Standards and Collaboration 7

  Quantitative and categorical data 9

  The many forms of data 10

 Data Quality 10

  Data screening and cleaning 13

  Why screen data? 14

  Concluding remarks 15

 Sources of Secondary Tourism Data 15

  International organisations 15

  Associations 16

  Private companies 16

 References 17

2 Testing Hypotheses and Comparing Samples 19

 Parametric and Non-Parametric Tests 22

Effect Size and Statistical Power 24
Sample Size and Significance 26
  Bootstrap 27
  Meta-analysis 30
A Summary of Statistical Tests 34
Similarity and Dissimilarity Measures 36
  Similarity measures for a single sample 37
  Similarity measures for two or more samples 39
Mahalanobis Distance and Multivariate Outlier Detection 41
References 45

3 Data Reduction 47
Factor Analysis 47
  Techniques for exploratory factor analysis 50
  Choosing the number of factors to extract 51
  Selecting variables 54
  Rotation and interpretation of factors 56
Using the Results of a Factor Analysis 70
Data Considerations and Other Issues in Factor Analysis 72
Cluster Analysis 74
  How cluster analysis works 74
  Using distance measures to represent similarity and
    difference in cluster analysis 76
  Partitioning 78
  Hierarchical cluster analysis 79
  Evaluating and improving cluster analysis solutions 82
Multidimensional Scaling and Correspondence Analysis 83
References 85

4 Model Building 87
Simple Regression 88
  The regression equation 88
  Initial inspection of the data: Is there evidence of a
    linear relationship? 89
A Solution for Non-Linearity: Transformation 89
  Measuring the quality of the linear regression model 90
  The statistical significance of the regression model 91

Assumptions that must be met for a valid linear
    regression model   93
Assessing the Validity of Assumptions   93
    More pitfalls: Influential values and outliers   96
    The extrapolation limitation   98
Multiple Regression   99
    Modelling categorical variables   99
    Assessing the quality of a multiple regression model   100
    The multicollinearity problem   101
    Choosing a multiple regression model   102
Logistic Regression   105
    The logistic regression model   106
    Assumptions of logistic regression   107
    Interpreting and reporting the results of logistic
        regression analyses   107
    Evaluating the quality of a logistic regression model   109
Path Modelling   110
    Comparing SEM and PLS   112
    The language of covariance-based structural equa-
        tion modelling   114
    Specifying a structural equation model   115
    Basic operations of SEM   116
    Measuring the fit of a structural equation model   116
    Assumptions of SEM and associated issues in estimation   118
    Measurement models and structural models   119
    Dealing with small samples   128
Mediation and Moderation in Model Building   128
    Mediation   130
    Moderation   132
Multilevel Modelling   134
    Hierarchically structured data   135
    Testing for multilevel effects   136
    Modelling multilevel effects   138
    Multilevel Regression Models   138
    Multi-Group Analysis in Structural Equation Modelling   140

Common Method Variance: A Special Case of
Multilevel Variance   143
The effects of CMV   145
Techniques for identification and remediation of CMV   145
References   148

5   Time-Dependent Phenomena and Forecasting   152
Basic Concepts of Time Series   153
Smoothing methods   158
Autoregressive integrated moving average models   160
Filtering Techniques   163
Hodrick–Prescott filter   164
Comparing Time Series Models   165
Combining Forecasts   166
Correlation between Series   168
Stationarity, Stability and System Representations   172
Predictability   176
Non-linearity (BDS test)   176
Long-range dependency (Hurst exponents)   177
References   179

Part 2: Numerical Methods   **183**

6   Maximum Likelihood Estimation   187
Estimating Statistical Parameters   187
Likelihood Ratio Test   197
References   198

7   Monte Carlo Methods   200
Numerical Experiments   200
Random and Pseudorandom Numbers   204
References   209

8   Big Data   210
Technology   213
Data collection tools   215
Some Statistical Remarks   215

Artificial Intelligence and Machine Learning   217
    Supervised learning   217
    Unsupervised learning   218
Concluding Remarks   220
References   221

9   Simulations and Agent-Based Modelling   223
    Jacopo A. Baggio
Complex Adaptive Systems and Simulations   223
Agent-Based Models   226
Issues with Agent-Based Models   231
Evaluation of an Agent-Based Model   233
ABM and Tourism   234
Concluding Remarks   241
References   241

Appendix: Software Programs   245
Software List   246
Statistical Packages   247
    Generic packages   247
    Specialised programs cited in this book   247
    Development environments and programming languages   248
References   249

Subject Index   251

Contributors

Rodolfo Baggio holds a 'Laurea' degree in Physics (MPhys) from the University of Milan, Italy, and a PhD from the School of Tourism at the University of Queensland, Australia. After working for leading information technology firms for over 20 years, he is currently a professor at the Bocconi University where he teaches courses in Computer Science and coordinates the Information and Communication Technologies area at the Master in Economics and Tourism. He is also Research Fellow at the 'Carlo F. Dondena' Centre for Research on Social Dynamics and Public Policy. Rodolfo has held several courses and lectures at national and international level and has carried out consulting activities for private and public tourism organisations. He has managed several international research projects and actively researches and publishes in the field of information technology and tourism. His current research combines complexity theory and network analysis methods with the study of tourism destinations.

Jane Klobas is an Education and Research Consultant, based in Australia and Italy. She is an Adjunct Professor at Murdoch University, Western Australia and a Visiting Professor to the University of Bergamo and other universities in Europe and Asia. She was previously at Bocconi University in Milan and the University of Western Australia. She supervises doctoral students for the University of Liverpool Online and teaches research methods to doctoral students and faculty at several universities. She is author or co-author of several books and book chapters, and has published widely across disciplines in journals including *The Internet and Higher Education, Computers in Human Behavior, Library and Information Science Research, Demographic Research, Journal of Organizational Behavior* and *Decision Support Systems*.

Jacopo A. Baggio holds a degree in Economic and Social Sciences from the University of Milan Bicocca, a Master in Development Economics and a PhD in International Development from the University of East Anglia, which was funded by the UK Economic and Social Research Council (ESRC). He subsequently worked as a postdoctoral research associate with the Center for Behavior, Institutions and the Environment (CBIE) at

Arizona State University, and is now Assistant Professor at the Department of Environment and Society, Utah State University. His research focuses on the analysis and modelling of social-ecological systems. His main interests can be divided into two macro areas. One focuses on the conditions under which collective action succeeds in human societies, analysing what drives collective action and how it is influenced by uncertainty. The other centres upon social-ecological networks, characterising interdependencies between biodiversity, food, water, energy and decision-making.

Foreword

The tourism subject continues to mature, evidenced by debates on research approaches and the ever-increasing sophistication of the techniques used to investigate the activity that is tourism. These debates are often focused around the quantitative versus qualitative debate, and as Rodolfo and Jane say in their introduction to the first edition of this book, statistics and the quantitative approach are often labelled as 'disagreeable'. Yet, if tourism is to mature effectively as a subject, we cannot hide from the demands of quantitative approaches.

At a stroke, the second edition of this book progresses the maturity of tourism while also removing the mystique surrounding numbers and tourism. This is not a quantitative methods textbook; rather, it is a manual to guide tourism researchers through the minefield of advanced quantitative methods and how to apply them to tourism research. The book is unusual because it is written by experts in mathematics and quantitative methods; experts who have since moved into the tourism subject area. As such, this is a 'grown up' book that makes a number of demands and assumptions of its readers, providing researchers with the practical tools necessary for the analysis of complex tourism data sets, without shying away from the word 'complex'. This book will considerably enhance the standing of tourism as a subject and I know that it will be a valuable addition to the researchers' armoury.

Chris Cooper
Oxford Brookes University, Oxford

Introduction to the Second Edition

Five years ago, when we wrote the first edition of this book, we thought of it as a one-time-only project. We were inspired by our experiences, as advisers to researchers, analysts and students, to provide an accessible, sensible and rigorous guide to useful methods for statistical inquiry into tourism matters of all but the most econometrically complex kind. We were delighted by the response to our book and happy to bask in the pleasure of a job well done. But, of course, quantitative methods, technological tools and sources of data continue to develop, and the expectations of supervisors, examiners and peer reviewers of research papers evolve. What was 'enough to know' five years ago, is not enough to know now. Thus, this second edition.

This edition retains the overall approach taken in the first edition. The first part of the book concerns common issues in the statistical analysis of data and the most widely used techniques. The second part describes and discusses several newer and less common approaches to data analysis that we believe are useful for tourism researchers and analysts, and which we encourage readers to consider. We have added material to both sections.

The first part of the book now includes sections on issues that, while always important, have become more transparent as software evolves and makes it easier to adopt and present the results of analyses undertaken using both older and newer techniques. We focus on techniques that, having become more accessible are, in the reports and papers we read, often applied without a great deal of thought, in a textbook sequence that does not necessarily fit the data and context of the project being described. We have added consideration of data screening and cleaning to Chapter 1 and methods for measuring similarity and dissimilarity to Chapter 2. Chapter 4 has been extended to include observations about the partial least squares (PLS) approach to path modelling (sometimes equated with structural equation modelling [SEM]). Chapter 4 also includes new sections on multilevel modelling and accounting for common method variance in SEM.

A new chapter on 'Big Data' has been added to Part 2. This chapter aims not only to inform readers about the many aspects that come together to make Big Data more than a data-based revolution, but also to consider controversies about whether Big Data means the end of statistics. The chapter guides users through decisions to be made about when and how to use Big Data and how to interpret and evaluate the findings of Big Data projects. The final chapter, on agent-based modelling and simulations, has been updated and revised.

Once again, many people have provided encouragement and support for this edition. We thank you all.

Introduction

*Data is like garbage. You had better know what you are going
to do with it before you collect it*
Mark Twain

Many people consider statistics a disagreeable discipline. Probably because
for centuries it has been used to allow power (whether public or private) to
achieve its objectives. Did a king want to declare war? His mathematicians
counted people fit for military service, their available means and their
equipment. Were funds for building a palace or a castle insufficient? Incomes
were calculated, and taxes were increased just enough, if the regency was
astute, to collect the amount of money required to satisfy all the wishes
without squeezing the taxpayers too much. Was a firm in need of increasing
production or profit levels? Statisticians were employed to count, measure,
highlight weak areas, rationalise costs, remove or add workers and suggest
possible solutions. Yet, with its methods, medicine, technology, economics
and many other disciplines have reached levels that have allowed us to
live longer and better, to work in more favourable conditions and to have a
deeper knowledge of the physical world.

Formally, statistics has the objective of collecting, analysing and
interpreting data collected in various ways and assessing methods and
procedures for performing these activities. The objective of a statistician is to
derive universally valid conclusions from a collection of partial observations.
With a very practical approach, knowing that measuring all the aspects of
a phenomenon can be impossible for many reasons, we employ well studied
and discussed scientific methods to do the work, and, more importantly, to
give some measure of the reliability of the conclusions drawn. In his book,
The Rise of Statistical Thinking 1820–1900, Theodore Porter states:

Statistics has become known in the twentieth century as the
mathematical tool for analysing experimental and observational data.
Enshrined by public policy as the only reliable basis for judgements as
to the efficacy of medical procedures or the safety of chemicals, and
adopted by business for such uses as industrial quality control, it is
evidently among the products of science whose influence on public and
private life has been most pervasive. Statistical analysis has also come
to be seen in many scientific disciplines as indispensable for drawing
reliable conclusions from empirical results. For some modern fields, such
as quantitative genetics, statistical mechanics, and the psychological

field of intelligence testing, statistical mathematics is inseparable from actual theory. Not since the invention of calculus, if ever, has a new field of mathematics found so extensive a domain of applications. (Porter, 1986: 3)

Tourism, like many other human activities, relies heavily on data of all sorts and the quantitative treatment of data and information collected in a wide variety of ways is a crucial endeavour for both academics and practitioners. Yet, numbers and formulas are not the most widely diffused objects in the tourism field and our experience in this area tells us that the application of mathematical and statistical concepts and procedures is far from common practice.

In its long history, statistics has implemented a large number of techniques for dealing with different situations and giving answers in different conditions. Very sophisticated, and sometimes complicated, procedures enable us to derive justified outcomes that, in many cases, prove to be crucial for decision-making, or for the implementation of development plans or policies, or simply for understanding how tourism activities unfold.

Many of these techniques, however, can only be found in scholarly journal papers or in advanced specialised books. There is, generally, little practical information on a variety of methods and, mainly, on the way they can be applied to tourism cases. Advanced quantitative methods are rarely described in tourism textbooks, and the treatment given in more standard statistical textbooks is, at times, too theoretical and gives little operational information. On the other hand, a quick survey of the tourism literature shows a certain limitation in the number of methods and techniques.

This book aims to fill this information gap by providing practical tools for the quantitative analysis of data in the tourism field. The main objective is to make available a usable reference book rather than a theoretical text discussing the methods. For a full treatment of the different methods described, the reader will be supplied with relevant references on the different topics. Most of the methods presented have been chosen after a survey of the tourism literature. We have also taken into account many current techniques used in journals and scientific publications as well as our experience in teaching these topics and the efforts spent in trying to find instructional materials with the right mix of arguments and the right balance between scientific rigour, practical usefulness and simplicity of language. This work has highlighted a number of approaches that have been shown to provide interesting outcomes. To these, a number of more recent topics have been added. They are well consolidated in other disciplines and their effectiveness allows us to see a promising future for their application in tourism studies.

Different from a standard statistics textbook, this work gives little space to the theoretical discussion of the methods presented. Rather, it aims at providing practical hints on their applicability and, where appropriate, a discussion on their advantages and disadvantages. Many examples are presented and references to similar studies are illustrated; they are an integral part of the text and, in many cases, replace the theoretical exposition of the methods discussed.

This book has been designed for graduate students at master and PhD level, researchers in both tourism and the social sciences and practitioners or industry consultants. It is assumed that the reader has at least a basic understanding and some (good) familiarity with elementary statistics (descriptive and inferential) and with concepts and terms such as confidence limits, significance levels, degrees of freedom, probability and probability distributions and so on. In any case, numerous references in the book will point the reader to noteworthy works in which he/she will find extensive mathematical and conceptual treatment for the different topics to satisfy his/her curiosity or need to explore all the nuances of the methods discussed here. Many of the techniques described definitely require the use of some software program, and in many cases, the standard statistical analysis programs do not contain dedicated functions for them. Nevertheless, these can be found without much effort on the internet as small executable programs or scripts for some widely used application development environments, such as Matlab or GAUSS. References have been given with the text and an appendix contains a list of these programs with their internet addresses. Needless to say, some familiarity with the use of a computer is an unavoidable skill today.

Many authors report, as diffuse wisdom, the fact that every equation included in a book would halve the sales. Caring much for the economic health of our publisher, we have tried to reduce mathematical expressions to a minimum. However, as the reader will understand, some of them are unavoidable when speaking the language of numbers.

Finally, it is important to remark here that, although it is commonly considered to be a scientific discipline, statistics might be more accurately thought of as a craft or an art, where experience plays a central role and numerous different interpretations of even basic concepts and procedures exist. What is presented in this book is the interpretation (grounded) of the authors. We have taken care to present the most widely accepted readings, but in some cases our views might be questioned and different versions may be found in the literature.

The book is divided into two parts. The first part deals with data analysis methods that are widely used by the tourism research community, but not described much in standard tourism books. The second part describes some numerical methods that, to date, have seen limited use in tourism studies.

These techniques are gaining wide attention and a reputation in many disciplines for the study of several types of systems, especially when the issues investigated are difficult or not tractable with analytical methods. They have been made practically usable through the operation of modern computer systems. Although, in some cases, highly computationally intensive, they have proved to be able to provide useful insights that can complement the conclusions attained by more traditional methods and may give, in the future, different perspectives to the field of tourism. An appendix describing some of the more used software tools closes the book.

All the chapters have been written to be independent of one another, and for this reason the references have been listed separately at the end of each chapter. In this way, the reader is not forced to go through the book with a predetermined sequence, but is free to hop here and there, following his/her own curiosity or needs.

As a final note, the authors wish to advise the reader that all the internet addresses contained in the book have been checked before releasing the final version of the text. However, nothing can guarantee that they will not change or disappear. Should this happen, an online search will surely enable the reader to find moved pages or similar contents.

The authors would like to thank a number of people who have helped and supported us in our work, but the list risks being quite long and tedious for the reader. All who have helped us are aware of the importance of their contributions, and to them our sincere thanks.

Part 1

The Analysis of Data

Introduction to Part 1

The first part of this book contains a discussion of standard methods in statistical data analysis: hypothesis tests, regressions, cluster and factor analysis and time series analysis. They have been chosen for their importance in the field of tourism studies, even though they are scarcely treated in general tourism textbooks.

We have avoided highly sophisticated methods that, usually, can only be applied well in special circumstances, but we have included some extensions to the standard techniques. These, although well diffused in other disciplines (e.g. non-linear analysis techniques for time series), have not had wide use in tourism studies. Their effectiveness has been demonstrated many times in other fields and we think they will prove useful in this area too.

The content of this part is organised as follows.

The Nature of Data in Tourism

Data are the main ingredient of all the methods discussed in this book and are examined from a general perspective. The various types are described and examined. The quality of data is then discussed and practical suggestions for assessing and evaluating the suitability of data in relation to the objective of an investigation are given. Finally, a list of electronic sources of tourism data is provided.

Testing Hypotheses and Comparing Samples

This chapter contains a review of the main concepts and techniques connected with statistical hypotheses testing. Issues regarding the power of tests and the effects of sample size are discussed. Also, bootstrap and meta-analysis as methods to improve the reliability of the outcomes are presented. A summary of the most commonly used statistical tests is included. The chapter closes with a description of different methods to assess similarity (or diversity) within and between samples.

Data Reduction

An analysis of multivariate data is presented here. Factor analysis and cluster analysis as well as multidimensional scaling techniques are also described and discussed along with the main issue, advantages, disadvantages and applicability.

Model Building

The chapter discusses regression models and structural equation modelling. Focusing on the tourism field, the chapter highlights the issues related to computational techniques and the reliability of the results in different conditions.

Time-Dependent Phenomena and Forecasting

This chapter contains a quick overview of time series analysis methods and their use for forecasting purposes. In addition, different uses of time series are discussed, such as simple non-linear analysis techniques to provide different ways of studying the basic characteristics of the structure and the behaviour of a tourism system.

1 The Nature of Data in Tourism

This chapter contains a brief review of the nature of data as used in tourism and hospitality, and discusses the main quality characteristics needed to obtain useful and reliable outcomes from data analysis. A list of the main sources of tourism data is provided.

The protagonist in the adventures described in this book is the datum, better known in its plural form, data. The original Latin meaning, something given (and accepted as true), defines it well. It is (usually) a number, the result of some observation or measurement process, objectively[1] representing concepts or other entities, put in a form suitable for communication, interpretation or processing by humans or automated systems. By themselves, and out of a specified context, data have no meaning at all; they are merely strings of symbols. Once organised or processed in some way, and associated with some other concepts or entities, they become useful information, assuming relevance and purpose, providing insights into phenomena, allowing judgements to be made and decisions to be taken (if interested in a discussion of these concepts, the review by Zins [2007] is a good starting point). All statistical techniques have exactly this objective.

Many disciplines, and tourism is no exception, require large quantities of data. The main challenge a researcher has today is that of managing a huge quantity, variety and complexity of data types, and of being sure to obtain useful and valid outcomes.

Data: A Taxonomy

It is possible to categorise data in several ways. One distinction is between primary and secondary data. Another classifies data by their level of measurement or measurement scale. Yet another is the medium or form from which the data are derived. We provide a brief overview of the key issues associated with data of each type here.

The distinction between primary and secondary data is made on the basis of the source of the data and their specificity to the study for which they are gathered. Each type of source has strengths and weaknesses, the focus of our discussion here.

Primary data

Primary data are those directly collected from the original or 'primary' source by researchers through methods such as direct observation (both human observation and automatic collection of data such as clicks on links in websites or through use of other information and communications technology), questionnaire surveys (online, printed or administered by telephone or computer), structured or unstructured interviews[2] and case studies. To be classified as primary data, the data elements collected using any one of these techniques will be unique and tailored to the specific purposes of the study conducted. The most used techniques and their strengths and limitations are well described in many books (Babbie, 2010; Creswell, 2003; Hair et al., 2005; Neuman, 2006; Phillimore & Goodson, 2004; Veal, 2006; Yin, 1994). Here, we concentrate on recent developments and issues of particular relevance to tourism research.

The main disadvantages are well known: cost and time. Collecting tailored information tends to be expensive in terms of resources needed (money and people) and it may take a long time to properly design the research and process the results. Recently, use of the internet and the world wide web has reduced the cost and time requirements for conducting surveys. However, unless used carefully, the use of online surveys can hide problems related to the representativeness of the sample and the technical characteristics of the medium used and individual differences among respondents can bias results. Of course, these concerns are not unique to electronic media, but can be exacerbated by the seductive ease and speed of online data collection. Indeed, many survey experts consider internet surveying (provided the sample is representative) to provide valid, reliable and relatively error-free results, among other reasons because data are captured directly from the respondent without the need for an interviewer or assistant to enter the data separately into a database for analysis (Dillman, 2007).

Regardless of the method used to capture primary data, the researcher should consider and understand well all issues associated with sampling (representativeness and sample size) and obtaining data of suitable quality. From a practical point of view, it is advisable to start any study by surveying a pilot sample and studying the responses obtained. Participants in the pilot study can be asked to identify any questions that they found difficult to understand or to answer and, using a technique known as cognitive interviewing, they can also be asked how they interpreted specific questions. The data collected from a pilot study can be used to estimate population parameters for the statistical models that will be used to draw conclusions from the final survey, information that can be used to determine the data distribution and sample size necessary or desirable for the larger-scale investigation to be conducted effectively (Dillman, 2007; Pan, 2010).

Secondary data

In many cases, collecting primary data is not within the reach of the investigator. Furthermore, it is not always necessary to have primary data to conduct a study. For example, very few researchers would start collecting primary data on the number of tourists visiting a country or on the gross domestic product (GDP) of some nations. When theoretical or practical reasons do not indicate direct collection of data, secondary data are used. Secondary data are data gathered, typically by someone else, for a purpose other than the study for which they will be used. The main sources of secondary data external to an organisation are government agencies (statistical bureaus, public tourism departments), international associations and institutions, private research companies and industry associations. Data from these sources are available directly from the provider (particularly in the case of those public institutions that have an obligation – often by law – to make public the outcomes of their activities) or from libraries and electronic databases. Often, they can be obtained from these sources over the internet. Useful data for some studies can also be found in previously published research or reports. Increasingly, secondary data are drawn from the databases (typically customer or visitor databases) maintained by individual organisations. A special case of secondary data is so-called Big Data, which we discuss in Chapter 8.

Secondary data tend to be readily available and they are often free or inexpensive to obtain. It is often possible to assemble large quantities of data and to draw together data from different sources. On the other hand, secondary data may be more difficult to use and to interpret because, typically, they were gathered by other researchers, or by practitioners, for other purposes. Extracting useful information from a source of secondary data requires an understanding of the structure of the data and the database as well as a good understanding of the characteristics and meaning of each data element. A careful reading of the data specifications is essential in order to judge the suitability of the data for the study under way as well as their reliability and trustworthiness.

When secondary data are drawn from databases in which individuals can be identified (examples include corporate customer databases and data extracted from online social networks), researchers need also to meet criteria for the ethical treatment of data. The most widely accepted criteria are outlined in the Declaration of Helsinki (http://www.wma.net/en/30publications/10policies/b3/), which is maintained by the authors, the World Medical Association, and adopted for research in most fields that use data obtained from humans.

As a final point, secondary data are often preprocessed to give summaries, totals or averages (e.g. by country or region) and the original details cannot be easily recovered. The dangers of drawing conclusions about individuals from such preprocessed data are nicely described in Simpson's paradox:

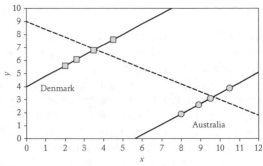

Figure 1.1 Illustration of Simpson's paradox (adapted from Wikipedia, 2010)

relationships observed at the aggregate level are not necessarily the same (or even in the same direction) as relationships observed at the level from which the data were aggregated. Figure 1.1 shows the relationship between two variables, let's say hours of sunlight (on the *x* axis) and visitor numbers (in thousands, on the *y* axis). The two lines show the relationship between hours of sunlight and daily visitor arrivals in four cities in two countries over Christmas (say, Australia and Denmark). Both lines show a positive relationship: the more sunlight in the city at Christmas time, the more visitor arrivals recorded. The dotted line shows, however, the relationship between the average number of hours of sunlight and the average visitor numbers to each city. On average, the cities in one country have around 10 hours of sunlight and around 3000 visitors while the cities in the second country have around 2 hours of sunlight and 7000 visitors. The dotted line shows a *negative* relationship between hours of sunlight and visitor arrivals. Which relationship is the right one? On which would one make plans?

Combining primary and secondary data

In many cases, the data used for a study come from different sources and a combination of primary and secondary data is quite common in tourism studies. In addition to the specific considerations of primary and secondary data, the researcher needs to keep in mind the nature of the sample and the level of aggregation of data from the different sources. Specific techniques may be needed to ensure that results are useful and to avoid errors.

Example: Use of primary and secondary data

Some examples of how the tourism and hospitality literature utilises primary and secondary data will better clarify the roles and the uses of them.

In their paper 'Information source usage among motive-based segments of travelers to newly emerging tourist destinations', Dey and Sarma (2010) interview a sample of people to assess the importance of word-of-mouth (WOM) suggestions and recommendations about an Indian destination. The data are collected through a questionnaire and their primary sources confirm the initial hypothesis, assigning to WOM the highest rank in the information sources used to gather some knowledge of the destination.

On some occasions, the data used should be technically defined as secondary, but the distinction may be blurred. An example is the paper by Woodside and Dubelaar (2002) on the derivation of a model for a tourism consumption system. This is, in the authors' idea: 'the set of related travel thoughts, decisions, and behaviors by a discretionary traveler prior to, during, and following a trip' (Woodside & Dubelaar, 2002: 120). In order to build this model, they to turn to a database containing the responses to a large number of interviews. This collection consists of raw data (the answers collected) never used before except for some preliminary analysis. In this case, even if collected by others, the authors possess the questionnaire used which fits well their needs, and they also have access to additional details on the specific questions in the questionnaire. Formally secondary, the data could well be considered as primary.

Very often, researchers combine both primary and secondary data in their studies. Chung and Law (2003) develop a performance indicator for hotel websites. Their primary source is a set of questionnaires expressly developed to measure the perceptions of hotel managers of the importance of a number of attributes of a hotel website and its performance. The results of this inquiry are then supplemented by information regarding hotel classification and tariffs in order to derive the desired indicator.

The same combined use can be found in a work by Hystad and Keller (2008): 'Towards a destination tourism disaster management framework: Long-term lessons from a forest fire disaster'. The basis for their assessment is a repeated series of interviews conducted after a major forest fire occurred in an area of Canada. In this way, the authors collect information on what the tourism industry experienced over the long term after the disaster, what strategies were implemented for the recovery and the lessons learned for improving disaster management practices. They combine these outcomes with secondary data consisting of outlook and travel intention surveys to assess the different roles of the destination stakeholders involved and the effectiveness of their recovery plans.

Data Harmonisation, Standards and Collaboration

Use of secondary data, particularly when they are obtained from multiple sources, can be greatly aided by harmonisation and standards. International organisations harmonise data they draw from different countries as best they can, and record any country-specific variations from the standard data definition (such as year of data collection or age groups from which data are collected) in data specifications or metadata, but there is no universally recognised or adopted standard for many of the concepts that are important for tourism studies. Many attempts exist and international institutions have published several recommendations (see for example Eurostat, 2000, 2002; UNSD, 2010; UNWTO, 2000), but in many cases, local variations make complete harmonisation very difficult if not impossible. A good example is the classification of hospitality structures. Almost all countries (and often even regions in the same country) have developed their own schemes and a comparison between hotels in different areas of the world can become a difficult task (see for example Cser & Ohuchi, 2008; Hotelstars, 2010; IHRA, 2004).

Moreover, when it comes to electronically distributed data, scarce adoption of even the existing technological standards makes data collection and comparison even more difficult. A key issue is that different software applications and heterogeneous computing platforms need a way to exchange data automatically without much human intervention. This interoperability between systems (or, better, the lack of) is a problem which is most obvious in large online commercial environments, but also has significant effects on the possibility to extract and use data for research purposes. Many international efforts try to overcome this problem by attempting to set standards for the representation and exchange of electronic data in tourism. Probably the most known and diffused is the proposal made by the Open Travel Alliance (OTA: http://www.opentravel.org/), a consortium of many important companies active both in the tourism and the information technology fields. The work is done at two levels. The first level concerns the semantic aspect, and standard definitions and names for the different objects (a trip, a destination, a hotel, a room etc.) involved are set by building an ontology (i.e. an agreed classification and definition scheme) (Gruber, 1993). The second regards the technical means to store and transfer data. One proposal is the use of a service-oriented architecture (Erl, 2005) based on eXtensible Markup Language (XML) standards (see http://www.w3.org/XML; Harold & Means, 2004). Commercial software also exists; the Nesstar system (http://www.nesstar.com) is used by a number of national and international bodies.

An associated development is the increasing attention being paid to making the data on which research results are based openly and publicly available. Several major publishers already offer authors the possibility of making their original data available as an online supplement to a published journal article and the Scholarly Publishing and Academic Resources Coalition (SPARC, http://www.sparceurope.org), which brings together major research libraries and peak university bodies, acts as an advocate of this open data model. Nonetheless, it is rare to find original data, not only in tourism, but also in many other fields. An old joke in the life science research community is that 'the data are mine, mine, mine' and papers have been written on the subject (Campbell *et al.*, 2002).

One more effect of the widespread use of computers in research concerns the increasing utilisation of computational models and simulations. This not only increases the types of data available, but also complicates the picture as specific information about the algorithms, the software and the different parameters used to set up a model run are important pieces of information required to repeat or evaluate results. The reproducibility of findings is central to the scientific enterprise, and one key constituent is the availability of the data and the procedures used for examination and inspection by the larger community of researchers. The increasing use of computer simulations, then, worsens the problem as software and algorithms that underlie these artefacts should be well verified and understood, not limited to a generic description such as the one that is normally put in a paper or a report. In some fields, particularly in the sciences, researchers are setting up environments known as collaboratories to share this critical information, but as yet there is no collaboratory for tourism data, software and routines (Sonnenwald, 2007).

We conclude this section with an example of how one journal has addressed the issue of replicability. The *Journal of Applied Econometrics* states: 'A special feature of the Journal is its emphasis on the replicability of results by other researchers. To achieve this aim, authors are expected to make available a complete set of the data used as well as any specialized computer programs employed through a readily accessible medium, preferably in a machine-readable form'. Hopefully, this example will be followed by many others and modern information technologies, standards for recording and making data available and the attitude towards using them, will help by increasing the visibility and accessibility of data and algorithms.

Quantitative and categorical data

Another fundamental distinction between types of data concerns the level of measurement of the data. This distinction is well covered in statistical textbooks, but it is so critical to the selection of appropriate statistical techniques and is so often ignored that we want to draw attention to it here. We will distinguish primarily between quantitative or metric data and categorical data. Quantitative data are data that are measured using a numerical scale that reflects a quantity such as temperature, height, cost, age (in years), percentage satisfaction with an experience and so on. Categorical data represent qualities or characteristics that can be used to categorise a person or object; examples are sex, age group, country, approval or disapproval of a policy or plan and so on. While categorical data can be included in statistical analyses, they often require special treatment if the results are to be meaningful.

The many forms of data

One more important element when considering data is the different forms in which they are recorded and expressed. Data can be found in forms such as simple numerical quantities, high-dimensional data (i.e. multivariate data that can only be defined by recording observations on several variables), geometric or spatial records, images, graphs, texts, maps and geographical representations (Shoval & Isaacson, 2010). Advances in modern technologies have led us to a world in which practically every object of interest can be put in digital form. Overlaid on any one of these there is often a temporal dimension that multiplies quantities and types to be managed by a factor equal to the number of time steps of interest; this may result in very large data sets.

Data Quality

As seen in the previous sections, the quantity and the types of data available for studying tourism matters are vast. Today, the issue of information overload is ever present. Even if, historically, it is a common complaint born with the invention of the printing press, the modern excess of data and information poses a serious challenge. In this regard, a foremost issue is data quality. As well put by Kent (2001):

> The statistics themselves are pointless unless the data on which they are performed are of good or at least acceptable quality. 'Garbage in, garbage out' (GIGO) is a phrase that is commonly heard, but whose implications are seldom given the attention or credence they deserve. If the data going into the analysis are of dubious quality, then no degree of statistical sophistication can prevent the ensuing analysis being similarly suspect. (Kent, 2001: 2)

In order not to attempt to perform miracles by trying to extract gems from rubbish, the researcher has an important responsibility in guaranteeing the quality of the sources used. The collection of high-quality data is a complicated task and many problems (not only scientific, but also administrative, political, interpersonal, etc.) that risk compromising the work performed may arise in a multifaceted field such as tourism. Moreover, the methods or the design of a published study cannot be modified. They must be evaluated and shortcomings taken into account to assess the impact of these problems on the data and the results of the analysis (Vannan, 2001).

The definition of quality is difficult and controversial, but it is useful to consider this concept relative to the specific situation. Many scholars and institutions have attempted to list the most important characteristics of high quality data. A general consensus has been reached on what they are and a wealth of conceptual practical techniques has been devised to assess most of them (Batini & Scannapieco, 2006).

Eurostat, the European statistical bureau, and the International Monetary Fund (IMF), to cite two important organisations for example, have dedicated specific activities and publications to this issue and defined the main dimensions of data quality along with indicators for their assessment (see Eurostat, 2005a, 2005b, or the website http://dsbb .imf.org/Pages/DQRS/Home.aspx). One common scheme, derived from the different views on the topic, leads to the identification of a number of aspects reputed to be essential for defining the quality of data (Laliberté et al., 2004). They are:

- *Relevance*: Importance of the data for the purpose for which they were collected and agreement with the expectations of the researcher.
- *Accuracy*: Reliability of the data, absence of errors in data sources, the measurement of such errors and the correctness of the survey methodology.
- *Comparability*: Application of international definitions of concepts and classifications and methodological guidelines.
- *Coherence*: Consistency of observations within the data set, with other data sets and over time.
- *Timeliness*: Amount of time between the reference period and the date of dissemination of the data.
- *Accessibility and clarity*: Conditions to access data (means, support, possible restrictions, etc.) and availability of accompanying information on data (documentation, explanations, limits, assistance to users, etc.).

Although quantitative indicators can be derived for assessing (at least partially) the characteristics of high quality data (the literature proposes some, typically based on the extent of variability in the values), probably the best practical advice consists of a checklist containing the most important features, and use of this list as a guide for a brief, but thorough, qualitative assessment before deciding whether and how to use the data collected. A useful proposal is the one made by Pipino et al. (2002), shown in Table 1.1 with some modifications and adaptations. It must be noted that in real situations not all of the features need to be used. Depending on the specific situation, the evaluation will be limited to those considered essential for the given objective. This series of features can be evaluated using some quantitative measure or by assigning a score (for example on a 1–10 scale), thus giving a rapid way of assessing the data collected or found in a secondary source, or comparing different sets of similar data in order to decide which are the most suitable for the purpose of the work being undertaken. As in many of these types of assessments, experience will be of guidance to judge the features.

Table 1.1 Main features defining the quality of data

Feature	Definition
Accessibility	Extent to which data are available and quickly retrievable
Amount	Extent to which the volume of data is appropriate for the task at hand
Believability	Extent to which data are regarded as true and credible
Completeness	Extent to which data are not missing and are of sufficient breadth and depth for the task at hand
Conciseness	Extent to which data are compactly represented
Consistency	Extent to which data are presented in the same format
Ease of manipulation	Extent to which data are easy to manipulate and apply to different tasks
Error free	Extent to which data are correct and reliable
Interpretability	Extent to which data are in appropriate language, symbols and units and definitions are clear
Objectivity	Extent to which data are unbiased, unprejudiced and impartial
Precision	Extent to which data are measured to the required level of specificity
Relevance	Extent to which data are applicable and helpful for the task at hand
Reputation	Extent to which data are highly regarded in terms of source or their contents
Security	Extent to which access to data is restricted appropriately to maintain their security
Timeliness	Extent to which data are sufficiently up to date for the task at hand
Understandability	Extent to which data are easily comprehended
Value-added	Extent to which data are beneficial and provide advantage from their use

Source: Adapted from Pipino *et al.* (2002).

Example: Selecting a data set

An example of a procedure to decide the best possible choice is discussed in the paper by Frank *et al.* (2004): 'Procedure to select the best dataset for a task'. The paper models a decision process to select the one most suitable data set from a number of possible candidates. The authors compare the requirements and data quality, noting: 'some general, common-sense knowledge about effects of errors, lack of precision in the data and the dilution of quality over time' (Frank *et al.*, 2004: 81). The quality is evaluated by considering only a few of the possible features, those deemed most important for the specific case. Then a 'utility' is defined which gives a quantitative answer to the initial question.

The practical example consists of the evaluation of two data sets for two different tasks. The data sets contain geographical information for studying navigation in a city (essentially they are maps).

The features assessed by the authors are the following:

• precision, judged by calculating the standard deviation of random errors;
• completeness, evaluated qualitatively by reading the collection methods;
• timeliness, measured in terms of the date on which the collection was performed.

Since the suitability of data for a task is a relative concept, the purpose of the study to be performed must be considered by analysing the information available from the data set and how it is influenced by the quality of the data. In the case under analysis, the data considered refer to a map. In order to assess the utility of the data, the specific use must be expressed, since different maps can be produced for different user groups (tourists, locals, emergency services, etc.). The utility is measured on a 0–1 scale and is defined in terms of some quality parameters. It can be measured as having gradual influence (essentially a linear relationship between quality and utility) or as a threshold (i.e. if the quality is above a certain level, utility=1, otherwise it is zero).

The main parameter used in the paper is precision (noting that lower values mean higher quality) which is used to derive the utility. Once the latter has been determined, completeness is used to correct it. The average utility for an incomplete data set is thus the result of multiplying utility by the completeness factor. Finally, when multiple tasks are combined, the overall utility is obtained by weighting the different tasks and using these values to weight the utilities calculated.

Data screening and cleaning

Statistics textbooks and software packages now pay quite a lot of attention to methods for testing the quality of a data set, repairing errors and dealing properly with shortcomings such as missing values and outliers. This puts more tools in the hands of researchers, which is a good thing – but only if the researcher uses the tools knowledgeably. Mechanistic 'paint-by-numbers' data screening and cleaning, where the researcher follows the steps listed in a textbook without thoughtfully setting evaluation criteria or weighing up the strengths and weaknesses of taking a certain action, are becoming more common. The risks of poor data screening and 'cleaning' range from removing valid cases and unnecessarily reducing sample size (and, thus, the amount of information available for analysis) to making poor decisions about data distributions and appropriate techniques for data analysis. In this section, we provide a brief overview of techniques for data screening and cleaning and the situations in which they are appropriate, leaving operational detail to generic texts (for example: DeSimone *et al.*, 2015; Furnham, 1986; Osborne, 2012).

Why screen data?

Data screening is a necessary step, undertaken before data analysis. Its primary goal is data quality and consistency assurance. A typical issue, for instance, concerns very extreme values (outliers) in the data that should be identified and assessed before running the analysis (see Chapter 2, this volume: Mahalanobis Distance and Multivariate Outlier Detection for an example).

If data problems are identified and they can be remedied, either the data are cleaned before analysis begins (e.g. missing values are replaced or social desirability bias is removed) or an analysis-specific remedy is applied (e.g. a latent common method variable can be defined in structural equation modelling). If the data problems cannot be remedied, the researcher must decide what constraints the data limitations place on the types of analyses that can be conducted and the interpretation of the results.

The data quality problems most commonly examined in the data screening step are listed in Table 1.2. The table emphasises that most problems

Table 1.2 Common data quality problems and their primary associations, highlighting the role of variables in diagnosis

Problem	Cases	Groups within cases	Variables
Missing values	P		d
Invalid responses	P		P, d
Data entry errors			d
Response bias			d
Dissimulation	P		d
Positive and negative affectivity	P		d
Social desirability	P	P	d
Common method bias	P	P	d
Floor and ceiling effects		P	P, d
Outliers	P		d

Note: P: problem is primarily associated with cases, groups or variables as indicated; d: diagnosis is based on analyses of variables.

are related to cases rather than variables, even though diagnosis of problems relies primarily on reports related to variables and their distribution.

Concluding remarks

Research in tourism, as in many other fields, uses quite large quantities of data coming from different sources and with different degrees of suitability for the specific purposes of a specific investigation. After a survey of the common classifications used for defining data and developments in standards and practices for sharing data and routines, this chapter has discussed the quality of data and some ways to assess it. The issue of data quality is highly relevant and well known in tourism research, as described by Smith (1988):

> ... Each of these measures has utility but they lead to different estimates and conclusions and, ultimately, to the impression that no one in tourism knows what they are talking about.
>
> Credibility problems in tourism data also arise from the quality of data sources, sample sizes, period of recall (i.e. whether a person is asked questions about a trip just completed, one taken three months ago or one taken one year ago), the wording of questions, and other methodological details affect the precision, accuracy, validity, and reliability of tourism statistics and, by association, the industry's credibility. (Smith, 1988: 33)

Sources of Secondary Tourism Data

Data at country or regional level are usually provided by the relevant organisations, typically the tourism boards or statistical bureaus of the area under study. Their websites outline the types and quantity of information provided and how they can be accessed or downloaded.

Sources of general data about tourism include the most important international organisations specialised in tourism or which have tourism as one of their interests, the main international associations and many private research companies. The availability of data is quite differentiated and may change even for the same provider according to types, quantities or specific investigations. Many offer data freely, but, especially for private companies, sometimes the cost may be very high. The reader is advised to check the costs and conditions of use carefully before selecting the data sources.

International organisations

- United Nations World Tourism Organisation (UNWTO): http://www. unwto.org/
- World Tourism Foundation (WTF): http://www.worldtourismfounda tion.org/

- United Nations Statistics Division (UNDATA): http://data.un.org/
- Organisation for Economic Co-operation and Development (OECD): http://www.oecd.org/
- European Travel Commission (ETC): http://www.etc-corporate.org/
- Statistical Office of the European Commission (Eurostat): http://epp.eurostat.ec.europa.eu/
- Organisation of American States (OAS): http://www.oas.org/
- The World Bank: http://www.worldbank.org/
- World Economic Forum (WEF): http://www.weforum.org/
- International Monetary Fund (IMF): http://www.imf.org/

Associations

- Council on Hotel, Restaurant and Institutional Education (CHRIE): http://www.chrie.org/
- International Hotel & Restaurant Association (IH&RA): http://www.ih-ra.com/
- Pacific Asia Travel Association (PATA): http://www.pata.org/
- South Pacific Tourism Organisation (SPTO): http://www.spto.org/
- Travel and Tourism Research Association (TTRA): http://www.ttra.com/
- World Association of Travel Agencies (WATA): http://www.wata.net/
- World Federation of Tourist Guide Associations (WFTGA): http://wftga.org/
- World Travel and Tourism Council (WTTC): http://www.wttc.org/

Private companies

- European Travel Monitor/IPK International: http://www.ipkinternational.com/
- Mintel (Travel & Tourism Intelligence): http://www.mintel.com/
- PhoCus Wright: http://www.phocuswright.com/
- Tourism Economics (an Oxford Economics company): http://www.tourismeconomics.com/
- eMarketer: http://www.emarketer.com/
- Forrester Research: http://www.forrester.com/
- The Nielsen Company: http://www.nielsen.com/
- The Gartner Group: http://www.gartner.com/

Notes

(1)   A long philosophical and epistemological discussion of the meaning of *objective* would be needed here, but the aim (and the space) of this book does not allow it. We assume then the word in its common connotation.

(2)   Common terms used to describe data collection methods that combine survey and interview are computer-assisted personal interviewing (CAPI), where the interviewer and survey respondent meet face to face and the interviewer records responses to questions directly onto a personal computer, and computer-assisted telephone interviewing (CATI). The term *computer-assisted self-interviewing* (CASI) is sometimes used (erroneously, when no interviewer is involved!) to describe data collection when the respondents complete a survey form on the computer themselves.

References

Babbie, E. (2010) *The Practice of Social Research* (12th edn). Belmont, CA: Wadsworth.

Batini, C. and Scannapieco, M. (2006) *Data Quality: Concepts, Methods and Techniques.* Berlin: Springer.

Campbell, E.G., Clarridge, B.R., Gokhale, M., Birenbaum, L., Hilgartner, S., Holtzen, N.A. and Blumenthal, D. (2002) Data withholding in academic genetics: Evidence from a national survey. *Journal of the American Medical Association* 287 (4), 473–480.

Chung, T. and Law, R. (2003) Developing a performance indicator for hotel websites. *International Journal of Hospitality Management* 22 (1), 119–125.

Creswell, J.W. (2003) *Research Design: Qualitative, Quantitative, and Mixed Methods Approaches* (2nd edn). Thousand Oaks, CA: Sage.

Cser, K. and Ohuchi, A. (2008) World practices of hotel classification systems. *Asia Pacific Journal of Tourism Research* 13, 379–398.

DeSimone, J.A., Harms, P.D. and DeSimone, A.J. (2015) Best practice recommendations for data screening. *Journal of Organizational Behavior* 36 (2), 171–181.

Dey, B. and Sarma, M.K. (2010) Information source usage among motive-based segments of travelers to newly emerging tourist destinations. *Tourism Management* 31, 341–344.

Dillman, D.A. (2007) *Mail and Internet Surveys: The Tailored Design Method* (2nd edn). Hoboken, NJ: John Wiley Co.

Erl, T. (2005) *Service-Oriented Architecture: Concepts, Technology, and Design*. Upper Saddle River, NJ: Prentice Hall.

Eurostat (2000) *Community Methodology on Tourism Statistics*. Luxembourg: Office for the Official Publications of the European Communities.

Eurostat (2002) *Methodology of Short-Term Business Statistics: Interpretation and Guidelines*. Luxembourg: Office for the Official Publications of the European Communities.

Eurostat (2005a) *Quality Measures for Economic Indicators*. Luxembourg: Office for the Official Publications of the European Communities.

Eurostat (2005b) *Standard Quality Indicators*. Luxembourg: Office for the Official Publications of the European Communities.

Frank, A.U., Grum, E. and Vasseur, B. (2004) Procedure to select the best dataset for a task. In M.J. Egenhofer, C. Freksa and H.J. Miller (eds) *Geographic Information Science* (pp. 81–93). Berlin: Springer.

Furnham, A. (1986) Response bias, social desirability and dissimulation. *Personality and Individual Differences* 7 (3), 385–400.

Gruber, T.R. (1993) A translation approach to portable ontology specifications. *Knowledge Acquisition* 5 (2), 199–220.

Hair, J.F., Babin, B.J., Money, A.H. and Samouel, P. (2005) *Essentials of Business Research Methods*. Hoboken, NJ: John Wiley & Sons.

Harold, E.R. and Means, W.S. (2004) *XML in a Nutshell* (3rd edn). Sebastopol, CA: O'Reilly Media, Inc.

Hotelstars (2010) Catalogue of Criteria 2010–2014. Brussels: Hotelstars Union – HOTREC (Hotels, Restaurants & Cafés in Europe). See http://hotelstars.eu/userfiles/files/en/downloads/Criteria_2010-2014.pdf (accessed June 2010).

Hystad, P.W. and Keller, P.C. (2008) Towards a destination tourism disaster management framework: Long-term lessons from a forest fire disaster. *Tourism Management* 29 (1), 151–162.

IHRA (2004) The Joint WTO & IH&RA Study on Hotel Classification. Geneva, CH: International Hotel & Restaurant Association. See http://www.ih-ra.com/marketplace/WTO_IHRA_Hotel_classification_study.pdf (accessed June 2010).

Kent, R.A. (2001) *Data Construction and Data Analysis for Survey Research*. Basingstoke: Palgrave.

Laliberté, L., Grünewald, W. and Probst, L. (2004) Data Quality: A Comparison of IMF's Data Quality Assessment Framework (DQAF) and Eurostat's Quality Definition. Paper presented at the IMF/OECD Workshop Assessing and Improving Statistical Quality, Paris, 5–7 November 2003. See http://www.imf.org/external/pubs/ft/bop/2003/dataq.pdf (accessed June 2010).

Neuman, W.L. (2006) *Social Research Methods: Qualitative and Quantitative Approaches* (6th edn). Boston, MA: Pearson.

Osborne, J.W. (2012) *Best Practices in Data Cleaning: A Complete Guide to Everything You Need to Do Before and After Collecting Your Data*. London: Sage.

Pan, B. (2010) Online travel surveys and response patterns. *Journal of Travel Research* 49, 121–135.

Phillimore, J. and Goodson, L. (2004) *Qualitative Research in Tourism: Ontologies, Epistemologies and Methodologies*. London: Routledge.

Pipino, L.L., Lee, Y.W. and Wang, R.Y. (2002) Data quality assessment. *Communications of the ACM* 45 (4), 211–218.

Shoval, N. and Isaacson, M. (2010) *Tourist Mobility and Advanced Tracking Technologies*. New York: Routledge.

Smith, S.L.J. (1988) Tourism as an industry: Debates and concepts. In D. Ioannides and K.G. Debbage (eds) *The Economic Geography of the Tourist Industry: A Supply-Side Analysis* (pp. 31–52). London: Routledge.

Sonnenwald, D. (2007) Scientific collaboration. *Annual Review of Information Science and Technology* 41, 643–681.

UNSD (2010) International Recommendations for Tourism Statistics 2008. New York: United Nations – Department of Economic and Social Affairs – Statistics Division. See http://unstats.un.org/unsd/trade/IRTS/IRTS%202008%20unedited.pdf (accessed June 2010).

UNWTO (2000) *Basic References on Tourism Statistics*. Madrid: World Tourism Organization.

Vannan, E. (2001) Quality data: An improbable dream? *Educause Quarterly* 24 (1), 56–58.

Veal, A.J. (2006) *Research Methods for Leisure and Tourism: A Practical Guide* (3rd edn). Harlow: Financial Times – Prentice Hall/Pearson Education.

Wikipedia (2010) Simpson's paradox. See http://en.wikipedia.org/w/index.php?title=Simpson%27s_paradox (accessed 12 October).

Woodside, A.G. and Dubelaar, C. (2002) A general theory of tourism consumption systems: A conceptual framework and an empirical exploration. *Journal of Travel Research* 41 (2), 120–132.

Yin, R.K. (1994) *Case Study Research, Design and Methods* (2nd edn). London: Sage.

Zins, C. (2007) Conceptual approaches for defining data, information, and knowledge. *Journal of the American Society for Information Science and Technology* 58 (4), 479–493.

2 Testing Hypotheses and Comparing Samples

This chapter contains a review of the main concepts and techniques connected with statistical hypotheses testing. Issues regarding the power of tests and the effects of sample size are discussed. Also, bootstrap and meta-analysis as methods to improve the reliability of the outcomes are presented. A summary of the most commonly used statistical tests is included. The chapter closes with a description of different methods to assess similarity (or diversity) within and between samples.

Hypothesis testing is probably the most important and used practice in the analysis of empirical data. Even if usually a handful of tests is employed, hundreds of them have been implemented (Kanji, 2006; Sheskin, 2000). Each one has its own characteristics and applicability. The essential aim is to decide whether, given a certain assertion (hypothesis), it is probable that what we observe is in agreement with it, and in addition, to determine the reliability of this conclusion.

More formally, as any statistical textbook reports (Langley, 1971; Shao, 1999; Triola, 2009), a statistical test is a procedure to calculate the probability (p-value) of observing a given value in a specified population. A low probability is typically considered evidence that the observed value is drawn from a different population, but of course, it is also possible that the observed value is drawn from the population of interest, and simply represents a rare case. Whether you report the estimated p-value or conduct a test of statistical significance, studies should be designed to obtain the most accurate p-value with the highest reliability, given the context of the research. The classical approach aims to minimise two types of error: the error (Type I error) of accepting a hypothesis on the data when it is false and the error of failing to accept a hypothesis when it is actually true. Researchers who adopt the logic of formal hypothesis testing establish a null hypothesis (H_0), for example, that the means of two measurements are 'equal' (i.e. they concern elements coming from the same population), then compute the probability that the observed data depart from H_0, for example that the two observed means differ from one another. If the probability of departure from H_0 is lower than a set limit (the significance level α), we can reject the null hypothesis, and conclude that the evidence supports a claim that the observations come from a different population. If, on the other hand, the p-value is at or above α, there is a higher than acceptable chance that the observations are from the (same) population, and we are unable to reject the hypothesis of no difference (H_0). The probability of falsely concluding that a value comes from a given population when it does not (Type II error) is β, and the quantity $1-\beta$ is termed the *power* of the test. Power represents how 'good' (reliable) the test is at discriminating between different populations. Rather obviously, accepting a hypothesis does not necessarily mean that the null hypothesis is true, it only suggests that there is no statistical evidence against it in the data used to conduct the test. The situation is depicted in Table 2.1.

The algorithms used to calculate these probabilities are based on a (limited) number of elements, not least of which is a method of summarising the distribution of values in the population. If the values follow a known population distribution, such as the normal, t, chi-square, binomial or Poisson distribution, only one or two elements, known as population parameters, are needed to describe the population.

Despite the great number of tests, all hypothesis testing procedures follow a common path:

(1) Set a null hypothesis H_0. In the great majority of cases this is a hypothesis of the equality of two or more values. For example: in my destination, are the average expenses of German tourists equal to those of American visitors?
(2) Choose a significance level α. If we opt (as customarily done in the social sciences) for a 95% value, it means that we are ready to accept a maximum of $\alpha=5\%$ probability to commit a Type I error (i.e. reject H_0 when it is true). Often, this is expressed as a proportion: $\alpha=0.05=1/20$.[1]
(3) Consider the assumptions being made in doing the test. These can be assumptions about the statistical independence of the variables considered, or about the type of distribution of the population and the data collected. The latter consideration is a very important one as it guides the choice of the family of tests used. If the observations exhibit the shape of a known distribution, it is possible to use a so-called parametric test to compare specific values to values expected given the population parameter(s). If the data do not follow the distribution of a known distribution, or we do not want to make any assumption about it, a non-parametric test must be used.

Table 2.1 Statistical tests and possible errors

Inference from test	H_0 is true	H_0 is false
Do not reject H_0	Correct conclusion: $p=1-\alpha$	Type II error: error rate=β
Reject H_0	Type I error: error rate=α	Correct conclusion: $p=1-\beta$=power

(4) Choose the test and compute the relevant test statistic (*TS*). This belongs to a family of distributions having the number of degrees of freedom (*df*) as the parameter (with the exception of the *z*-test), that is the number of independent observations in a sample of data available to estimate a parameter[2] of the population from which that sample is drawn. For example, in a set of *n* observations, since one value (the arithmetic mean) has been calculated, *df*=*n*-1 when testing a hypothesis about the mean.

(5) Once *TS* and *df* have been calculated, it is possible to calculate (or read on an appropriate table) the *p*-value (the probability) associated with the test distribution for the given *df*.

(6) Now there are two ways to come to a conclusion, using *TS* and *CV* or using the *p*-value. H_0 is not rejected if *TS*<*CV* or the *p*-value is >α. If the opposite applies, H_0 can be rejected.

Although observed *p*-values (e.g. *p*=0.052) are increasingly reported, tests of statistical significance, based on the *p*-value, are common. Levels of significance may also be summarised by putting asterisks close to the *TS* calculated. Symbols commonly used in the social sciences, when α=0.05, are shown in Table 2.2.[3]

Table 2.2 *p*-Values and their interpretation, with α=0.05

p-Value	*Meaning*	*Symbol*
≥0.05	Not significant	ns
0.01 to <0.05	Statistically significant	*
0.001 to <0.01	Moderately significant	**
<0.001	Highly significant	***

The procedure described above can also provide a guide to reporting the results of a test. Besides means and standard deviations (SD), all the important values should be given. One example is the following (following the *APA Manual* [5th edn]., 2001):

A study compared the average expenses made by German and American tourists at the destination and found that there is a significant difference (*t*=2.22, *df*=40, *p*=0.03). German tourists spent 79.71 (*SD*=11.57) euro while Americans spent 70.92 (*SD*=13.64) euro.

With complete information about the sample size (in the above example *n*=*df*+2) and the statistics calculated, it is also possible to rework the test calculations if needed (Appendix 1 contains the formulas for the most commonly used statistical tests).

Reporting actual, rather than summarised, *p*-values is particularly useful in limit cases, i.e. cases where the *p*-value is ≈α. If the *p*-value is much higher or much lower than α, it is easy to decide if a value is likely to differ from expected population values. When, however, the p-value is $\approx\alpha$, such a decision can be disputed, and the actual p-value gives a clearer indication of the reliability of possible conclusions. The actual value might also suggest ways to improve reliability, for example, by increasing the sample size or by performing several different tests to check their agreement.

One important issue in performing a statistical test is whether to use a one-tailed or a two-tailed test of significance. The controversy on this issue is quite passionate, and many papers and books have analysed and discussed the problem. A full discussion is outside the scope of this work, but it is important to note a few key points. The distinction has important practical implications. The probability that A and B are only different (two-tailed) is twice as large as the probability that A is higher (or lower) than B (one-tailed). To be equivalent, the significance level set for a one-tailed test must be one half of that which would be used in a two-tailed test. For example, sentences such as: 'difference in means was significant at $\alpha=0.05$ for the one-tailed test', translated into a two-tailed wording would imply a 0.1 significance level. The hypothesis set by the researcher will guide in choosing the type of test, but it is advisable to use a one-tailed test only when a statistically significant change in the opposite direction would not have any influence at all (which is seldom the case). Moreover, the 'p-value' interpretation is generally simpler in a two-tailed test, the outcomes are more conservative and the meaning when more than two variables are compared is inappropriate.

Parametric and Non-Parametric Tests

Usually, the most stringent assumption on the data concerns their distribution. As noted earlier, when data are normally distributed, parametric tests are used. Actually, parametric tests are often robust enough to provide meaningful results even when the normality of the data is questionable. Non-parametric tests are normally considered to have lower discrimination power, particularly when the sample size is small. In any case, the use of modern statistical software makes it relatively easy to perform both types of tests on the same data and compare the results. All widely used parametric tests have their non-parametric equivalent (see Table 2.3). For a thorough discussion of non-parametric tests, the reader may browse Siegel and Castellan (1988) or Sheskin (2000).

One more possibility is the transformation of the original variables via a suitable function (often logarithmic or square root) in order to increase the 'normality'. It is thus possible to use (if the results of the transformation are favourable) a parametric test. However, it must be noted that the test outcomes will apply to the transformed variables rather than the actual measurements, and the back transformation of the results and its interpretation might be problematic.

Table 2.3 Common parametric tests and non-parametric equivalents

Type of test	Parametric test	Non-parametric test
1-Sample	t-test	Wilcoxon signed rank
2-Sample	t-test	Wilcoxon 2-sample rank-sum, Mann–Whitney U
Paired sample	Paired t-test	Wilcoxon signed rank
>2 Samples	1-Way ANOVA	Kruskal–Wallis
Distribution	Chi-square	Kolmogorov–Smirnov
Correlation	Pearson's r	Spearman's rho, Kendall's tau-b

Example: Statistical hypothesis testing

Let us consider the following data. We begin with a set of observations of the satisfaction of tourists before and after the refurbishment of a hotel. Satisfaction is assessed through a questionnaire and evaluated on a scale from 1 (minimum) to 10 (maximum). The question we want to answer is whether satisfaction has increased or our refurbishment had no effect.

The null hypothesis is that the average satisfaction levels are the same before and after (H_0: mean$_{BEFORE}$=mean$_{AFTER}$).

The mean evaluation *Before* is mean$_{BEFORE}$=6.97 with SD=0.99; the mean evaluation *After* is mean$_{AFTER}$=7.02 with SD=1.06; in both cases, 109 evaluations were collected.

A look at the distributions creates doubts about the normality of the two distributions (Figure 2.1); therefore, two tests are performed: a paired samples *t*-test (parametric) and a Wilcoxon signed rank test

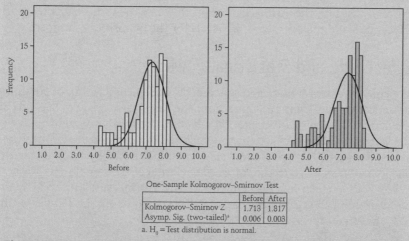

One-Sample Kolmogorov–Smirnov Test	Before	After
Kolmogorov–Smirnov Z	1.713	1.817
Asymp. Sig. (two-tailed)[a]	0.006	0.003

a. H_0 = Test distribution is normal.

Figure 2.1 Frequency distributions for the *Before* and *After* evaluations. A reference normal curve is superimposed and the results of a Kolmogorov–Smirnov normality test are reported (non-parametric). All calculations are done with SPSS (note that SPSS uses the term Sig. or Asymp. Sig. to report the p-value).

As can be seen (Figure 2.2), both tests agree in suggesting the rejection of H_0 and allow us to conclude that the difference in evaluations is significant (at the 95% level) and that the satisfaction of our customers really increased after the refurbishment.

When the results of the two tests do not agree, the most appropriate to the situation should be chosen (i.e. a non-parametric test for non-normally distributed data, a parametric one for normal data).

Paired Samples t-test					Wilcoxon Signed Ranks Test Statistics	
	t	dt	Sig. (two-tailed)			Before – After
Pair 1 Before – After	–2.576	108	0.011		Z	–2.320
					Asymp. Sig. (two-tailed)	0.020

Figure 2.2 Test results

It must be noted here also that a number of issues have been raised on the use of p-values alone in measuring the strength of evidence against a null hypothesis (see e.g. Halsey et al., 2015 or Nuzzo, 2014). The American Statistical Association (ASA) has even released a statement on statistical significance and p-values, clearly affirming that by itself, a p-value does not provide a good measure of evidence regarding a model or hypothesis (Wasserstein & Lazar, 2016), and some journals, mainly in the field of medicine and psychology, have announced that they would no longer publish papers containing p-values alone. The common suggestion is to complete the analysis with the estimation of the power of the tests conducted, their effect sizes and the confidence intervals for the quantities examined.

Effect Size and Statistical Power

The power of a statistical test is, essentially, the probability of obtaining statistically significant outcomes from the calculations. Power depends on the statistical significance criterion adopted, the reliability and the size of the sample used and the extent to which the phenomenon to be measured exists. This latter is called effect size and is computed by normalising the phenomenon assessed to the standard deviation of the sample data (Cohen, 1988). For example, in a one sample t-test, if the measured mean is $\bar{x}$, the population mean is μ and the data standard deviation of the sample means is $s_{\bar{x}}$, the effect size is

$$ES = \frac{\bar{x} - \mu}{s_{\bar{x}}}$$

Being normalised, *ES* varies between 0 (no effect) and 1, and usually the terms small, medium and large are assigned to effect sizes of, respectively, 0.2, 0.5, 0.8. Several methods for calculating effect sizes for the most used statistical tests have been proposed. The reader can consult Cohen's (1988) book: *Statistical Power Analysis for the Behavioral Sciences* for more details.

Larger effect sizes are more readily detected than smaller ones giving greater statistical power.

The statistical power is the probability (therefore measured on a scale from 0 to 1) of rejecting the null hypothesis when it is false. In essence, it measures a test's ability to reject H_0 when it should be rejected. For example, when we consider a situation in which we want to assess whether a certain segment of tourists prefers to engage in a certain activity while visiting a resort. To do so, we compare the time that tourists in the segment of interest spent in performing this activity with the average of all the other visitors. The power of the test we perform is the probability of finding a significant difference between the two groups. If, for example, we find a power of 0.75, it means that conducting the same study several times, in 75% of the cases we are likely to find a statistically significant difference. On the other hand, 25% of the tests will give a non-significant result. The commonly accepted standard for power is 0.8 (Fisher, 1935).

The actual statistical power of an analysis can only be calculated once all data have been obtained. Nonetheless, statistical power calculations are very useful when done before conducting a study. Pre-study power calculations are particularly useful for identifying the size of the sample needed to achieve the objective of each analysis, given the expected effect size and the statistical test that will be used. Because most studies use multivariate data and include multiple analyses, it is important to estimate the minimum sample size for the most complex analysis with the smallest expected effect size. When multiple analyses are to be conducted, the minimum sample size calculated for a single analysis should be adjusted (upwards) because multiple analyses increase the probability of Type I error.

Statistical power calculations can be performed using software available for this purpose.

Example: Statistical power calculation

The following calculation has been worked out by using *G*Power 3*, a freeware program available at: http://www.psycho.uni-duesseldorf.de/abteilungen/aap/gpower3/.

Let us consider the study reported about the spending of German and American tourists at a destination. The results were: German tourists' mean expenditure €79.71 (SD=11.57), American tourists' mean expenditure €70.92 (SD=13.64), a *t*-test with *df*=40 was used.

$G*Power$ 3 allows calculation of the effect size from these values: $d=0.52$ (a medium effect) and the power $p=0.89$ for the calculated $t=2.02$. In this case, we conclude that, even with a relatively small sample, the test is powerful enough to discriminate between the two groups (see Figure 2.3).

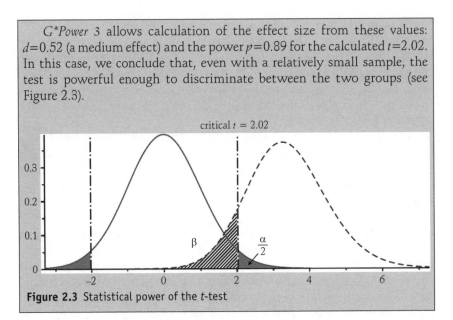

Figure 2.3 Statistical power of the t-test

Sample Size and Significance

A major determinant of the statistical power of a test is the size of the sample used. And generally, the sample size is crucial in ensuring the possibility of finding statistically significant results. Moreover, a reasonable sample size will provide a low margin of error to the confidence limits of the quantity measured in an empirical investigation. It is important to note that 'statistically significant' is not to be confused with the common language meaning of significance. It is possible to find two samples which are (statistically) significantly different from each other but with a difference so small as to be of no practical value.

Sample size calculations are well described in many textbooks (Cochran, 1977; Triola, 2009), where formulas and tables can be found which help in planning an experiment or in evaluating the significance and the margin of error of the calculated statistics. For example, a quick calculation can be performed by using the values reported in Table 2.4. Besides that, a prior power calculation will give a good estimate of the size of the sample needed to achieve a desired result.

Collecting data can be a long, hard and expensive task. It is not always possible to reach the ideal size, and cost, opportunity or feasibility may hinder the assembly of the desired number of observations. This problem is well known in many disciplines, mainly in those where the replicability of the measurements is problematic (astronomy and astrophysics, for example). In these cases, several methods to derive confidence levels for

Table 2.4 Sample size calculation for a normally distributed population with mean µ and standard deviation σ, for margin of error E

	α			
	0.10	0.05	0.01	0.001
z_α	1.6449	1.9600	2.5758	3.2905
Parameter	*Estimate*	*Sample size (n)*		
µ	$\bar{x}$	$n = \left(\dfrac{z_\alpha \cdot \sigma}{E} \right)^2$		
$\mu_1 - \mu_2$	$\bar{x}_1 - \bar{x}_2$	$n_1 = n_2 = \dfrac{(z_\alpha)^2 \left(\sigma_1^2 + \sigma_2^2 \right)}{E^2}$		

Source: Adapted from Zwillinger and Kokoska (2000: 204).

observations with a very limited number of events have been formulated (Gehrels, 1986; Regener, 1951). There are several practical possibilities to increase the confidence levels of the statistics calculated from a series of observations. Two examples are discussed in the following sections. The first one derives the confidence levels from the data collected, the second one involves the gathering of similar data from different studies.

Bootstrap

Bootstrapping, introduced by Bradley Efron (1979; Efron & Tibshirani, 1993), is a method for estimating the sampling distribution of a parameter[1] by resampling with replacement from the original sample. The method allows a researcher to obtain an approximation of the distribution of the parameter, in the absence of prior information about its true distribution or of the original data (Davison & Hinkley, 1997).

The basic idea is that, in the absence of any other information about a population, the values in a random sample are the best approximation to the population's distribution. Resampling the sample is therefore the best approximation to what can be expected when resampling the population. In other words, the uncertainty of an estimate is assessed by the uncertainty calculated from estimates obtained by resampled sets of data. Given a sample of size n, a large number (usually 1500–2000) of new sets are generated by drawing, with replacement, m observations from the original sample (m can also be equal to n, but that would defeat the purpose of the bootstrap). It must be noted that since the new sets are sampled with replacement, some observed values can appear more than once, and some can be missing. For each new data set, the parameter is calculated.

The resulting empirical distribution of the values is used to approximate its true distribution.

In other words, given a set of independent observations x_1, x_2,... x_n, a parameter that can be defined as some function Φ (mean or median, for example) of the values in the population and a statistic that is the same function of the observations, the bootstrap procedure estimates the sampling distribution of that function. Bootstrap samples are repeatedly drawn and the parameter (e.g. mean or median) is evaluated for each bootstrap sample, giving a set of values Φ'_{B1}, Φ'_{B2},..., Φ'_{Bn}. The empirical distribution of these bootstrap values is an estimate of the theoretical sampling distribution and is used to estimate standard errors or to construct a confidence interval.

Standard parametric confidence intervals can provide a measure of significance. They require, however, the acceptance of normality assumptions and a large sample size for their validity. With the bootstrap method, it is possible to calculate the confidence interval of the parameter estimated from the distribution generated by the replications, without being forced to accept other assumptions (e.g. normality). Usually, the percentile confidence interval method is used. The $1-\alpha$ confidence interval for the parameter is given by the $\alpha/2$ and $1-\alpha/2$ quantiles of the distribution calculated.

Bootstrap methods have seen many applications in several fields and have proved a useful means for sample size determination based on pilot experiments in the preparation of large surveys (Mak, 2004). In tourism studies, these techniques have been successfully used in the determination of tourist spending (English, 2000; Pol et al., 2006) in evaluation of the quality characteristics of websites (Antonioli Corigliano & Baggio, 2006).

Example: Bootstrap calculations

Let us consider a situation in which the evaluations for a certain resort were collected from a small sample of visitors (50 observations). The evaluations are calculated by averaging the answers to a questionnaire and are measured on a scale from 1 (minimum) to 10.

The sample mean is 5.89, with SD=1.95, the median is 5.8; Figure 2.4 shows the frequency distribution of the evaluations.

Now, let us apply a bootstrap procedure. The data are resampled (with repetition) 1000 times. In other words, 1000 different arrangements of the original sample are generated. For each sample, the arithmetic mean and the variance of the values obtained are calculated. Figure 2.5 shows the frequency distribution of the 1000 means. As can be seen, the resulting histogram (Figure 2.5) follows a normal distribution well. The mean calculated is 5.88 with SD=0.27 and a standard error=0.0087. The 0.05 confidence interval is [5.34, 6.43], with a standard error=0.042.

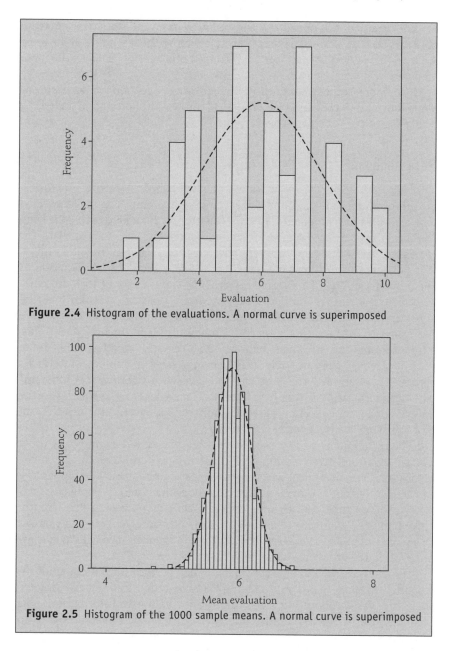

Figure 2.4 Histogram of the evaluations. A normal curve is superimposed

Figure 2.5 Histogram of the 1000 sample means. A normal curve is superimposed

The bootstrap procedure is sometimes described as computationally intensive, although with modern computers an example such as the one discussed above requires only a few seconds. It is true, however, that without appropriate software the method is practically unusable.

Bootstrap options or add-ons can be found in several statistical software packages such as SPSS. SPSS users can also refer to the Raynald's SPSS Tools Archive (http://www.spsstools.net/) to find other scripts to perform these analyses.

One more source, containing an extensive selection of both stand-alone and online programs for statistical analyses (bootstrap included), is available at http://statpages.org/.

Meta-analysis

There are many cases in which the published literature provides a wealth of studies on the same subject and several empirical investigations assess similar measurements. In this situation, it may be worth collecting these results and deriving a summary measurement. The idea is that, if it is possible to find several different investigations using different samples, it is possible to think of having a *mega sample*, which is a combination of the different studies. This would increase the significance of the outcomes.

Obviously, things are not that easy and a number of issues must be considered. A series of statistical methods, known as meta-analysis, have been devised to face this problem. Combining experimental results has long interested statisticians (Cochran, 1937; Fisher, 1935; Newcomb, 1886; Pearson, 1904), but only relatively recently have a number of scholars thoroughly examined the problem and devised a rigorous methodology. The term *meta-analysis* was first used by Gene Glass (1976) to refer to the analysis of a large collection of results from individual studies with the aim of integrating the findings.

The technique is widely used in health sciences, but examples in other disciplines are relatively common, mainly in all those cases in which the replication of an experiment with large sample sizes is impossible or impractical. In the field of tourism, meta-analytic methods are not very popular even if a few good examples exist (Brander *et al.*, 2007; Brons *et al.*, 2002; Crouch, 1995; Lim, 1999). However, taken with some precautions, meta-analysis can be a powerful tool to synthesise results from different studies which, in some areas, often tend to replicate the same lines of investigation.

Two main issues must be considered when performing a meta-analysis. The first one is that by 'averaging' simple numerical representations, there is a risk of obscuring some important qualitative information. The second concerns the availability and the choice of the research reports to be considered.

A meta-analysis follows, by and large, the same steps as primary research. Once the objective of the investigation has been set, the researcher locates and selects a set of studies that meet the specified criteria for inclusion. Normally, this means including comprehensive reviews or deep empirical investigations on the topic of interest. After that, data are collected from the published works and the outcomes are transformed to some common metric in order to ease the comparison. A metric often used is the effect size. Finally, statistical methods are used to assess the relationships among study characteristics and findings, their homogeneity and the overall significance of the combined results.

The final combination of the results is typically a weighted average of the collected values. Several weighting criteria are available (Hartung *et al.*, 2008; Hedges & Olkin, 1985; Rao, 2004).

The choice of studies to be included in a meta-analytic study is a crucial point. Obviously, all the important numerical values must be present or it must be possible to deduce them from the published data (effect sizes, for example).

One major problem is the so-called file-drawer effect. There can be a bias in published studies because people performing a study and failing to find significant outcomes are much less likely to publish their results than if they find statistically significant results. The effect is important. Significant usually means that there is a probability ($p<0.05$) that the results are due to pure statistical fluctuations (and therefore they do not show a 'real' effect). Therefore, we may expect (over a large number of cases) that 5% of the studies will show a significant effect even if that effect does not exist. Besides conducting thorough investigations before gathering works to be used in a meta-analytic study, a simple graphical test can be done to assess the completeness of the data collected. Publication biases or systematic heterogeneities can be highlighted by using a funnel plot. This consists of a scatter plot showing the empirical data collected against some measure of the study size. If the resulting picture is symmetric, it is possible to conclude that the set of data collected is 'well-behaved' and biases are unlikely. On the contrary, if strong asymmetries (or heterogeneities) are present, there is a high probability that some kind of relationship between effects and study size exist, suggesting the possibility of a file-drawer effect or systematic differences between smaller and larger studies. Whatever the cause, asymmetric funnel plots indicate that simple meta-analyses can be problematic for the significance of their outcomes and recommend deeper investigations.

Many possible measures of study size have been proposed, such as sample size, standard error of the effect or inverse variance of the effect. Sterne and Egger (2001), after having compared several metrics, recommend the standard error as best choice. In this case, straight lines may be drawn as guidance to the eye. The effect reported is usually standardised to ease the comparison. Funnel plots are traditionally drawn with the effect measure on the horizontal axis. An example is provided in Figure 2.6, which shows a symmetric funnel plot along with an example of a *problematic* diagram.

Figure 2.6(a) shows a situation which can be considered ideal: the plot is highly symmetric meaning that the data collected do not suffer from biases and can be used as a basis for some combination study. Figure 2.6(b), however, shows a marked asymmetry. Clearly, many values are missing on the left-hand portion of the plot. When using these data for a meta-analysis, the results risk suffering from a biased view of the phenomenon under study.

If a rigorous scrutiny of the literature has not provided a way to overcome this situation, the missing data can be interpolated by using some simulation technique. A practical proposal, for example, is the one put forward by Duval and Tweedie (2000). The authors use a *trim-and-fill* method which allows the missing values to be inferred in order to obtain a reasonable sample of values to examine. After having estimated the number of studies in the asymmetric part of the funnel plot, the asymmetric outlying part is trimmed off. Then, the symmetric remainder is used to estimate the true centre of the plot. The trimmed studies and their missing counterparts are finally replaced around the centre. The final estimate of the true mean and its variance are based on the filled plot. This technique uses only minimal symmetry assumptions and an iterative approach which is relatively easy to put into practice to estimate the number of missing studies.

Although the calculations involved in a meta-analysis (such as those of the example which follows) can be implemented with little difficulty in a standard spreadsheet program, a number of dedicated programs exist. Examples are Meta-Stat by Rudner, Glass, Evartt and Emery, available at: http://echo.edres.org:8080/meta/metastat.htm; Meta-Analysis by Schwarzer, available at: http://userpage.fu-berlin.de/health/meta_e.htm; MIX (an Excel add-in) by Bax, Yu, Ikeda, Tsuruta and Moons, available at: http://mix-for-meta-analysis.info. Additionally, scripts and macros can be found online for the major commercial statistical software such as SPSS, STATA and SAS.

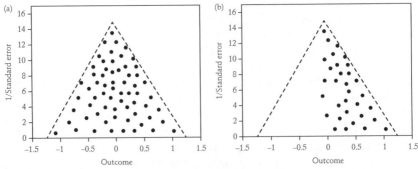

Figure 2.6 Funnel plots showing standardised outcomes and the inverse of standard errors: (a) a symmetric, unbiased collection of data; (b) a plot showing clear asymmetry

Example: Combining observations

Let us now work out an example. Suppose the objective of the study is to assess whether a certain series of marketing activities can improve the length of stay of tourists at a destination. A survey of the literature locates a number of studies which are judged to be quite similar to the objective of the study. Table 2.5 shows the data collected. For each study, the following values have been reported: effect (MD: mean difference of the length of stay before and after the actions), standard error (SE), p-value from the t-tests (p: significance of the result) and the effect size (ES). All the values have been transformed to bring them to a common scale; in a few cases, effect sizes were not explicitly reported and were calculated from the available data.

A funnel plot drawn by using the inverse standard error and the standardised (to the sample collected) value of the effect shows no particular asymmetry. Therefore, our data can be directly used for a meta-analysis without further treatment (Figure 2.7).

For the whole analysis, values will be calculated as weighted averages where the weights are based on the standard errors of the observed values:

$$w = \frac{1}{SE^2}$$

First of all, the overall effect is calculated as: $MD_{all} = (\sum_i w_i MD_i / \sum_i w_i) = 1.75$. Its standard error will be $SE_{MD} = \sqrt{1/\sum_i w_i} = 0.13$. To calculate the overall p-value in order to establish the significance of the combined effect, it is possible to use Fisher's test (Rao, 2004). If k independent studies report $p_1, p_2, \ldots, p_k$ p-values, the quantity $P = \sum_{i=1}^{k} -2\ln p_i$ is χ^2 distributed with $2k$ degrees of freedom. For our example, this gives $P=51.31$, which corresponds to a p-value $<10^{-4}$ giving a very good significance level for our combined result.

Table 2.5 Data collected for the meta-analysis

Study	Effect (MD)	Std error (se)	p-Value (p)	Effect size (ES)
1	1.56	0.42	0.23	0.27
2	1.78	0.40	0.05	0.28
3	1.85	0.44	0.58	0.36
4	2.16	0.45	0.04	0.44
5	1.43	0.45	0.05	0.29
6	1.73	0.42	0.09	0.31
7	1.70	0.45	0.01	0.35
8	1.73	0.37	0.04	0.23
9	1.96	0.42	0.10	0.34
10	1.66	0.38	0.15	0.25

The same weighted calculation can be performed to obtain the overall effect size:

$\mathrm{ES}_{\mathrm{all}} = (\sum_i w_i \mathrm{ES}_i / \sum_i w_i) = 0.31$ with a standard error $\mathrm{SE}_{\mathrm{ES}} = 0.13$. The 95% confidence interval for the combined effect size will be $\mathrm{ES}_{\mathrm{all}} \pm 1.96\ \mathrm{SE}_{\mathrm{ES}}$, that is: $0.05...0.57$. The z-test for the combined effect size gives: $z = \mathrm{ES}_{\mathrm{all}} / \mathrm{SE}_{\mathrm{ES}} = 2.32$, which gives a p-value (two-tailed)$=0.02$.

The homogeneity test assesses the hypothesis that the effect sizes are estimating the same population. In other words, the set of studies used can be assumed to be a series of studies conducted on different samples from the same population. If this assumption is accepted, the calculated overall ES can be considered a good estimator of the distribution.

The Q-test can be used in our example (Hedges & Olkin, 1985). The Q-statistic for a set of k effect sizes is $Q = \sum_{i=1}^{k} w_i \mathrm{ES}_i^2 - ((\sum_{i=1}^{k} w_i \mathrm{ES}_i)^2 / \sum_{i=1}^{k} w_i)$. Q is χ^2 distributed with $k-1$ degrees of freedom. In our example, $Q=11.02$, $df=9$, the critical value at $p=0.05$ is $\chi^2=16.92$; therefore, the examined set of values can be considered to be homogeneous.

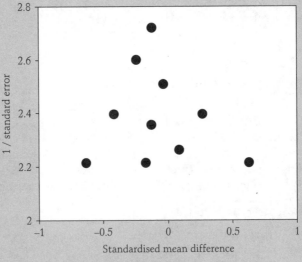

Figure 2.7 Funnel plot for the data in Table 2.5

A Summary of Statistical Tests

The most commonly used statistical tests are summarised below (adapted from Wikipedia, Statistical hypothesis testing: http://en.wikipedia.org/wiki/Statistical_hypothesis_testing).

Name	Formula	Assumptions or notes
One-sample z-test	$$z = \frac{\bar{x} - \mu_0}{\sigma / \sqrt{n}}$$	Normal population or $n > 30$; σ known
Two-sample z-test	$$z = \frac{(\bar{x}_1 - \bar{x}_2) - (\mu_1 - \mu_2)_0}{\sqrt{\dfrac{\sigma_1}{n_1} + \dfrac{\sigma_2}{n_2}}}$$	Normal population; independent observations; both σ_1 and σ_2 known
One-sample t-test	$$t = \frac{\bar{x} - \mu_0}{s / \sqrt{n}}; \quad df = n - 1$$	Normal population or $n > 30$; σ unknown
Paired t-test	$$t = \frac{\bar{d} - d_0}{s_d / \sqrt{n}}; \quad df = n - 1$$	Normal population of differences or $n > 30$; σ unknown
Two-sample pooled t-test, equal variances	$$t = \frac{(\bar{x}_1 - \bar{x}_2) - (\mu_1 - \mu_2)_0}{s_d \sqrt{\dfrac{1}{n_1} + \dfrac{1}{n_2}}}$$ $$s_d^2 = \frac{(n_1 - 1)s_1^2 + (n_2 - 1)s_2^2}{n_1 + n_2 - 2}$$ $$df = n_1 + n_2 - 2$$	Normal populations or $n_1 + n_2 > 40$; independent observations; $\sigma_1 = \sigma_2$
Two-sample unpooled t-test, unequal variances	$$t = \frac{(\bar{x}_1 - \bar{x}_2) - (\mu_1 - \mu_2)_0}{\sqrt{\dfrac{s_1^2}{n_1} + \dfrac{s_2^2}{n_2}}}$$ $$df = \frac{\left(\dfrac{s_1^2}{n_1} + \dfrac{s_2^2}{n_2}\right)^2}{\dfrac{\left(\dfrac{s_1^2}{n_1}\right)^2}{n_1 - 1} + \dfrac{\left(\dfrac{s_2^2}{n_2}\right)^2}{n_2 - 1}}$$	Normal populations or $n_1 + n_2 > 40$; independent observations; $\sigma_1 \neq \sigma_2$

Chi-square test	$$\chi^2 = \sum_i \frac{(o_i - e_i)^2}{e_i}; \quad \chi^2 = \frac{(n-1)s^2}{\sigma_0^2}$$	Expected counts are at least 5 or expected counts are >1 and no more that 20% of expected counts are less than 5
Definition of symbols in this table	suffix 0 refers to H_0 α, probability of Type I error n=sample size n_1=sample 1 size n_2=sample 2 size $\bar{x}$ =sample mean μ_0=hypothesised population mean μ_1=population 1 mean μ_2=population 2 mean σ=population standard deviation σ^2=population variance s=sample standard deviation s^2=sample variance s_1^2 =sample 1 variance s_2^2 =sample 2 variance t=t statistic df=degrees of freedom d=sample mean of differences d_0=hypothesized population mean difference s_d=standard deviation of differences χ^2=Chi-square statistic o_i=observed values e_i=expected values	

Similarity and Dissimilarity Measures

Besides testing hypotheses, there are times when it is useful or important to assess the uniformity of values in a group of measurements or the similarity between different groups. A seemingly bewildering number of metrics is available. Most come from the biological and ecological sciences, where it is important to gauge the number and diversity of species present in an ecosystem, and their variations, and are then adopted in other fields (see e.g. Boriah, 2008; Boyle, 1990; Cha, 2007; Choi, 2010; Wolda, 1981).

In general terms, a similarity index is used to assess the uniformity of the measurements in a single series of data, to compare different partitions (clusterings) of a data set or to find matches between different series of measures (e.g. preference profiles for customers, patterns in pictures and semantic content of texts). Similarity indexes are often interpreted in terms of diversity, difference, distance or variation between cases, so the very same index might be described as a similarity index, a diversity index, a distance measure or another term suited to the context in which it is used and the manner in which it is calculated. Here, we provide a limited set of examples for the most widely known and used metrics.

Similarity measures for a single sample

The first group of measures provides an evaluation of the homogeneity (similarity) of measurements in a single sample.

Gini coefficient: Widely used in economics to measure the inequality of the distribution of a value or score. It is used by statistical agencies to measure income inequality in a country, but it can be used to measure inequality (or similarity) on any metric variable in any situation. It is typically calculated so that values for different populations or groups can be compared on a scale from 0 (perfect equality) to 100 (complete inequality), e.g. in 2013, the income inequality for Iceland was 24 (low) (OECD, 2016) and for South Africa 62.5 (CIA, 2016). This Gini index is calculated as the relative (average) mean difference, i.e. the mean of the differences between every possible pair of data points in the sample, divided by the sample size and mean:

$$G = \frac{\sum_i \sum_j |x_i - x_j|}{2n^2 \mu}$$

where x_i and x_j are the data values, n is the number of cases in the sample and μ is the sample mean (G is naturally normalised).

Herfindahl–Hirschman index (HHI): Typically used for measuring concentration (e.g. market share). Its raw form is given on a 0–10,000 scale, where 0 means that all cases (e.g. businesses) have equal share and higher values indicate different degrees of concentration, interpreted according to the context (e.g. values below 1500 unconcentrated; 1500–2500 moderately concentrated; above 2500 concentrated [US DOJ, 2010]). In this form, the HHI is calculated as

$$HHI = \sum_i (q_i \cdot 100)^2$$

where q_i are the shares possessed by the i elements under consideration.

HHI can be normalised to permit comparison. Given by N values with mean μ and standard deviation σ, the normalised HHI (HHI*) is

$$HHI^* = \frac{1}{N-1} \frac{\sigma^2}{\mu^2}$$

In this form, HHI* is actually a squared coefficient of variation divided by the adjusted sample size, N–1.

Shannon index: Accounts for both the abundance and evenness (equality of distribution) of the values considered. Although derived from information theory, it is widely used in the biological and environmental sciences, e.g. abundance can be interpreted as the richness of an environment in terms of total number of species present and evenness is interpreted as the relative number of members of each species. It is typically calculated as a normalisation of Shannon entropy so that its values range from 0 (uniformity) to 1 (maximum diversity). The formula is

$$\text{SH}^* = 1 - \frac{\sum_i p(x_i) \cdot \ln p(x_i)}{\ln N}$$

where $p(x_i)$ is the proportion (or the probability) of each value, x_i (species, group) is the sample under consideration and N is the number of observations.

Example: Assessing seasonality

Let us consider the seasonality of a tourism destination. For planning purposes, we are interested in assessing to what extent a place receives tourists uniformly throughout the year. This can be done by using one or more of the indices defined above. Figure 2.8 and Table 2.6 provide the

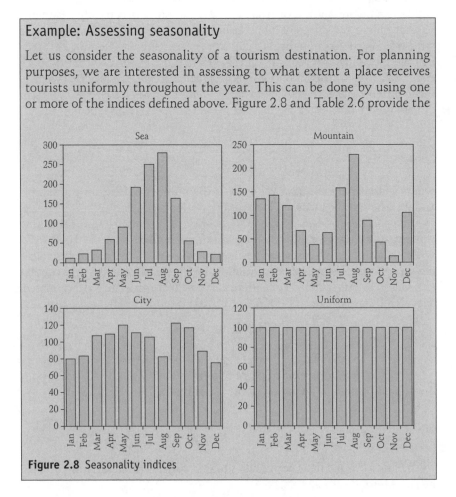

Figure 2.8 Seasonality indices

seasonality indices for three destinations (a seaside location, a mountain destination and a city) along with a uniform distribution used as a comparison.

Using the above formulas (SH* is calculated by using the values provided divided by their sum), we calculate the different indices. Results are shown in Table 2.7. It can be easily seen that the indices have different sensitivity to the distributions considered. They allow, however, the same conclusions to be derived.

Table 2.6 Seasonality indices

	Sea	Mountain	City	Uniform
Jan	10	135	79	100
Feb	22	143	83	100
Mar	32	120	107	100
Apr	58	67	109	100
May	90	37	120	100
Jun	192	62	111	100
Jul	250	158	106	100
Aug	280	229	82	100
Sep	164	89	122	100
Oct	55	42	117	100
Nov	27	13	89	100
Dec	20	105	75	100

Table 2.7 Diversity indices

	Sea	Mountain	City	Uniform
G	0.492	0.327	0.092	0
HHI*	0.077	0.031	0.002	0
SH*	0.164	0.072	0.006	0

Similarity measures for two or more samples

Besides evaluating the uniformity of a sample of values, we may be interested in comparing different samples. Similarity (distance) measures are also used to group similar cases or samples into clusters, as outlined in Chapter 4.

The general idea is to define a series of features or attributes for an element (traveller, hotel, market segment, destination) and assign values (no matter what type: ordinal, categorical or scale) for each attribute to each case or group of cases (groups are represented by summary statistics appropriate to the level of measurement). The series of values can be seen as the coordinates of a point that locates each case or group in an n-dimensional space. It is then possible to define distances between the points or between the points and a central position.[4] The smaller the distance between cases or groups, the more similar they are. A distance d can be transformed to a similarity score s by using $s=1/(1+d)$.

In the following, we consider two vectors: $x_1=(x_{11}, x_{12}, x_{13},..., x_{1p})$ and $x_2=(x_{21}, x_{22}, x_{23},..., x_{2p})$. The following are the most used and known similarity (distance) metrics.

Euclidean distance: It is the basis for many other metrics. The distance is given by

$$ED = \sqrt{\sum_p (x_{1p} - x_{2p})^2}$$

A similarity score can be calculated as: EDs=1/(1+ED). The formula makes no adjustment for differences in scale between values or vectors; therefore, when scales differ, it is advisable to use standardised values.

Cosine similarity: Measures the similarity between two vectors by calculating the cosine of the angle between them. Two vectors with the same orientation have a cosine similarity of 1, two vectors at 90° have a similarity of 0 and two vectors diametrically opposed have a similarity of –1, independent of their magnitude. Cosine similarity is calculated as

$$COs = \frac{\sum_p x_{1p} \cdot x_{2p}}{\sqrt{\sum_p x_{1p}^2} \sqrt{\sum_p x_{2p}^2}}$$

Jaccard index: Assesses the diversity in content between two sets of elements. It is calculated as

$$JC = \frac{X \cap Y}{X \cup Y}$$

where the numerator is the intersection between the two sets (i.e. the number of elements belonging to both sets) divided by the union of the sample sets (i.e. the number of elements common to both sets). When the two sets are vectors of real numbers, a generalised form can be used:

$$JCs = \frac{\sum_p \min(x_{1p}, x_{2p})}{\sum_p \max(x_{1p}, x_{2p})}$$

Example: Similarity of tourist profiles

Three groups of tourists have expressed their interest in a number of activities on a 1–5 scale (5=max) as shown in Table 2.8.

Similarity between the groups can be assessed by calculating index scores for all possible pairs: (A,B), (A,C) and (B,C), as shown in Table 2.9.

As Table 2.10 shows, the ranking across the indices is homogeneous, only the range of scores and the proportional difference between them change.

Table 2.8 Interest in tourism activities, three groups of tourists

Group	Culture	Events	Food & Wine	Nature	Relax	Shopping	Sport
A	5	1	4	3	2	5	4
B	2	1	5	5	4	4	5
C	4	3	2	1	2	5	1

Table 2.9 Three indices of similarity between three groups of tourists

(Values)	EDs	COs	JCs
AB	0.141	0.788	0.500
AC	0.179	0.886	0.679
BC	0.164	0.841	0.571

Note: Higher values indicate higher similarity.

Table 2.10 Similarity between three groups of tourists, ranked

(Ranks)	EDs	COs	JCs
AB	3	3	3
AC	1	1	1
BC	2	2	2

Note: 1 is most similar.

Mahalanobis Distance and Multivariate Outlier Detection

The Mahalanobis distance, d^2, is used in many fields to model the distances (or similarities) between objects (cases) measured on multiple attributes (variables). In tourism and management research, it is often used to identify multivariate outliers, i.e. cases which vary so greatly from the other cases in a data set across a set of variables of interest that they should be treated as outliers.

More formally, the Mahalanobis distance is a measure of multivariate normality, calculated by comparing the vector of case values on each variable (p) with a multivariate normal distribution with a vector of the variable means (μ) and the associated covariance matrix (Σ). Multivariate outliers identified with the Mahalanobis distance are, therefore, assumed to be outliers from the population multivariate normal distribution, unless your software package specifies a different basis of comparison.

Several forms of calculation are available. Like the other multiple sample indices we have already discussed, the basis of calculation is the distance between pairs of elements in the data set. The following equation shows how d^2 is calculated for a pair of variables, x_{1p} and x_{2p}.

$$d_p^2 = (x_{1p} - x_{2p})^T S^{-1} (x_{1p} - x_{2p})$$

where T indicates that the matrix of differences between scores is transformed and S^{-1} is the inverse covariance matrix.

The probability distribution of Mahalanobis scores takes the shape of a cumulative chi-square distribution with degrees of freedom (df) equal to the number of variables (not cases) in the set. This allows outliers to be identified with a given level of probability, p. Although the researcher is free to set p, software packages such as the AMOS structural equation modelling (SEM) tool, have established a default level of $p<0.001$. Cases with a Mahalanobis value greater than the critical value of chi-square for the appropriate degrees of freedom and chi-square for the analysis should be flagged as outliers.

Example: Using the Malahanobis distance to identify multivariate outliers in a data set

An example comes from the work of Mary D., who asked 648 travellers 78 questions, which formed the basis of a set of scales that she later used to study their response to a tourism destination. She screened her data for multivariate outlier cases by calculating the Mahalanobis distance using the linear regression procedure in SPSS.

Before beginning, Mary calculated the critical value for outliers. Using the Microsoft Excel function, CHISQ.INV(0.001,78), she determined that the critical value of chi-square for a distribution with $df=78$ at $p=001$ is 45.01. Thus, any case with a Mahalanobis distance greater than 45.01 would be flagged as an outlier.

Mahalanobis distances can be calculated in SPSS by setting up a linear regression model with all variables to be included in data analysis for the study entered as independent variables and any variable chosen as the dependent variable (e.g. the case identification number). Save the Mahalanobis distance. When the procedure is run, a new variable is created in the data file to record the Mahalanobis distance for each case and descriptive statistics are reported with the table of residuals statistics. Table 2.11 shows that the maximum Mahalanobis distance is 131.54, higher than the critical value of chi-square of 45.01 for 78 variables, so Mary needed to examine her file for multivariate outliers.

Table 2.11 SPSS residuals statistics table with summary statistics for saved Mahalanobis distances

Residuals statistics[a]	Minimum	Maximum	Mean	Std. Deviation	N
Predicted value	2.19	144.39	72.59	24.795	648
Std. predicted value	−2.839	2.895	0.000	1.000	648
Standard error of predicted value	1.886	14.169	7.361	1.819	648
Adjusted predicted value	1.91	148.39	72.58	24.895	648
Residual	−99.188	101.497	0.000	34.788	648
Std. residual	−2.787	2.852	0.000	0.978	648
Stud. residual	−2.834	2.970	0.000	1.001	648
Deleted residual	−103.390	110.036	0.014	36.475	648
Stud. deleted residual	−2.847	2.985	0.000	1.002	648
Mahal. distance	**1.350**	**131.541**	**36.956**	**18.720**	**648**
Cook's distance	0.000	0.020	0.001	0.002	648
Centred leverage value	0.002	0.157	0.044	0.022	648

[a]Dependent variable: A_RaterID.

Mary plotted the Mahalanobis scores and found that they followed the shape of a chi-square distribution, so she decided to retain all cases in the data set, but to assess each analysis that she conducted for the effects of influential cases (Figure 2.9).

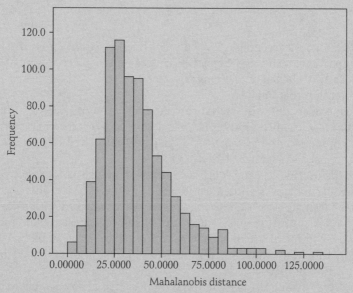

Figure 2.9 Distribution of Mahalanobis scores (distances)

A common error in using the Mahalanobis distance is to adopt a critical value that has been used by another researcher or included in a textbook example. Instead, the critical value of the Mahalanobis distance is specific to the number of variables you include in your own analysis. For example, if Mary (in the above example) decides to drop two items from her analyses, she will be working with 76 variables, and df for the determination of the critical value of the Mahalanobis distance would also be 76.

Another common error is to rely on the Mahalanobis distances reported in AMOS SEM to identify multivariate outliers for analyses other than AMOS models. No matter which statistical package is used, the key issue in the identification of multivariate outliers is the selection of the variables. If variables used in some analyses (such as exploratory factor analysis), but not in AMOS SEM, are omitted from tests for multivariate outliers, the tests are not valid.

Researchers can be confused by the two p values reported against Mahalanobis distances in AMOS output. The first value, $p1$, is the chi-square probability of observing the reported Mahalanobis distance in a sample with df equal to the number of observed variables in the structural equation model. The second value, $p2$, reports the results of a non-parametric test, the probability of observing the reported d^2 in a set of n ordered values, where the cases are ordered by d^2 and n equals the total number of cases in the data set). All cases with $p2 < 0.001$ are usually considered to be outliers on the set of observed items in the AMOS model, although $p1$ is also valid.

Notes

(1) The highest acceptable level of significance varies across disciplines. In particular, the significance level is often set in economics at $\alpha = 0.1$, i.e. a 1/10 chance of rejecting H_0 when it is true. This is a less stringent condition than $\alpha = 0.05$.

(2) Remember that, in statistical parlance, a *parameter* is a numeric quantity, usually unknown, that describes a certain characteristic of a population and a *statistic* is a quantity, calculated from a sample of data, used to estimate a *parameter*.

(3) In fields that accept <0.1 as sufficient evidence to reject H_0, the p-value for non-significance is $p \geq 0.1$. In some cases, this is marked with a single asterisk, although it can also be marked with a dagger (†) to avoid confusion with the system of symbols presented in Table 2.2. We recommend use of the dagger for p-values between 0.05 and 0.1.

(4) Any function d that satisfies the following conditions is called distance function or metric:
  - $d(x,y) \geq 0$ and $d(x,y) = 0$ if and only if $x = y$ (d is positive between two different points, and is zero only from a point to itself);

- $d(x,y)=d(y,x)$ (the distance between x and y is the same in either direction);
- $d(x,z) \leq d(x,y)+d(y,z)$ (known as triangle inequality: the distance between two points is the shortest distance along any path).

References

Antonioli Corigliano, M. and Baggio, R. (2006) On the significance of tourism website evaluations. In M. Hitz, M. Sigala and J. Murphy (eds) *Information and Communication Technologies in Tourism 2006: Proceedings of the International Conference in Lausanne, Switzerland* (pp. 320–331). Wien: Springer.

Boriah, S. (2008) Similarity measures for categorical data: A comparative evaluation. In C. Apte, H. Park, K. Wang and M.J. Zaki (eds) *Proceedings of the 2008 SIAM International Conference on Data Mining*, Atlanta, GA, 24, 26 April (pp. 243–254). Philadelphia: Society for Industrial and Applied Mathematics (SIAM).

Boyle, T.P., Smillie, G.M., Anderson, J.C. and Beeson, D.R. (1990) A sensitivity analysis of nine diversity and seven similarity indices. *Research Journal of the Water Pollution Control Federation* 62, 749–762.

Brander, L.M., Van Beukering, P. and Cesar, H.S.J. (2007) The recreational value of coral reefs: A meta-analysis. *Ecological Economics* 63 (1), 209–218.

Brons, M., Pels, E., Nijkamp, P. and Rietveld, P. (2002) Price elasticities of demand for passenger air travel: A meta-analysis. *Journal of Air Transport Management* 8 (3), 165–175.

Cha, S.-H. (2007) Comprehensive survey on distance/similarity measures between probability density functions. *International Journal of Mathematical Models and Methods in Applied Science* 1 (4), 300–307.

Choi, S.S., Cha, S.H. and Tappert, C.C. (2010) A survey of binary similarity and distance measures. *Journal of Systemics, Cybernetics and Informatics* 8 (1), 43–48.

CIA (2016) Country comparison: Distribution of family income. The World Factbook. See https://www.cia.gov/library/publications/the-world-factbook/rankorder/2172rank.html (accessed 26 April 2016).

Cochran, W.G. (1937) Problems arising in the analysis of a series of similar experiments. *Journal of the Royal Statistical Society* 4 (Suppl), 102–118.

Cochran, W.G. (1977) *Sampling Techniques* (3rd edn). New York: John Wiley.

Cohen, J. (1988) *Statistical Power Analysis for the Behavioral Sciences* (2nd edn). Hillsdale, NJ: Lawrence Erlbaum Associates.

Crouch, G.I. (1995) A meta-analysis of tourism demand. *Annals of Tourism Research* 22 (1), 103–118.

Davison, A.C. and Hinkley, D.V. (1997) *Bootstrap Methods and Their Application*. Cambridge: Cambridge University Press.

Duval, S. and Tweedie, R. (2000) Trim and fill: A simple funnel-plot-based method of testing and adjusting for publication bias in meta-analysis. *Biometrics* 56 (2), 455–463.

Efron, B. (1979) Bootstrap methods: Another look at the jackknife. *The Annals of Statistics* 7, 1–26.

Efron, B. and Tibshirani, R.J. (1993) *An Introduction to the Bootstrap*. New York: Chapman & Hall.

English, D.B.K. (2000) A simple procedure for generating confidence intervals in tourist spending profiles and resulting economic impacts. *Journal of Regional Analysis and Policy* 30, 59–74.

Fisher, R.A. (1935) *The Design of Experiments*. Edinburgh: Oliver and Boyd.

Gallego et al., (2013) On the Mahalanobis distance classification criterion for multidimensional normal distributions. *IEEE Transactions on Signal Processing* 61 (17), 4387–4396.

Gehrels, N. (1986) Confidence limits for small numbers of events in astrophysical data. *Astrophysical Journal* 303, 336–346.

Glass, G.V. (1976) Primary, secondary and meta-analysis of research. *Educational Researcher* 5, 3–8.

Halsey, L.H., Curran-Everett, D., Vowler, S.H. and Drummond, G.B. (2015) The fickle P value generates irreproducible results. *Nature Methods* 12 (3), 179–185.

Hartung, J., Knapp, G. and Sinha, B.K. (2008) *Statistical Meta-Analysis with Applications*. Hoboken, NJ: Wiley.

Hedges, L.V. and Olkin, I. (1985) *Statistical Methods for Meta-Analysis*. Orlando, FL: Academic Press.

Kanji, G.K. (2006) *100 Statistical Tests* (3rd edn). London: Sage Publications.

Langley, R. (1971) *Practical Statistics*. New York: Dover.

Lim, C. (1999) A meta-analytic review of international tourism demand. *Journal of Travel Research* 37 (3), 273–284.

Mak, T.K. (2004) Estimating variances for all sample sizes by the bootstrap. *Computational Statistics & Data Analysis* 46, 459–467.

Newcomb, S. (1886) A generalized theory of the combination of observations so as to obtain the best result. *American Journal of Mathematics* 8 (4), 343–366.

Nuzzo, R. (201) Statistical errors. *Nature* 506, 150–152.

OECD (2016) Income inequality (indicator). http://www.oecd-ilibrary.org/social-issues-migration-health/income-inequality/indicator/english_459aa7f1-en (accessed 25 July 2016).

Pearson, K. (1904) Report on certain enteric fever inoculation statistics. *British Medical Journal* 3, 1243–1246.

Pol, A.P., Pascual, M.B. and Vazquez, P.C. (2006) Robust estimators and bootstrap confidence intervals applied to tourism spending. *Tourism Management* 27 (1), 42–50.

Rao, C.R. (2004) Combining information from different sources to estimate a common effect and use of multiple measurements for ecological assessment. *Environmetrics* 15, 415–422.

Regener, V.H. (1951) Statistical significance of small samples of cosmic ray counts. *Physical Review* 84, 161–162.

Shao, J. (1999) *Mathematical Statistics*. Heidelberg: Springer.

Sheskin, D.J. (2000) *Handbook of Parametric and Nonparametric Statistical Procedures*. Boca Raton, FL: Chapman & Hall/CRC.

Siegel, S. and Castellan, N.J.J. (1988) *Nonparametric Statistics for the Behavioral Sciences* (2nd edn). New York: McGraw-Hill.

Sterne, J.A.C. and Egger, M. (2001) Funnel plots for detecting bias in meta-analysis: Guidelines on choice of axis. *Journal of Clinical Epidemiology* 54 (10), 1046–1045.

Triola, M.F. (2009) *Elementary Statistics* (11th edn). Boston, MA: Addison Wesley.

US DOJ (2010) Horizontal Merger Guidelines. See https://www.justice.gov/atr/horizontal-merger-guidelines-08192010 (accessed 26 April 2016).

Wasserstein, R.L. and Lazar, N.A. (2016) The ASA's statement on p-values: Context, process and purpose. *The American Statistician* 70 (2), 129–133.

Wolda, H. (1981) Similarity indices, sample size and diversity. *Oecologia* 50 (3), 296–302.

Zwillinger, D. and Kokoska, S. (2000) *CRC Standard Probability and Statistics Tables and Formulae*. Boca Raton, FL: Chapman & Hall/CRC.

3   Data Reduction

The analysis of multivariate data is presented here. Factor analysis and cluster analysis as well as multidimensional scaling (MDS) techniques are also described and discussed along with the main issue, advantages, disadvantages and applicability.

A number of techniques exist for reducing large or complex sets of data to smaller sets that are easier to manage and to interpret. Two of the most important families of such techniques are factor analysis and cluster analysis. Factor analysis is most often used to identify common patterns in sets of *variables*, while cluster analysis is most often used to identify common patterns in sets of *cases*. For example, you might use factor analysis to classify a large number of possible reasons (say, 10 or even 30 or more) for visiting a destination into two or three categories based on visitors' ratings of the destination, while you might use cluster analysis to classify visitors themselves into two or three categories based on similarities in their reasons for visiting.

While some of the techniques in these families allow some testing of hypotheses about how well the derived classification fits the original data, the techniques themselves are based primarily on correlation and other types of pattern matching. Because the techniques are primarily descriptive rather than inferential, decisions about the number of categories to use and whether they provide a good enough representation of the original data are left largely to the investigator, who is aided by 'rules of thumb' rather than statistical testing. There is therefore much art, as well as science, in the application of these techniques. In this chapter, we provide an overview of the science, but emphasise the art of factor analysis and cluster analysis. In the final section, we introduce MDS and correspondence analysis, two techniques that produce, often in a single analytical step, both a set of dimensions (i.e. factors) that underlie evaluations of cases and a comparison of the cases along those dimensions in such a way that the similarities between the cases – and their attributes – can be seen.

Factor Analysis

Factor analysis can be used either to identify underlying factors or dimensions in a data set or to confirm that a set of factors defined *a priori* can be used to summarise the data. When using factor analysis to identify underlying factors, we speak of *exploratory factor analysis* (EFA); when attempting to confirm a proposed factor structure, we use *confirmatory factor analysis* (CFA). This section focuses on EFA, but we make some brief comments on CFA at the end.

Suppose you have a set of data structured as in Figure 3.1, which we will call an **X** matrix. You have a large number, p, of variables, x, which you want to reduce to a smaller set of factors. You have taken observations from a sample with size n of individuals or cases, i. (The cases might be people or other objects, such as locations or performance indicators.) For each variable, x, you therefore have an observation for each case, i. These values are represented in Figure 3.1 as x_{np}. (Of course, you might not have values for every variable, x, for every case, i, in which situation you have some missing values.) The goal of EFA is to find a way to represent this data structure in fewer variables, by collapsing the p original (also called observed) x variables to c factors, where $c<p$.

The approach is fundamentally quite simple: We look for subsets of variables that are (quite) strongly correlated with one another but weakly correlated with other variables in the data set. Each of the inter-correlated sets of variables forms a factor, which is mathematically – and, if all goes well, meaningfully – separate from the others. This process

$$
\begin{array}{l}
x_1 \; x_2 \; x_3 \; ... \, x_p \\
i_1 \; x_{11} x_{12} x_{13} ... \; x_{1p} \\
i_2 \; x_{21} x_{22} x_{23} ... \; x_{2p} \\
i_3 \; x_{31} x_{32} x_{33} ... \; x_{3p} \\
\vdots \quad \vdots \quad \vdots \\
i_n \; x_{n1} x_{n2} x_{n3} ... \; x_{np}
\end{array}
$$

Figure 3.1 The goal of factor analysis is to reduce a large data matrix, **X**, to a smaller one

$$
\begin{array}{ll}
x_1 \; x_2 \; x_3 \; ... \, x_p & \quad F_1 \;\; F_2 \;\; ... \;\; F_c \\
x_1 & \quad x_1 \; b_{11} \; b_{12} \; ... \; b_{1c} \\
x_2 \, r_{21} & \quad x_2 \; b_{21} \; b_{22} \; ... \; b_{2c} \\
x_3 \, r_{31} \, r_{32} & \Longrightarrow \quad x_3 \; b_{31} \; b_{32} \; ... \; b_{3c} \\
\vdots \quad \vdots \quad \vdots & \quad \vdots \quad \vdots \quad \vdots \quad \vdots \quad \vdots \\
x_p \, r_{p1} \, r_{p2} \, r_{p3} ... \, r_{p(p-1)} & \quad x_p \; b_{p1} \; b_{p1} \; ... \; b_{pc} \\
\qquad\quad R & \qquad\qquad B
\end{array}
$$

Figure 3.2 Data reduction from a $p{\times}p$ correlation matrix (**R**) to a (smaller) $p{\times}c$ factor matrix (**B**)

is illustrated in Figure 3.2, where the left-hand panel shows the $p \times p$ matrix of correlations (**R**) between the observed (x) variables, and the right-hand panel shows the $p \times c$ (smaller, because $c < p$) factor matrix, **B**, extracted from it. Each observed variable, x_p, is correlated with each factor, F_c; this correlation is known as a factor loading, b_{pc}. (It is also possible to conduct factor analysis from a covariance matrix. This results in some differences in analytical detail, but the fundamental approach, and the structure and interpretation of results remain the same, so we will consider only the most common approaches to EFA in detail in this chapter.)

This is a good place to point out that the art in EFA comes from deciding at least four things: the factor analytic technique to use, how many factors to select, which sets of variables to combine in each factor and how to interpret the factors so that they are meaningful for our purpose. We will deal with each of these decisions in turn, but signal first that the key to meaningful interpretation is to obtain a factor matrix in which each variable has a high factor loading on one and only one factor. With this 'simple structure', each factor can be interpreted on the basis of the meaning of the variables that load strongly on it.

Example: Factor analysis in tourism research

There are many examples of factor analysis in tourism research, including Lankford and Howard's (1994) widely cited work to develop the Tourism Impact Attitude Scale (TIAS). Lankford and Howard (1994) asked 1436 residents their views about the impact of tourism on 50(!) issues that might affect their community.

Using principal components analysis (PCA; a factor analytic technique), they found two factors could be used to represent 27 of these issues in a simple structure (the other 23 issues/variables did not contribute to the solution). We reproduce their results, in a form that emphasises simple structure, in Table 3.1. In this example, we see that Lankford and Howard decided that the best way to summarise attitudes to the impact of tourism, based on the available data, was to use just two factors and draw on 27 of the original variables. They further interpreted the two factors as representing concerns about the role of government in local tourism development, and personal and community benefits, respectively. In the rest of this section, we will examine how such choices are made.

Table 3.1 A simple structure representation of Lankford and Howard's (1994) Tourism Impact Attitude Scale

	Factor 1: Concern for local tourism development	Factor 2: Personal and community benefits
Against new tourism development	0.844	
Encourage tourism in community	0.840	
Should not attract more visitors	0.810	
Should encourage tourism in [location]	0.803	
Encourage more intensive development	0.769	
Tourism vital for community	0.759	
Council right in promoting tourism	0.753	
Community should become destination	0.746	
Negatively impacts environment	0.742	
Noise level not appropriate	0.730	
More litter from tourism	0.725	
Tourists are valuable	0.723	
Limit outdoor recreation development	0.702	
Crime has increased	0.699	
Benefits outweigh consequences	0.666	
Like to see tourism be main industry	0.510	
Planning can control impacts	0.484	
Will provide more jobs in community	0.416	
Better roads due to tourism		0.807
Public service improved due to tourism		0.791
Have more money to spend		0.789
Has increased my standard of living		0.762
More recreation opportunities		0.640
Provides highly desirable jobs		0.601
Shopping opportunities are better		0.559
Support local tax levies for tourism		0.487
Will play major economic role		0.463

Note: Factor loadings below 0.4 are suppressed to emphasise the simple structure and aid interpretation of the factors. Factor names have been taken from Lankford and Howard (1994).

Techniques for exploratory factor analysis

A number of techniques for EFA are available, but the primary distinction is between PCA and common factor techniques. Some authors do not classify PCA with factor analysis, but it is sufficiently similar to common factor techniques that we can simply consider it a special case here. What makes PCA a special case is its assumption that there is no error in the measurement of the variables from which factors (or, technically, in the case of PCA, 'components') are drawn. On the other hand, common factor techniques assume, and then allow for the existence of measurement error. PCA is therefore a suitable approach to data reduction when the variables are indicators that can be measured with little or no error, for example, different indicators of financial performance drawn from accounting and economic statistics. On the other hand, when there is likely to be some error of measurement – typically the case when you ask humans to give their opinions or to report their attitudes to certain objects or activities, where their responses can be affected by a recent critical incident, their general mood or even whether they feel well or unwell at the time of answering a survey – common factor techniques are more appropriate. Both approaches proceed in the same way, based on an estimate of the amount of variance each variable has in common with the other variables in the data set. For PCA, the beginning estimate is 1.00 or 100% of common variance, while the initial estimate of common variance for common factor techniques is the squared multiple correlation (SMC) of each variable. The SMC of each variable is the variance explained (R-squared) of a regression equation in which all other variables in the data set are used to predict the variable.

For readers familiar with matrix algebra, the fundamental operation underlying classical factor analysis is quite straightforward: the determinant of the correlation matrix, $\mathbf{R}$, is used to decompose it into matrices of eigenvalues ($\mathbf{L}$) and eigenvectors ($\mathbf{V}$). (The factor loading matrix, $\mathbf{B}$, is estimated as $\mathbf{B}=\mathbf{VL}^{0.5}$.) It is important to note that the determinant must be positive, otherwise this operation cannot be completed and a solution cannot be reached. In practical terms, this means that, while it is important that each of the variables included in a factor analysis is correlated with some of the other variables (otherwise no sets of inter-correlated variables could be identified), no pair of variables can be so strongly correlated that the determinant of the correlation matrix is 0. Our student of matrix algebra might point out that simply decomposing the correlation matrix does not reduce the number of variables, and he/she would be correct: the initial solution of a factor analysis contains as many factors as variables. Once the investigator (or, usually, the computer software) has decomposed the correlation matrix with the help of some matrix algebra, the investigator must make his/her first foray into the realm of art – guided by some statistics and rules of thumb – and make his/her first (but necessarily final) choice of the number of factors to extract.

Choosing the number of factors to extract

Several rules of thumb are available to help choose the number of factors to extract. Two of these rules use eigenvalues, on the basis that the eigenvalues represent the variance explained by each of the decomposed factors. Indeed, the percentage of variance explained by each factor can be calculated by dividing the eigenvalue by the number of factors in the initial solution (i.e. the number of variables in the observed data set). The most common of the eigenvalue-based rules is called the latent root criterion or

Kaiser's rule, after Henry Kaiser (1960) who popularised Guttman's (1954) earlier recommendation that investigators extract all factors that have an eigenvalue greater than 1 in the initial solution. The rationale is that factors with eigenvalues less than 1 explain less variance than a single variable on its own and therefore fail to simplify the data set. Several decades of practice has shown that Kaiser's rule often provides a good starting point, although fewer factors may provide more meaningful solutions, particularly when the number of observed variables is quite small (say, under 10) and more factors might be useful, particularly when the number of observed variables is quite large (say, over 30) (Hair *et al.*, 2009; Tabachnick & Fidell, 2006).

The second rule that uses eigenvalues was proposed by Cattell (1966) who suggested that inspecting a plot of eigenvalues would enable the detection of a point of diminishing returns. The optimum number of factors to select would be the number above the elbow or point of inflexion in this so-called 'scree plot' (named after the sloping piles of rocks that can be found at the base of rock falls or cliffs). After this point, each additional factor included in the solution would explain relatively little additional variance. Often, the scree plot points to the same number of factors as Kaiser's rule. Nonetheless, using the scree plot in practice is not as simple, or as reliable, as it might seem because there is often no clear point of inflexion. Critics of the scree plot also question why the plot should present the eigenvalues rather than, for example, the square

Example: Scree plots

An example of a straightforward scree plot is provided in Figure 3.3. Here, there is a clear point of inflexion at Factor 5, indicating that four factors should be extracted. This is the same solution as suggested by the

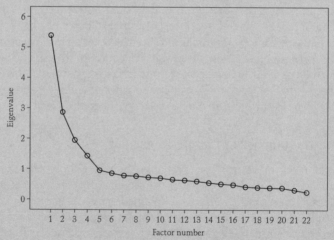

Figure 3.3 A scree plot for the initial solution from a factor analysis of 22 variables from data set A

latent root criterion: the four variables above the point of inflexion in the scree plot are the only variables with an eigenvalue greater than 1.

Next, consider the scree plot for 26 variables taken from a different data set in Figure 3.4. This plot suggests that one, four or even eight factors might be selected. In this case, the scree plot is helpful only as an indication that the first factor extracts a very large amount of variance relative to the others.

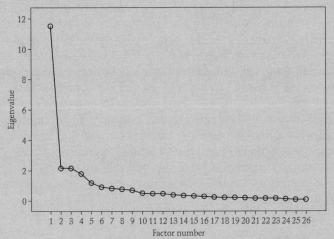

Figure 3.4 A scree plot for the initial solution from a factor analysis of 26 variables from data set B

roots or the logarithms of the eigenvalues, which are then in comparable units of measurement, but which would produce plots of a different shape (Darlington, 1968, 1997).

Other approaches to choosing the number of factors to extract include deciding on a minimum amount of variance in the original data set that should be accounted for by a meaningful set of factors, typically 50%, and choosing a set number of factors to extract based on either prior information about the number of factors that might meaningfully summarise the data set or a decision about the number of factors that would permit a description of the data that is both manageable and meaningful. While the total variance explained by the extracted factors can be determined from the initial solution, the meaningfulness of the extracted factors can only be determined from a complete solution, usually after the processes of rotation and interpretation that will be discussed below. It is sufficient to say at this point that the meaningfulness of a factor is usually considered in terms of both the ability to interpret the meaning of the factor from the variables that load strongly on it and the total amount of variance the factor explains in the complete solution. The amount of variance a factor explains in a complete solution is not the same as the amount of variance it explains in the initial solution; this value is instead the sum of the squared loadings of each variable in the solution on the factor:

$$\mathrm{Var}(F_c) = \sum_{p=1}^{p} b_{pc}^{\ 2}$$

No rule of thumb is available for a 'meaningful' amount of variance explained by a factor in the final solution, but experienced practitioners of factor analysis typically compare the amount of variance explained by each factor with that explained by each of the others, and consider reducing the number of factors in the solution if any factor explains a very low proportion of variance relative to the others (a kind of informal, completed factor solution scree test) or if the absolute amount of variance explained by any factor in the complete solution is low (e.g. below 5% of total variance in the data set).

Another approach, becoming quite common, is to produce several complete factor solutions based on different numbers of factors and select the solution that is most readily interpretable. Experienced users of factor analysis usually draw on all of these approaches, using their judgement to decide on the most useful and meaningful solution – art, indeed, although some guidance is available.

Selecting variables

Before proceeding to the final steps of factor analysis, we consider how variables are selected for inclusion in the final solution. We have already said that our observed data set must include sets of inter-correlated variables. While, in some special cases, a single factor solution is of interest, investigators usually look for solutions in which two or more factors represent the original set of observed variables. It is not necessary, however, to have large numbers of variables loading on factors: If a useful and meaningful interpretation can be obtained from as few as three variables, then that is sufficient to define a factor. This means that it is not necessary to include all variables in the original data set in the factor solution. Furthermore, some variables might need to be discarded anyway. Variables are commonly discarded for one of two reasons: Either they are not sufficiently correlated with any other variables in the data set, i.e. they do not share sufficient common variance with any other variables to form a factor; or they are correlated with several other variables that load on different factors and thus have a moderate or strong loading on more than one factor, i.e. they do not contribute to a solution that has a simple structure. As noted earlier, a variable might also be discarded if it is collinear (very strongly correlated, say 0.8 or 0.9) with one or more other variables and therefore results in a correlation matrix with a determinant of 0.

Two rules of thumb are available to screen variables for sufficient common variance. The first uses the Kaiser–Meyer–Olkin (KMO) measure of sampling adequacy (MSA), and is used before extracting factors. (The MSA does not actually concern the sample itself, but is an estimate of the variance a variable has in common with all other variables in the data set [its SMC] relative to the total shared variance among all variables in the data set.) Rather than using a formula to illustrate the MSA, we refer to Figure 3.5 which shows the MSA of a variable ($X1$) in three different data sets. In the top panel, the variance that $X1$ (always the top left-hand ellipse) has in common with the other two variables is half of the total variance shared among the three variables; an MSA of 0.5 is considered just sufficient for inclusion of a variable in a factor analysis solution. In the middle panel, there is a high proportion of shared variance between $X1$ and the other two variables, while in the lower panel, $X1$ shares insufficient variance with the other two variables to contribute meaningfully to a factor analysis solution.

The second statistic used to screen variables for inclusion in factor analysis is the amount of variance in a variable that is explained by the *extracted* factor solution. This statistic, known as communality, is calculated as the sum of the squared loadings of the variable on each factor in the extracted factor solution, i.e.

$$h_p{}^2 = \sum_{c=1}^{c} b_{pc}{}^2$$

(Some software packages, such as Stata, report 'uniqueness', which is $1-h^2$.) Communality varies with the number of extracted factors. If, for

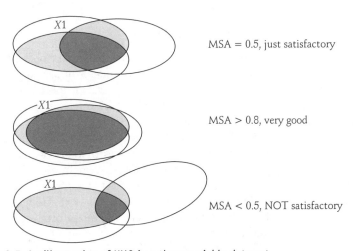

MSA = 0.5, just satisfactory

MSA > 0.8, very good

MSA < 0.5, NOT satisfactory

Figure 3.5 An illustration of KMO in a three variable data set

example, few factors are selected, a variable with satisfactory MSA might not have sufficient communality to be included in the solution while, if more factors are selected, communality might increase to be sufficient. Of course, we need a test of sufficiency, and you might not be surprised by now to read that the test is based on a rule of thumb, typically 0.4 (indicating that 40% of the variable's variance is explained by the extracted factors).

Satisfactory communality can be obtained if a variable has moderate or strong loadings on several factors, but its communality alone does not guarantee that the variable contributes to a satisfactory factor solution. If we are to be able to interpret the factors that emerge from factor analysis, we need a simple structure in which each variable's communality is derived primarily from its loading on one factor only, not from relatively weak loading across several factors. To obtain such a structure, we need to apply a little more art, but before doing so, it is worth considering how strong a factor loading needs to be to be satisfactory. It is possible to set up hypotheses for factor loadings (e.g. that they differ from 0). This is, however, rarely done. Instead, researchers typically use yet another rule of thumb and generally choose 0.4 as the cut off for a factor loading to be large enough to be meaningful. This approach makes some sense because, as the factor loading is a correlation, we can be guided by the usual considerations for the interpretation of correlation coefficients – and, if necessary, the estimation of the statistical significance of the correlation coefficient in a sample of the size used in the analysis. While this decision is typically governed by the rule of thumb, it is good practice to remember that factor loadings may be unreliable in small samples. Hair *et al.* (2006: 128) point out, for example, that for a factor loading of 0.4 and a typical standard error, a sample of 200 is likely to be needed for statistical significance at 0.05 with power of 0.8. With a sample of only 50, the statistically significant factor loading under these conditions is 0.75.

Rotation and interpretation of factors

Mathematically, the number of factor solutions that can be obtained from EFA is infinite. This is known as the problem of indeterminacy, and is dealt with in each factor analytic method by applying a rule to obtain the initial solution (Guttman, 1955; Krijnen *et al.*, 1998). For example, in PCA and the most commonly used common factor method, principal axis factoring (PAF), when a correlation matrix is decomposed to produce the matrixes of eigenvalues and eigenvectors of the initial factor solution, the first factor extracted is the strongest factor, i.e. the factor that joins together the most highly inter-correlated subset of variables and explains the highest amount of the common variance in the data set. The next factor extracted is the next strongest factor, and so on. However the initial solution is reached, it rarely produces a factor solution that is meaningful, so the final step in producing a complete factor solution is to rotate the factors geometrically in c dimensional space to identify a set of coordinates (factor loadings) that exhibits a simple structure.

Example: Rotation

A simple example of rotation is shown in Figure 3.6, which shows the rotated and unrotated factor solutions for two dimensions used to evaluate a computer-synthesised tour guide on the world wide web (we base this example on data described in Haddad and Klobas [2002]).

The left-hand panel shows the unrotated solution. In this solution, the variable *expert* has factor loadings of −0.49 on Factor 1 and 0.7 on Factor 2 and the variable *understd* (understandable) loads −0.45 on Factor 1 and 0.25 on Factor 2, while the variable *incomptnt* (incompetent) has factor loadings of 0.55 on Factor 1 and −0.4 on Factor 2. Three variables that concern the quality of the guide's voice (all preceded by *vc*) also have a range of (non-zero) loadings on both factors.

The right-hand panel shows the same factor solution rotated approximately 40 degrees to the right. The pattern of relationships between the variables remains the same, but now each variable has a loading close to 0 on one of the factors: the three variables associated with the perceived voice quality of the guide have loadings with absolute values above 0.5 on Factor 1 and near 0 loadings on Factor 2, while the three variables associated with the perceived expertise of the guide all have loadings with absolute values of around 0.5 and above on Factor 2 and near 0 loadings on Factor 1.

By rotating the factors, we have achieved a simple structure from which the interpretation of the factors emerges clearly: Factor 1 represents the perceived voice quality of the guide, while Factor 2 represents the perceived expertise of the guide.

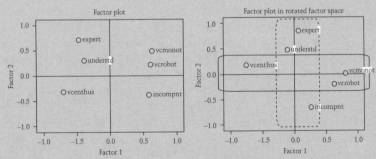

Figure 3.6 Rotation of a two-factor solution to achieve simple structure

There are two arts to master here: that of rotation and that of interpretation, but interpretation should follow relatively easily from satisfactory rotation. Two basic types of rotation can be used: *orthogonal* rotation, which keeps the factors at 90 degrees from one another (as in the original solution), thereby minimising the correlation between the rotated factors; and *oblique* rotation, which permits the factors to be rotated at different angles thereby permitting them to be correlated with one another.

If the factor solution is a means in itself, and the investigator believes that the factors are likely to be correlated – a common situation when people are asked to evaluate, or to express their opinions about or attitudes to objects, places or other people – the most satisfactory solutions are usually obtained from oblique rotation. If, on the other hand, the goal is to reduce the original set of variables to a smaller set of variables (i.e. the factors) for inclusion in statistical analyses that assume little or no correlation between variables, orthogonal rotation may be called for, even if interpretation may be more difficult.

Extended example: Evaluating a destination website

As we have seen, factor analysis involves several steps and several decisions, many of which, while guided by statistics, require the judgement of the investigator. Here, we present an example that shows how an investigator used factor analysis to evaluate the website for a destination. (This example is adapted from Klobas & McGill [2010]). In this case, the investigator asked 244 visitors to the website to evaluate it using criteria that were developed in the information systems field for the evaluation of the success of computer applications (DeLone & McLean, 1992, 2004; McGill *et al.*, 2003). The criteria were expected to cover four categories of response to the website, reflecting the quality of the information in the site (six variables, labelled InfQual1 to InfQual6); the technical quality of the site including such characteristics as speed of page loads, quality of images and page layout (nine variables, labelled SysQual1 to SysQual9); the quality of the services available from the site, including booking services, requests for information and requests for help with using the site (seven variables, labelled ServQ1 to ServQ7); and the benefits users reported from using the site, including saving time and locating information quickly (four variables, labelled NetBen1 to NetBen4). While the investigator could have used CFA to confirm the existence of these four factors, she was really unsure whether four factors would emerge from her analysis and whether all of the original variables were needed to evaluate the destination website, so she chose to use EFA.

Because the data had been obtained from human evaluators, the investigator chose to use the PAF method of common factor analysis. Although she had used the information systems literature to guide her development of variables, she did not wish to limit her initial analysis to four factors, but instead decided to accept her software's default setting, which extracts all factors with an eigenvalue greater than 1 (Kaiser's rule), as a starting point for her investigation. Finally, because her data had been obtained from humans and her ultimate goal was to evaluate the website using a manageable set of categories, she used oblique rotation in her search for an interpretable factor solution.

The SPSS syntax for her initial exploration of a factor solution is shown in Figure 3.7. (This analysis can also be run from the Windows pull-down menus in SPSS as Analyze – Dimension reduction – Factor.) This syntax first describes which variables to use (the /VARIABLES command) and how to treat missing values (the /MISSING command). In this case, the default of deleting all cases that contain missing values 'listwise' has been accepted. This approach makes computation simpler and, provided relatively few cases contain missing values or values are missing at random, it will result in a solution that can be generalised beyond the subset of the sample included in the analysis. It is also possible to produce a correlation matrix for factor analysis with 'pairwise' deletion of missing values. With this approach, every case is included in the

```
FACTOR
   /VARIABLES InfQual1 InfQual2 InfQual3 InfQual4 InfQual5 InfQual6
SysQual1 SysQual2 SysQual3
     SysQual4 SysQual5 SysQual6 SysQual7 SysQual8 SysQual9 ServQ1
ServQ2 ServQ3 ServQ4 ServQ5 ServQ6
     ServQ7 NetBen1 NetBen2 NetBen3 NetBen4
   /MISSING LISTWISE
   /ANALYSIS InfQual1 InfQual2 InfQual3 InfQual4 InfQual5 InfQual6
SysQual1 SysQual2 SysQual3
     SysQual4 SysQual5 SysQual6 SysQual7 SysQual8 SysQual9 ServQ1
ServQ2 ServQ3 ServQ4 ServQ5 ServQ6
     ServQ7 NetBen1 NetBen2 NetBen3 NetBen4
   /PRINT INITIAL DET KMO AIC EXTRACTION ROTATION
   /FORMAT SORT BLANK(.4)
   /PLOT EIGEN
   /CRITERIA MINEIGEN(1) ITERATE(25)
   /EXTRACTION PAF
   /CRITERIA ITERATE(25) DELTA(0)
   /ROTATION OBLIMIN
   /METHOD=CORRELATION.
```

Figure 3.7 Sample SPSS syntax for principal axis factoring with oblimin rotation

solution, and each correlation in the correlation matrix is calculated only from those cases where values are available for both variables. Pairwise deletion enables more cases to be retained in the factor analysis, but can render the solution unstable or make it impossible to reach a solution.

The SPSS syntax in Figure 3.7 continues with instructions for the output to be reported. The /PRINT command asks for three solutions to be reported: the INITIAL factor solution, the EXTRACTED solution (i.e. the solution for the number of factors extracted according to the criterion for extraction) and the ROTATED solution (i.e. the complete solution, which will be consulted for interpretation and meaningfulness). It also requests three diagnostic reports: DET requests the determinant of the correlation matrix; KMO requests statistics about the amount of correlation in the data set as a whole; and AIC produces an anti-image correlation matrix from which the KMO MSA for individual variables can be inspected.

Other available descriptive reports, not requested here, produce the sample size, mean and standard deviation of all variables included in the analysis (the only way to find out the size of the sample included in the analysis if you have missing values!); the correlation matrix (useful for identifying multicollinearity if the determinant is 0 or inspecting the data to see if there are sufficient correlations between variables to produce a factor solution); and the reproduced correlation matrix, a correlation matrix reproduced from the factor solution, useful for inspection of how closely the factor solution maps back to the original data set.

The /FORMAT command helps with the interpretation and assessment of a simple structure: SORT sorts the variables by strength of loading on the factor on which they load most strongly, while BLANK allows investigators to select a value of the factor loading below which they consider the loading of a variable on a factor to be too low to be meaningful. In this case, the investigator has chosen 0.4.

The final five lines of the syntax specify the technical details of the factor analysis: /EXTRACTION specifies that the technique to be used in identifying factors is PAF; the first /CRITERIA command specifies that the criterion for selection of the number of factors in the extracted solution is Kaiser's rule (minimum eigenvalue of 1) and allows the default 25 iterations in order to reach a solution; /ROTATION specifies that an oblique method of rotation, oblimin, will be used; and the second /CRITERIA command indicates that the default amount of correlation between variables will be accepted (delta=0, where delta is an indicator of the amount of permitted correlation) and, again, the default number of 25 iterations will be permitted to seek a solution. The /METHOD=CORRELATION command, also a default, instructs SPSS to use a correlation matrix to produce a solution.

Once the analysis is run, the requested output is first inspected to ensure that a factor solution is possible. In this case, the reported determinant is very small (8.13E-011, or 0.0000000000813), but not 0. While in some cases, such a small determinant might indicate a problem with multicollinearity, we do not worry about it unless problems are encountered in reaching a solution. The statistics produced from the /PRINT KMO command are shown in Table 3.2. This output includes a statistical test for correlation among the variables in the data set, Bartlett's test of sphericity. Bartlett's test tests the null hypothesis that there are no significant correlations in the data set (in matrix algebra terms, it tests if the matrix is an identity matrix with all off-diagonal values not significantly different from 0). Where $p<0.05$, we accept the alternative hypothesis, and conclude that there is sufficient correlation (at least somewhere) within the correlation matrix to proceed with factor analysis. Table 3.2 also shows that the KMO MSA for all variables taken together is 0.903, well above the rule of thumb of 0.5, indicating that the data set contains at least some variables that share a substantial amount of common variance, and thus that factors can be formed.

While different factor analysis practitioners proceed in slightly different steps, the sequence of the SPSS output guides the investigator to next consider two aspects of the contribution of individual variables to the solution. The two relevant outputs for our example are in Tables 3.3 and 3.4. The KMO MSA for each variable is shown in the diagonal of the anti-image correlation matrix (Table 3.3). While only an extract is shown here, in fact the MSA for all variables in the analysis was high (above 0.8), indicating that each variable has the potential to contribute to a factor in the initial solution.

The initial and extraction communalities for each variable are shown in Table 3.4. The important column in this output is the extraction communalities column, which shows the amount of variance in each variable that is explained by the extracted number of factors. Here, we see that three variables (SysQual5, SysQual7 and ServQ5) have communality below 0.4. These variables are potential candidates for omission from the final solution – but a decision should not be made until after the complete solution has been inspected: this default factor

Table 3.2 KMO MSA and Bartlett's test results for a test that a factor solution is possible in the example problem

KMO and Bartlett's test

Kaiser–Meyer–Olkin measure of sampling adequacy		0.903
Bartlett's test of sphericity	*Approx. Chi-square*	*4379.49*
	df	325
	Sig.	0.000

solution might be considered inadequate and a solution with a different number of factors from a different subset of variables might be preferred, in which case one or more of these variables might then have sufficient communality to be included in the final solution while variables that have sufficient communality in this solution might be better omitted.

We next consider the number of factors to be extracted. The relevant outputs for initial inspection are the reports of variance explained by each of the solutions – initial, extracted and rotated (Table 3.5), and the scree plot, which we have already seen for this problem in Figure 3.4. The initial solution appears on the left-hand side of Table 3.5. Here, we can see that the initial solution contains as many factors as variables (26). The factors are numbered in order of eigenvalue (which, recall, is proportional to the amount of variance they explain). Five variables have eigenvalue >1. Details of the variance explained by only the extracted factors (in this case, set to be those with eigenvalue >1) are shown in the central columns of the output.

The total amount of variance explained by the five extracted factors is a respectable 66.01%, but before rotation, this variance is concentrated on Factor 1. The final column shows the sums of squared factor loadings for each of the factors when the solution is rotated. The variance is now spread more evenly. These values can be converted to percentages of variance

Table 3.3 Extract from the anti-image correlation matrix for the example problem

		InfQual1	InfQual2	InfQual3	InfQual4	InfQual5	InfQual6	SysQual1
Anti-image correlation	InfQual1	0.930[a]	−0.350	0.011	−0.083	−0.036	−0.040	0.045
	InfQual2	−0.350	0.939[a]	−0.245	−0.276	−0.083	0.001	0.049
	InfQual3	0.011	−0.245	0.934[a]	−0.351	0.017	−0.305	0.060
	InfQual4	−0.083	−0.276	−0.351	0.916[a]	−0.243	−0.064	−0.050
	InfQual5	−0.036	−0.083	0.017	−0.243	0.909[a]	−0.504	−0.001
	InfQual6	−0.040	0.001	−0.305	−0.064	−0.504	0.888[a]	−0.073
	SysQual1	0.045	0.049	0.060	−0.050	−0.001	−0.073	0.913[a]
	SysQual2	0.071	−0.007	−0.126	0.022	−0.126	0.251	−0.565
	SysQual3	0.247	0.024	0.050	−0.089	0.112	−0.069	0.181
	SysQual4	−0.180	0.009	0.008	0.029	−0.098	0.029	0.000
	SysQual5	−0.041	0.062	−0.015	−0.006	0.044	−0.176	0.196
	SysQual6	−0.349	0.029	0.035	0.085	−0.156	0.022	−0.108
	SysQual7	0.118	−0.016	−0.098	0.071	−0.021	−0.084	0.032
	SysQual8	0.032	0.012	0.065	−0.127	0.037	−0.096	−0.092

[a]KMO MSA for each individual variable in the diagonal.

Table 3.4 Initial communalities (SMC) and extraction communalities for the example problem

Communalities	Initial	Extraction
InfQual1	0.699	0.622
InfQual2	0.772	0.733
InfQual3	0.767	0.765
InfQual4	0.778	0.769
InfQual5	0.758	0.720
InfQual6	0.766	0.732
SysQu l1	0.801	0.803
SysQual2	0.795	0.784
SysQual3	0.524	0.420
SysQual4	0.456	0.449
SysQual5	0.366	0.285
SysQual6	0.651	0.550
SysQual7	0.326	0.228
SysQual8	0.687	0.590
SysQual9	0.728	0.641
ServQ1	0.797	0.815
ServQ2	0.866	0.859
ServQ3	0.895	0.929
ServQ4	0.704	0.642
ServQ5	0.557	0.373
ServQ6	0.719	0.826
ServQ7	0.656	0.619
NetBen1	0.885	0.839
NetBen2	0.885	0.804
NetBen3	0.669	0.636
NetBen4	0.709	0.729

Note: Extraction method: Principal axis factoring.

explained by dividing by the sum of squared factor loadings for each factor by the total number of variables in the solution. SPSS does not do this for oblique rotations (it does for orthogonal rotations) because the sum of the variance explained by each factor in an obliquely rotated solution is greater than the total variance explained by the solution itself. This is because the factors are correlated with one another and therefore share some variance.

A word is required about the scree plot for this problem (Figure 3.4). We have already noted that it could be interpreted as supporting a one-, four- or eight-factor solution, but Kaiser's rule suggested a five-factor solution. While the five-factor solution explains a satisfactory amount of total variance, we still need to inspect the factor loadings in the complete

Table 3.5 Table of variance explained in the initial solution (columns headed Initial eigenvalues), the extracted solution (Extractions sums of squared loadings columns) and the complete rotated solution (Rotation sums of squared loadings columns) for the first solution produced for example problem

Factor	Initial eigenvalues			Extraction sums of squared loadings			Rotation sums of squared loadings[a]
	Total	% of Variance	Cumulative %	Total	% of Variance	Cumulative %	Total
1	11.468	44.106	44.106	11.172	42.969	42.969	7.842
2	2.170	8.345	52.451	1.889	7.266	50.235	5.557
3	2.112	8.123	60.575	1.811	6.964	57.199	8.261
4	1.762	6.775	67.350	1.456	5.600	62.799	6.285
5	1.192	4.584	71.934	0.834	3.209	66.008	5.695
6	0.888	3.415	75.349				
7	0.815	3.135	78.484				
8	0.761	2.928	81.413				
9	0.688	2.647	84.060				
10	0.503	1.933	85.993				
11	0.469	1.802	87.796				
12	0.453	1.744	89.539				
13	0.365	1.404	90.944				
14	0.336	1.294	92.238				
15	0.296	1.139	93.376				
16	0.275	1.059	94.435				
17	0.218	0.837	95.272				
18	0.202	0.776	96.048				
19	0.188	0.724	96.771				
20	0.180	0.690	97.462				
21	0.148	0.568	98.030				
22	0.142	0.547	98.577				
23	0.131	0.502	99.080				
24	0.113	0.435	99.514				
25	0.069	0.266	99.780				
26	0.057	0.220	100.000				

Note: Extraction method: Principal axis factoring.

[a]When factors are correlated, sums of squared loadings cannot be added to obtain a total variance.

rotated solution to decide how many factors might be best (as well as whether we should include all variables in the final solution).

Table 3.6 compares the extracted (and unrotated) five-factor solution (the Factor Matrix panel) with the rotated five-factor solution (the Pattern

Table 3.6 Comparison of extracted factor solution (Factor Matrix) with oblique rotated factor solution (Pattern Matrix)

| | Factor matrix[a] | | | | | | Pattern matrix[b] | | | | | |
| | Factor | | | | | | Factor | | | | | |
		1	2	3	4	5		1	2	3	4	5
InfQual2		0.767					ServQ3	0.987				
ServQ3		0.761					ServQ2	0.940				
InfQual3		0.748					ServQ1	0.914				
ServQ7		0.742					ServQ4	0.733				
ServQ2		0.737					ServQ7	0.533				
SysQual1		0.737					SysQual7					
SysQual2		0.734					NetBen4		0.846			
InfQual4		0.733		0.413			NetBen1		0.807			
ServQ1		0.723			0.401		NetBen3		0.804			
InfQual5		0.722					NetBen2		0.801			
InfQual1		0.711					InfQual6			0.886		
ServQ6		0.697				0.562	InfQual4			0.881		
NetBen1		0.696	0.576				InfQual3			0.848		
SysQual9		0.693					InfQual5			0.826		
SysQual8		0.690					InfQual2			0.756		
InfQual6		0.683		0.455			InfQual1			0.571		

(Continued)

Table 3.6 (Continued)

	Factor matrix[a]						Pattern matrix[b]				
	Factor						Factor				
	1	2	3	4	5		1	2	3	4	5
ServQ4	0.679					SysQual1				-0.773	
NetBen2	0.668	0.585				SysQual2				-0.738	
SysQual6	0.600					SysQual4				0.729	
SysQual5	0.476					SysQual9				-0.625	
SysQual7	0.462					SysQual3				0.617	
SysQual3	-0.456					SysQual8				-0.563	
ServQ5	0.448					ServQ6					0.831
NetBen4	0.552	0.612				SysQual6					0.58
NetBen3	0.493	0.591				ServQ5					0.522
SysQual4				0.403		SysQual5					

Note: For factor matrix: extraction method=principal axis factoring; for pattern matrix: extraction method=principal axis factoring and rotation method=Oblimin with Kaiser normalisation.
[a] Five factors extracted. Thirteen iterations required.
[b] Rotation converged in nine iterations.

Matrix panel). The order of variables is that defined by the /FORMAT SORT command and all factor loadings below 0.4 have been suppressed to assist with the identification of those variables that load most strongly on each factor. It is clear to see that the unrotated solution does not present a simple structure and cannot be interpreted while the rotated solution is much closer to a simple structure and permits interpretation of the results.

A close look at the rotated solution in Table 3.6 does, however, indicate some difficulties. While five ServQ variables load (moderately) strongly (between 0.987 for ServQ3 and 0.533 for ServQ7) on Factor 1, a sixth variable is also listed with them. This sixth variable, SysQual7, loads most strongly on Factor 1 (according to the SORT rule) but has a loading below the cut-off for display of 0.4. Furthermore, this variable is drawn from the SysQual pool, and so is less likely to be about the quality of services offered on the website than the other variables that load most strongly on Factor 1. In addition, it has low communality (recall our discussion of Table 3.4). If we retain a five-factor solution, this variable should be omitted unless its omission causes other problems with the results. It is also worth looking at the set of variables that load most strongly on Factor 5. Only one of these variables, ServQ6, has a strong factor loading, three variables have modest factor loadings of above 0.4 but below 0.6, and the fifth variable that loads most strongly on Factor 5 has a factor loading below 0.4 (and is therefore suppressed). This factor looks to be weak relative to the others, and because it combines both ServQ and SysQual items, appears also to be difficult to interpret.

At this stage, the investigator needs to invoke the art of factor analysis once again. Might a different rotation produce a more satisfactory solution (options include an orthogonal rather than an oblique rotation, oblique rotation using oblimin but with a different value of delta or oblique rotation using a different rotation method)? Might a four-factor solution more meaningfully and usefully permit a summary of users' evaluations of the website? A glance back at Table 3.5 shows that, at least in the initial solution, a four-factor solution explained 67.35% of the variance in the data set. The scree plot also suggested that a four-factor solution was feasible. Perhaps a combination of a different rotation method and a four-factor solution might be more satisfactory. Using the principle of Ockam's razor, we suggest reducing the number of factors (and thus simplifying both the final solution and the number of possible solutions to be tested before reaching a final solution) before inspecting different rotations.

The investigator ran several additional factor analyses after the example shown here, first fixing the number of factors to be extracted to four (in SPSS syntax, /CRITERIA FACTORS(4)), and then progressively removing variables that did not contribute to the solution (on the basis of their MSA, communality and factor loadings). For each run, she checked all the diagnostic statistics that we have described in this example to ensure that changes in the number of factors extracted and the set of variables included in the analysis did not introduce new problems. Her final solution is shown in Table 3.7 (table of variance explained) and Table 3.8 (pattern, i.e. oblique rotated solution, matrix). Not shown are that the determinant, Bartlett's test, KMO MSA for all variables and for each individual variable, and the extraction communalities for all variables were all satisfactory.

Table 3.7 Table of variance explained for the investigator's final solution to the example problem

	Initial eigenvalues			Extraction sums of squared loadings			Rotation sums of squared loadings[a]
Factor	Total	% of Variance	Cumulative %	Total	% of Variance	Cumulative %	Total
1	9.798	51.571	51.571	9.548	50.253	50.253	6.927
2	2.054	10.813	62.384	1.808	9.518	59.771	5.449
3	1.877	9.878	72.261	1.629	8.576	68.347	7.412
4	1.363	7.174	79.435	1.119	5.892	74.239	6.696
5	0.584	3.073	82.508				
6	0.501	2.635	85.143				
7	0.442	2.326	87.469				
8	0.359	1.890	89.359				
9	0.345	1.815	91.174				
10	0.280	1.475	92.649				
11	0.256	1.347	93.996				
12	0.228	1.199	95.196				
13	0.190	0.999	96.195				
14	0.170	0.893	97.088				
15	0.156	0.820	97.908				
16	0.139	0.729	98.637				
17	0.127	0.668	99.305				
18	0.072	0.380	99.686				
19	0.060	0.314	100.000				

Note: Extraction method: Principal axis factoring.
[a] When factors are correlated, sums of squared loadings cannot be added to obtain a total variance.

Table 3.8 Comparison of extracted factor solution (Factor Matrix) with oblique rotated factor solution (Pattern Matrix)

| | Factor matrix[a] | | | | | Pattern matrix[a] | | | |
| | Factor | | | | | Factor | | | |
	1	2	3	4		1	2	3	4
InfQual2	0.780				ServQ3	0.966			
ServQ3	0.778				ServQ2	0.938			
InfQual3	0.761		−0.429		ServQ1	0.898			
InfQual4	0.753		−0.447		ServQ4	0.753			
ServQ2	0.750				ServQ7	0.536			
ServQ7	0.746				NetBen4		0.867		
ServQ1	0.742				NetBen1		0.850		
InfQual5	0.737		−0.414		NetBen2		0.847		
SysQual1	0.732			0.482	NetBen3		0.804		
SysQual2	0.724			0.414	InfQual6			−0.902	
NetBen1	0.711	0.552			InfQual4			−0.872	
InfQual1	0.703				InfQual3			−0.863	
InfQual6	0.696		−0.469		InfQual5			−0.823	
SysQual8	0.696			0.410	InfQual2			−0.783	
SysQual9	0.695			0.480	InfQual1			−0.664	
NetBen2	0.683	0.581			SysQual1				0.885
ServQ4	0.673				SysQual9				0.841
NetBen4	0.545	0.597			SysQual2				0.807
NetBen3	0.497	0.569			SysQual8				0.744

A total of 19 variables was included in the final four-factor solution. The four factors explained 74.239% of the variance in the 19 variables. Each of the four factors in the rotated solution was readily interpretable: Factor 1 represents the quality of the services available on the destination's website; Factor 2 represents the users' perceptions of the benefits they can obtain from using the site; Factor 3 represents the users' perceptions of the quality of the information that the site contains; and Factor 4 represents the users' perceptions of the technical quality of the site.

For interest, we also include Table 3.9, the correlations between these four factors (produced by default in SPSS for obliquely rotated solutions).

Table 3.9 Correlation between factors in the rotated solution shown in Table 3.8

Factor correlation matrix

Factor	1	2	3	4
1	1.000	0.417	−0.555	0.599
2	0.417	1.000	−0.467	0.454
3	−0.555	−0.467	1.000	−0.581
4	0.599	0.454	−0.581	1.000

Note: Extraction method: Principal axis factoring. Rotation method: Oblimin with Kaiser normalisation.

Using the Results of a Factor Analysis

Unless discovery of the factor structure is an end in itself (a rare situation), more work needs to be done to evaluate the quality of each factor and, usually, to estimate a value on each factor that can be used in subsequent analyses. For example, to be able to say something about the quality of the destination website, the researcher in our example needs a single, reliable value for each of the four factors of interest (perceived quality of services offered, perceived benefits of using the site, perceived information quality and perceived technical quality). To do this, she needs to create a new variable for each factor. To avoid confusion with the new (sometimes called the 'latent' variable) and the original observed variables, the observed variables are often called 'items'. Together, the items form a 'scale' that will be used to measure the new variable.

Several options for creating new variables to represent factors are available. The most mechanical of these options is to accept the software's default of calculating a 'factor score'. A number of methods are available, but the common approach is to calculate the factor score as a weighted sum of the contribution of every variable included in the factor analysis on the factor. While the weight is derived from the factor loadings, it is *not* the factor loading, but a product of the factor loadings and the inverse of the correlation matrix. Furthermore, the factor scores for each case are the product of the factor loading and the *standardised* value of the item. All in all, it is not easy to see exactly how a factor score is derived from the factor model. In addition, while creating new variables in this way is quick and easy using statistical software, the variables themselves have only limited use. Because they are based on correlations found in a specific sample, they cannot be used to compare results across samples. Thus, in the example, factor scores for information quality after the website has been redesigned could not be compared with those obtained before the redesign, so it would not be possible to conclude that the redesign has improved (or reduced) information quality.

The simplest, and most common, way to obtain a score that can be compared across samples is to calculate the average (mean) value of the variables that load most strongly on each factor. This approach is most satisfactory when the variables are inter-correlated and additive. Inter-correlation is an indicator of internal consistency or reliability of measurement. The most common indicator of internal consistency is Cronbach's alpha (Cronbach, 1951), a value from 0 to 1 which is usually reported for each factor with the results of the factor analysis (although most software requires you to generate alpha using a separate 'Reliabilities' function). Cronbach's alpha, calculated as

$$\alpha = \frac{k \cdot \bar{r}}{1 + (k-1) \cdot \bar{r}}$$

can be interpreted as the average correlation among the items in a scale ($\bar{r}$), adjusted for the number of items in the scale (k). The rule of thumb is that α should be greater than 0.7 for satisfactory reliability. Because of the difficulty of achieving this value in many situations, it has become common to cite Robinson *et al.* (1991) as supporting values as low as 0.6 when research is exploratory. Rather a lot of authors retrospectively describe their research as exploratory when they discover that α is between 0.6 and 0.7, so beware of this in reading research results. Use of the lower threshold might be justified when a scale has been developed for a specific study or used for the first time, but a lower value is still an indication of lower reliability, and therefore more error, in measuring a variable. When a latent variable with low reliability is included in a subsequent analysis and is found not to have a significant effect, it can be difficult to determine if the lack of significance is a true lack of significance or simply a result of poor measurement. Cronbach's alpha increases with n and, because it does not account for chance correlations, can overestimate scale quality, so it is always important to look at the actual items that make up the scale to fully evaluate if a scale with a satisfactory alpha is logically as well as mathematically satisfactory (Cronbach & Shavelson, 2004).

Example: Dimensions of wine tourism

Most of the studies that use factor analysis in tourism use it in order to form new variables which will be used to address the main problem of interest. For example, Cohen and Ben-Nun (2009) used data from interviews with 373 adult tourists in Israel to differentiate between the interests of different tourist market segments in wine tourism. They asked interviewees to rate the importance of 42 features of wine tourism.

Because of the complexity of characterising the differences in market segments on the basis of 42 variables, they first used factor analysis (PAF with oblimin oblique rotation) to reduce the data to a smaller set of factors. Twenty-two of the 42 features formed three factors, all with satisfactory reliability as indicated by Cronbach's alpha above 0.7. They labelled the factors: winery atmosphere, cultural activities and family activities, and calculated a factor score for each of these factors for each interviewee. As a result of this preliminary data reduction, they were able to compare market segments defined in different ways (recent visitor to a winery, level of involvement in wine, with or without children) on each of the three factors.

Among their observations were that families with children rated family activities as more important than other features of wine tourism, and people who had not recently visited a winery were less interested in winery atmosphere than those who were already wine tourists. They directed their conclusions to the promoters of wine tourism, recommending that features should be planned to appeal to different groups of potential tourists.

Data Considerations and Other Issues in Factor Analysis

How large a sample is required to produce a meaningful and stable factor model? J.P. Guilford (1954), known for his work on the development of factor analysis as he developed his theory of the structure of intelligence, suggested that the minimum number of cases should be 200, but he was working with complex factor structures, and recent works suggest that fewer cases are often sufficient, depending on the number of variables in the model and how strong the factor model is. Several rules of thumb have been proposed, based on the number of cases per variable and an absolute minimum. Summarising them, Hair et al. (2006) proposed that as few as 5 cases per variable and 50 cases altogether could be sufficient in some cases, but noted that 10–20 cases per variable is the norm. A more conservative guide, based on Guadagnoli and Velicer (1988) and often quoted, is that a sample of 150 should be sufficient provided the factor model is strong, i.e. that each factor in the final model has at least one variable that loads 0.8 or above on it. In any case, the goal should be to obtain sufficient observations to avoid over-fitting the model to the sample (and therefore reducing the probability that it can be considered reflective of the population). Whatever the available sample size, the effect on the reliability of the factor loadings should also be considered when evaluating the results.

While the techniques described here are quite robust to different distributions of the underlying variables, they tend to work best for numeric data that are normally distributed. Software, such as MPlus (Muthén & Muthén, 2010), is now available to deal with categorical data. This software has the advantage that it also produces some measures of the quality of the fit of the solution to the original data set and can be used for CFA as well as EFA. For now, though, it can only be used by writing syntax and offers no simple pull-down menu-based interface.

Finally, given developments in statistics over the more than 100 years since factor analysis was first described by Spearman (1904), it is worth asking if it is still a valid and useful technique. Many questions were considered by leading psychometricians at the University of North Carolina in 2004, and the book that brings their considerations together shows that factor analysis is alive and well, even if (or, perhaps, especially because) its shortcomings are well known (Cudeck & McCallum, 2007). Nonetheless, given developments in CFA using structural equation models, in particular, there is much debate about whether EFA is still relevant. Statisticians and psychometricians take sides in this debate with religious fervour (see, for example, Hurley et al. [1997]). In favour of using structural equation modelling for CFA are arguments that structural equation modelling provides robust models in which hypotheses about factor structure can be tested statistically, and this is the case – provided you have a factor structure (hypothesised set of factors and hypothesised simple structure in which each observed variable measures or reflects only one factor) to test. CFA is, however, very cumbersome for exploration and, while it might be argued that exploration in the absence of prior theory or argument for a given factor structure or a set of alternative factor structures to be compared is statistically weak, it is hard to imagine that there will never be situations in which the need for exploration and discovery outweighs the need for statistical testing. While controversial, there is still considerable support for the use of EFA to simplify factor structures before conducting structural equation modelling. For example, Timothy Brown (2006: 209), the author of the most complete modern text on CFA using structural equation modelling methods, describes EFA and 'E/CFA' as 'important precursors to CFA for developing and refining a measurement model'.

Cluster Analysis

Having dealt with the use of factor analysis to reduce a large set of *variables* to a smaller set of factors, we now turn to the use of cluster analysis to identify classes or clusters of similar *cases* in a data set. Perhaps the most common use of cluster analysis in tourism is for market segmentation.

Example: Tourist market clusters

Market segmentation studies use cluster analysis to identify groups of tourists who are similar in terms of one or more characteristics or points of view. The characteristics or points of view are entered into the cluster analysis as variables and similar groups are uncovered by the analysis. This is a different approach to that used by Cohen and Ben-Nun (2009) (see example above) who used predefined market segments. There are many examples of cluster analysis in tourist segmentation, but sadly many contain quite basic errors. Here, we describe one study that can be used as an example of good practice.

Hudson and Ritchie (2002) used cluster analysis to identify and profile five clusters of domestic tourists in the Alberta region of Canada. They began with some qualitative research to identify important influences on domestic tourism, and found 13 influences covering a wide range of issues such as the quality of accommodation, the variety of activities offered, holiday periods and weather conditions. Questions about the importance of each of these influences were then put to 3017 residents in telephone interviews. On the basis of their answers to the questions, the residents could be clustered into five groups, each with quite a different domestic tourism profile. By looking at the common demographic characteristics of the people in each cluster, as well as their preferences for each of the influences on tourism, five market segments were identified: the young, urban outdoor market; the indoor leisure traveller market; the children-first market; the fair-weather friends market; and the older cost-conscious market.

How cluster analysis works

Our starting point is an **X** matrix of the same structure as that described in Figure 3.1, but our goal now is different: Instead of reducing the p variables to c factors where $c<p$, we now aim to summarise the n cases using k clusters where $k<n$. Again, we begin with statistics that represent similarity, but in cluster analysis we are concerned with the similarity between cases. Again, many techniques are available, but they share some elements. And again, while there is a mathematical basis, the final solution owes much to the art of the investigator.

Formally, when used to classify cases, cluster analysis is a method of identifying groups within a sample or population based on measured characteristics of the sample or population itself. Cases are thus grouped on the basis of the information provided in variables. The goal is to identify a set of clusters in which each case is as similar as possible to the other cases in the cluster while being as different as possible from the cases in the other clusters. Put more formally, we seek to simultaneously minimise the dissimilarity (maximise the similarity) between cases within each cluster and maximise the distances (differences) between clusters.

Example: Clusters

Two simple examples of cluster formation are shown in Figure 3.8. In both situations, 50 cases are plotted in terms of their scores on two variables, x_1 and x_2. The distinction between clusters appears to be quite clear in the left-hand panel (even though the most distant case from the axis in the lower left-hand cluster and the most distant case from the upper right-hand corner of the plot in the upper-right hand cluster are nearer to one another than to the most distant cases in their cluster). In the right-hand panel, two clusters have been formed by defining a line that has been rotated about the mean of both variables, but there is no 'natural' division into two clusters here and the investigator might just as readily have decided to distinguish between three or even four clusters if a solution with more clusters better served his/her purposes.

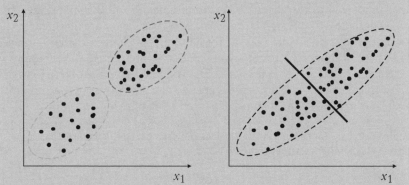

Figure 3.8 Two cluster solutions derived from two different distributions of cases on two variables

There are too many cluster analytic techniques for us to provide a thorough overview here. Instead, we begin by discussing one issue that all have in common: the representation of the similarity (or difference) between pairs of cases and between pairs of clusters. We then focus on one technique, hierarchical cluster analysis, which allows us to illustrate additional questions that arise in almost all cluster analyses.

Using distance measures to represent similarity and difference in cluster analysis

In all cluster analysis techniques, clusters are formed on the basis of the similarity or difference between pairs of objects. By convention, measures of both similarity and difference are described as *distance measures*. Distances might be calculated between pairs of cases, pairs of clusters or between a case and the centroid or centre of a cluster. In general, distances between pairs of cases, c_i and c_j, or pairs of clusters, C_i and C_j, are denoted d_{ij}. Any measure of distance between a pair of points can be used. There are a great many of these, and researchers continue to invent more as they seek to cluster cases on the basis of increasingly complex sets of characteristics. In this chapter, we provide an overview of those distance measures that it is most commonly assumed an investigator using or reading the results of a cluster analysis would know.

The fundamental measure of distance for variables measured on a binary scale is simple matching, which can be presented as either the count of attributes that are common to two cases, or the proportion or percentage agreement. Table 3.10 provides a simple example. Three variables, sex, income and completion of tertiary studies, are used to characterise five individuals (cases). The distance between each pair of cases is calculated by adding up the number of characteristics the individuals have in common. So, the distance between Cases 1 and 2, which have no characteristics in common is 0, the distance between Cases 2 and 3, which have two characteristics in common is 2 and so on. These values are often converted to proportions by dividing by the total number of characteristics (variables) that have been matched, and lower values are interpreted as representative of greater difference. The result is a matrix, known as a proximity matrix, shown in Table 3.11. Many approaches to cluster analysis use a proximity matrix to represent the distance between pairs of cases.

Table 3.10 Data for calculation of distance between pairs of individuals based on shared characteristics across three variables

Case (individual)	x_1 Male(1)/female (0)	x_2 High (1)/low (0) income	x_3 Has (1)/ does not have (0) tertiary degree
1	0	0	0
2	1	1	1
3	0	1	1
4	1	1	1
5	1	0	0

Table 3.11 Proximity matrix for distances between cases in Table 3.10

Case	1	2	3	4	5
1	1.00	0.00	0.33	0.00	0.67
2	0.00	1.00	0.67	1.00	0.33
3	0.33	0.67	1.00	0.67	0.00
4	0.000	1.00	0.67	1.00	0.33
5	0.67	0.33	0.00	0.33	1.00

Note: Proximity expressed as a proportion of simple match of shared attributes. Lower values indicate greater distance.

A similar approach can be used for variables with more than two response categories. Chi-square or related measures of the difference between two distributions are usually used to represent the distance between each pair of cases when the variables are categorical.

Finally, many distance measures are available when the variables on the basis of which distance is calculated are measured on metric variables. The base distance measure is the Euclidean distance, familiar in the two variable situation from high school geometry. The general formula is

$$d_{ij} = \sqrt{\sum_{p=1}^{p} \left(x_{ip} - x_{jp} \right)^2}$$

where x_{ip} and x_{jp} are scores on variable x_p for cases i and j, respectively.

In the familiar two variable situation, the sum is of the squared distance between cases on two variables. In the p variable situation, the sum is of the squared distance between cases on all p variables. To reduce computational load, the squared Euclidean distance is often used.

The Mahalanobis distance, introduced in Chapter 2, is effectively a standardised form of the squared Euclidean index which takes the covariances between variables into account (Mahalanobis, 1936). This is useful when the variables from which clusters are formed are correlated because it avoids inflation of similarity by extracting the variance shared among the variables.

Some cluster analysis methods allow (and some require) specification of the points within each cluster between which distances are calculated. The four main options are illustrated in Figure 3.9. Nearest neighbour or single linkage distances are most useful in distinguishing between clusters when clusters form 'chains', e.g. when values of all variables increase across clusters. Furthest neighbour or complete linkage distances are most useful when clusters fall together in 'clumps' rather than chains. Average linkage distances are calculated as the average distance between every pair of cases within a cluster and have the advantage that they characterise clusters on

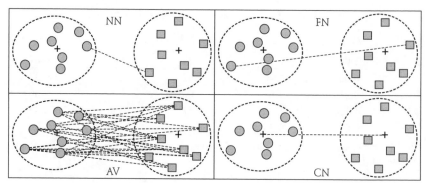

Figure 3.9 Different bases for calculating the distance between two clusters (crosses indicate their centroids): NN=nearest neighbour (also termed single linkage), FN=furthest neighbour (complete linkage), AV=average linkage, CN=centroids

the basis of all cases within the cluster rather than a single case. Finally, Figure 3.9 illustrates centroid distance, the distance between the defined midpoints of two clusters.

Partitioning

Techniques for cluster analysis are typically divided into two types: partitioning and hierarchical. Partitioning methods can be used to identify clusters in a 'single' pass based on set criteria, such as jointly maximising the covariance between clusters at the same time as minimising the covariance within clusters. (In reality, a series of iterations is almost always required to identify satisfactory partitions.) Many partitioning methods have been invented, and many of these have been developed for the specific problems of specific disciplines, including biology (e.g. Li *et al.*, 2008) and population dynamics (e.g. Piccarreta & Billari, 2007).

The most widely available partitioning technique is k-means clustering. As its name implies, it is suitable for use with quantitative variables for which the mean is a suitable summary statistic. With k-means clustering, the analyst first decides on the number of groups, k, that would be useful for the purpose of the study. The k-means procedure makes an initial partition of cases into k clusters, determines the mean value (centroid) for the cases in each cluster on each of the variables of interest and calculates the distance of each case from each cluster mean; a statistic is selected to represent the total distance of cases from the centroids of the clusters in which they have been placed. If a case that has been placed in one cluster is closer to the mean of another cluster than to the mean of its own cluster, it is moved to the nearer cluster and the cluster means and distances are calculated again. Cases continue to be moved until the sum of within-group variances is minimised. There are many variations on this technique that are well summarised by Everitt *et al.* (2001).

With partitioning techniques, the most important choices for the investigator to make are the basis on which partitions will be made, and usually, the number of partitions or clusters that are required. These decisions are often based on prior knowledge of the data and the problem, or on theoretical predictions. When such information is not available, an investigator might begin with a hierarchical method before partitioning.

Hierarchical cluster analysis

Hierarchical clustering methods can be either divisive or agglomerative. Divisive techniques begin by placing all cases into a single large cluster and progressively subdividing one cluster at a time into two clusters according to the rules that focus on maximising the differences between the clusters obtained from each division. The results are often displayed in a tree diagram which helps the investigator to decide which branches describe meaningful and useful clusters. Agglomerative techniques work in the opposite direction, beginning by characterising each case as a single cluster, and progressively joining the most similar pairs of clusters until all cases and clusters are joined together in a single large cluster. While stopping rules might be invoked in hierarchical cluster analysis, typically the investigator permits the process to proceed until its conclusion, then he/she uses one or more diagnostic reports to decide on the number of clusters that might best distinguish between groups of cases. We will focus here on agglomerative hierarchical cluster analysis to illustrate the most important decisions and how they are commonly made.

The first decision to be made is the clustering method to be used. Some agglomerative hierarchical clustering methods are suitable for both categorical and metric variables, while others (including those offered by SPSS and other general software packages) are suitable for metric or categorical data but not both. A common method is the unweighted pair-group method using arithmetic averages (UPGMA). Average distances between clusters are calculated and clusters are joined (one pair at a time) to maximise the mean distance between cases. This method is equally suited to clusters in chains or clumps, and can work with a wide variety of distance measures, so it is the default method in most software programs (in SPSS, it is called the between-groups method). Median clustering is often used for categorical data: The median or centroid of each cluster is the point that represents the most common value among all cases in the cluster of the attributes (variables) that characterise them, and distances are calculated on the basis of matching or Euclidean distance. Ward's method is a useful method when the variables which characterise clusters are all metric: At each stage, the pair of clusters that is joined is the pair whose agglomeration will result in the minimum increase in total within-cluster variance.

Once a clustering method and distance measure have been chosen, hierarchical cluster analysis is normally entrusted to the computer, which produces the proximity matrix and then proceeds, according to the rules of the clustering method, to join clusters. The nearest (least distant) clusters are identified from the proximity matrix and joined first. Joining continues until the most distant (and therefore most different) clusters are joined together. Decisions about how many clusters are likely to represent the groups in the data well are based on the distances at which clusters are joined: The further apart the clusters that are joined in the later stages of the cluster analysis are, the more likely they are to form meaningfully distinct clusters. Reports and plots are available to help investigators decide how many meaningful clusters might be formed. The following example focuses on one report, the agglomeration schedule, and one plot, the dendrogram.

Example: Using reports and plots to guide selection of the number of clusters

Table 3.12 shows the agglomeration schedule from SPSS for a cluster analysis of the tourism infrastructure available in 13 European countries, measured with three metric variables. The UPGMA method was used to form clusters. The coefficients reported in the centre column are the Euclidean distances between pairs of countries.

The schedule shows which clusters were combined at each stage. The last three columns allow each case and cluster to be tracked forward and backward according to the sequence in which it was joined with another. A 0 in one of the 'Stage cluster first appears' columns indicates that the 'cluster' was at that stage a single case. Thus, we can see that in Stage 1, countries 7 and 10 were joined together. The tourism infrastructure of these countries is very similar, with a Euclidean distance of 1.221. This cluster (consisting now of both Cases 7 and 10) next appears in Stage 2, where we can see that Cluster 7 (clusters are given the lowest number of the case or cluster in the join) has been combined with Case 11, a country whose tourism infrastructure is similar (Euclidean distance of 2.022) to the 'average' of the countries in Cluster 7.

Looking now to the final stages in the agglomeration schedule (the final lines of Table 3.12), we can see a very large increase in the size of the coefficient for agglomeration in Stage 12 compared to the coefficient for Stage 11. This indicates that there is a large distance between the clusters joined in Stage 12 (Clusters 1 and 6). Working back we can see, however,

Table 3.12 The agglomeration schedule shows which pairs of clusters are combined at each stage, and how distant the combined clusters are from one another

| | Cluster Combined | | | Stage Cluster First Appears | | Next |
Stage	Cluster 1	Cluster 2	Coefficients	Cluster 1	Cluster 2	Stage
1	7	10	1.221	0	0	2
2	7	11	2.022	1	0	4
3	4	9	2.100	0	0	5
4	6	7	2.385	0	2	12
5	2	4	3.059	0	3	11
6	5	13	4.061	0	0	7
7	3	5	6.161	0	6	8
8	1	3	6.177	0	7	9
9	1	12	6.264	8	0	10
10	1	8	7.308	9	0	11
11	1	2	7.440	10	5	12
12	1	6	15.835	11	4	0

that the coefficients for agglomeration in Stages 10 and 11 are quite similar. On this basis, it would seem that there are two quite distinct clusters of countries in this data set, but no more.

While it is possible to trace which cases have been joined in each cluster from the agglomeration schedule, it is rather tiresome to do so. Cluster analysis software provides various tree diagrams to assist with tracing. Figure 3.10 presents the SPSS-produced dendrogram for the tourism infrastructure analysis. Distances are rescaled to a minimum of 0 and a maximum of 25, and labels can be placed to the left of each bar. The 'Num' is the SPSS case number, which allows tracing back to the detail in the agglomeration schedule. The bars for each case are connected at the rescaled distance where the cases were joined into clusters, and each bar is then extended to the distance at which the cluster was joined with another cluster.

For example, we can see that the two nearest cases, Hungary (Case 7) and Latvia (Case 10), were joined together in a cluster, then at a greater distance they were joined with Lithuania (Case 11) and (later – Stage 4, according to the agglomeration schedule) with Greece. We can also see that France and Italy are similar to one another. An idea of the suitable number of clusters can be obtained from the dotted bars drawn (by the investigator) on the dendrogram. The line furthest to the right shows a clear distinction between the two clusters that were joined in the last stage: one small cluster, consisting of Hungary, Latvia, Lithuania and Greece, and a large cluster, consisting of the other

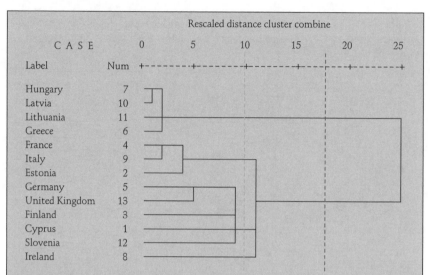

Figure 3.10 The dendrogram provides a graphical illustration of the distance between clusters combined at each stage

countries in the analysis. The dotted line just below distance 10 helps identify another possible division of clusters. It shows that the larger cluster could be further divided into a cluster consisting of France, Italy and Estonia, and a cluster of one country (Ireland), with the other countries in a single cluster.

Clearly, this process can be continued to produce smaller clusters of even more similar cases, but the investigator needs to find the balance between having meaningful and distinct clusters and having a small enough set of clusters to convey their meaning to others. In some situations, it might be useful to have a cluster of one case, where that case represents a special case, while in others the analyst might prefer a solution in which each cluster consists of at least two cases.

Evaluating and improving cluster analysis solutions

Few cluster analysis methods offer objective measures or statistical tests of quality. When the sample size is large enough, it can be split into subsamples and the results of running the same cluster analysis on the different subsamples compared. If they are similar, we can conclude that the method reliably reproduces a similar set of clusters across the whole sample. But, different clustering methods (and different distance measures) applied to the same data set can produce different solutions. Another test of the quality of a cluster solution is to run the analysis using different clustering methods and distance measures with the same sample; if the results are similar, our cluster solution is likely to offer a stable representation of the groups in the sample. Still, neither of these tests is really sufficient. We also need to ask if the results make sense (do they have 'face validity'?). Does it make sense, for example, to group Greece with Hungary, Latvia and Lithuania? Perhaps – but, the nature, quality and value of the cluster analysis solution depend on whether the variables which were used to form the clusters represent the dimensions along which clusters might be formed or interpreted sufficiently well. Adding another variable, or removing one, might change the formation of clusters markedly. Care needs also to be taken to ensure that each variable used for the formation of clusters carries an appropriate weight in the analysis. Variables that have a wider range, or that are highly correlated with others in the analysis can bias the solution in favour of clusters based on these influential variables. This might be desirable, but if not, one or more techniques must be used to remove their influence, for example by transformation of one or more variables, or by using clustering methods that remove the influence of correlated or influential variables. (The main pitfalls in cluster analysis and potential solutions to them are discussed by Everitt *et al.*, 2001.)

Ultimately, it is the investigator's judgement, based on knowledge of the context in which the analysis is conducted and the use to which the results will be put, that governs the final set of variables to be used to form clusters, and the final set of clusters chosen to represent a set of cases. Cluster analysis therefore remains very much an art – something worth taking into account the next time you read a newspaper article that classifies young people on the basis of their behaviour or consumers on the basis of the products they prefer!

Multidimensional Scaling and Correspondence Analysis

MDS and correspondence analysis enable objects (cases) to be placed in a multidimensional space, using two or more dimensions (similar to factors) derived from variables that represent the attributes of the objects. In marketing, where these techniques are commonly used, they are often used to evaluate and compare products and services (including hotels and restaurants) by mapping people's perceptions of actual products and services to their ideal. We refer the reader to Hair *et al.* (2006) for a good step-by-step guide to the conduct of correspondence analysis and MDS. Here, we provide an example to illustrate the techniques and the results that can be obtained when they are used with a different type of problem.

Example: Preferences of tourists

In our example, we have data for the clients of a tour booking service, including their preferences for certain types of activities (city tours, hiking, wine tasting, extreme sports, etc.) and some basic demographic information (sex, age, etc.). MDS allows us to map the similarities between clients on dimensions that represent their preferences. With correspondence analysis, it is also possible to classify clients on the basis of one or more characteristics.

Figure 3.11 shows the map obtained from correspondence analysis. The circles represent the positions of each activity relative to each dimension. These positions have coordinates or loadings on each dimension that can be read in the same way as factor loadings. So, for example, sightseeing has a high positive loading (near 1.8) on Dimension 1 but a loading of almost 0 on Dimension 2, while extreme sports have a high negative loading on Dimension 1 and a high positive loading on Dimension 2.

The solid diamond, on the other hand, overlays the age (group) of the clients onto the map. The location of each category is drawn from the activity preferences of the people in it. We can see some clusters of activities around or near different age groups, indicating that certain activities are preferred by clients in certain age groups, e.g. gourmet tours, wine tasting and cooking classes appeal to 35–54 year olds while extreme

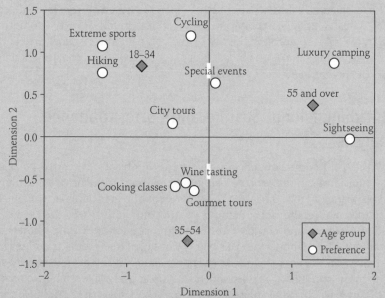

Figure 3.11 Two-dimensional map showing activity preferences of clients of different age groups

sports and hiking, and to a lesser extent, cycling, are most preferred by 18- to 34-year-old clients. Activities that do not cluster near to a specific category can be interpreted either as having a wide appeal or little appeal (you need to look at the actual responses to know which).

One weakness of MDS and correspondence analysis relative to factor analysis is that the dimensions are not rotated as part of the common procedure (although sufficient data are provided for rotation, if necessary). This means that they can be difficult to interpret. In this example, we might interpret Dimension 1 as distinguishing more active activities (negative values, left-hand side of the map) from more passive activities (positive values, right-hand side) and Dimension 2 as distinguishing outdoor activities (positive values, upper half of the map) from indoor activities (negative values, lower half of the map), although this interpretation is somewhat imperfect. Furthermore, while these techniques provide an attractive graphical representation in two dimensions, the results are difficult to visualise and interpret in more than three dimensions.

References

Brown, T.A. (2006) *Confirmatory Factor Analysis for Applied Research*. New York: The Guilford Press.

Cattell, R.B. (1966) The scree test for the number of factors. *Multivariate Behavioral Research* 1, 245–276.

Cohen, E., & Ben-Nun, L. (2009). The important dimensions of wine tourism experience from potential visitors' perception. *Tourism and Hospitality Research*, 9(1), 20-31.

Cronbach, L.J. (1951) Coefficient alpha and the internal structure of tests. *Psychometrika* 16 (3), 297–334.

Cronbach, L.J. and Shavelson, R.J. (2004) My current thoughts on coefficient alpha and successor procedures. *Educational and Psychological Measurement* 64 (3), 391–418.

Cudeck, R. and McCallum, R.C. (2007) *Factor Analysis at 100: Historical Developments and Future Directions*. Mahwah, NJ: Lawrence Erlbaum Associates.

Darlington, R.B. (1968) Multiple regression in psychological research and practice. *Psychological Bulletin* 69 (3), 161–182.

Darlington, R.B. (1997) Factor analysis. Ithaca, NY: Department of Psychology, Cornell University. See https://msu.edu/course/psy/818/deshon/Readings/Darlington%20()%20-%20Factor%20Analysis.pdf (accessed February 2017).

DeLone, W.H. and McLean, E.R. (1992) Information systems success: The quest for the dependent variable. *Information Systems Research* 3 (1), 60–95.

DeLone, W.H. and McLean, E.R. (2004) Measuring e-commerce success: Applying the DeLone & McLean information systems success model. *International Journal of Electronic Commerce & Business Media* 9 (1), 31–47.

Everitt, B.S., Landau, S. and Leese, M. (2001) *Cluster Analysis*. New York: Arnold.

Guadagnoli, E. and Velicer, W.F. (1988) Relation of sample size to the stability of component patterns. *Psychological Bulletin* 103 (2), 265–275.

Guilford, J.P. (1954) *Psychometric Methods* (2nd edn). New York: McGraw Hill.

Guttman, L. (1954) Some necessary conditions for factor analysis. *Psychometrika* 19 (2), 149–161.

Guttman, L. (1955) The determinacy of factor score matrices with implications for five other basic problems of common-factor theory. *The British Journal of Statistical Psychology* 8, 65–81.

Haddad, H. and Klobas, J.E. (2002) The relationship between visual abstraction and the effectiveness of a pedagogical character-agent. *The First International Joint Conference on Autonomous Agents & Multi-Agent Systems*, Bologna, Italy. See http://www.vhml.org/workshops/AAMAS/papers/Haddad.pdf. (accessed February 2017)

Hair, J.F., Black, W.C., Babin, B.J., Anderson, R.E. and Tatham, R.L. (2006) *Multivariate Data Analysis* (6th edn). Upper Saddle River, NJ: Prentice Hall.

Hair, J., Anderson, R., Tatham, R. and Black, W.R. (2009) *Multivariate Data Analysis* (7th edn). Upper Saddle River, NJ: Prentice-Hall.

Hudson, S. and Ritchie, B. (2002) Understanding the domestic market using cluster analysis: A case study of the marketing efforts of Travel Alberta. *Journal of Vacation Marketing* 8 (3), 263–276.

Hurley, A.E., Scandura, T.A., Schriesheim, C.A., Brannick, M.T., Seers, A., Vandenberg, R.J. and Williams, L.J. (1997) Exploratory and confirmatory factor analysis: Guidelines, issues, and alternatives. *Journal of Organizational Behavior* 18, 667–683.

Kaiser, H.F. (1960) The application of electronic computers to factor analysis. *Educational and Psychological Measurement* 20, 141–151.

Klobas, J.E. and McGill, T.J. (2010) The role of involvement in learning management system success. *Journal of Computing in Higher Education* 22 (2), 114–134.

Krijnen, W.P., Dijkstra, T.K. and Gill, R.D. (1998) Conditions for factor (in)determinacy in factor analysis. *Psychometrika* 63 (4), 359–367.

Lankford, S.V. and Howard, D.R. (1994) Developing a tourism impact attitude scale. *Annals of Tourism Research* 21 (1), 121–139.

Li, C., Lu, G. and Ortí, G. (2008) Optimal data partitioning and a test case for ray-finned fishes (*Actinopterygii*) based on ten nuclear loci. *Systematic Biology* 57 (4), 519–539.

Mahalanobis, P.C. (1936) On the generalised distance in statistics. *Proceedings of the National Institute of Sciences of India* 2 (1), 49–55.

McGill, T., Hobbs, V. and Klobas, J. (2003) User-developed applications and information systems success: A test of DeLone and McLean's model. *Information Resources Management Journal* 16 (1), 24–45.

Muthén, L.K. and Muthén, B.O. (2010) *Mplus User's Guide* (6th edn). Los Angeles, CA: Muthén & Muthén. See http://www.statmodel.com/ugexcerpts.shtml. (accessed February 2017)

Piccarreta, R. and Billari, F.C. (2007) Clustering work and family trajectories by using a divisive algorithm. *Journal of the Royal Statistical Society Series A* 170 (4), 1061–1078.

Robinson, J.O., Shaver, P.R. and Wrightsman, L.S. (1991) *Measures of Personality and Social Psychological Attitudes*. New York: Academic Press.

Spearman, C. (1904) General intelligence, objectively determined and measured. *American Journal of Psychology* 15, 201–293.

Tabachnick, B.G. and Fidell, L.S. (2006) *Using Multivariate Statistics* (5th edn). Needham Heights, MA: Allyn & Bacon, Inc.

4 Model Building

This chapter discusses regression models and structural equation modelling (SEM). Focusing on the tourism field, the chapter highlights the issues related to computational techniques and the reliability of the results in different conditions.

Modelling means generating abstract representations of some real system, process or phenomenon. It is an essential component of any scientific endeavour. The term is used (and often abused) in a wide range of circumstances and applied to the production of a large variety of models: graphical, physical, mathematical, conceptual. The goal is to build a model that reflects the 'real world' with sufficient accuracy that evaluations, explanations and predictions can be drawn and transferred accurately and validly back to the real world. Useful, insightful and reliable models based on sound assumptions and implemented with rigorous methods are powerful tools to describe the functioning of real systems or events, uncover aspects that may have been neglected and attempt predictions about future behaviours. Models are also used when it is impossible, for theoretical or practical reasons, to create experimental conditions that make direct measurement possible.

A great many methods can be employed for the building of quantitative models to represent phenomena in the social sciences. Many of these are well known and used in the tourism field. Usually, a model is built by first making some simplifying hypotheses about the object of study, or about the relationships between specific elements of it, or about both. Then, a representation is built (a set of mathematical relationships, a numerical simulation program, a physical object, a graphical element, etc.) and a validation of the outcomes is performed by comparison with real data. The suitability of a model is judged in terms of its capacity to explain past observations, its ability to predict future behaviours, its simplicity and sometimes even its aesthetic appeal (Silvert, 2001).

For the purposes of this work, we introduce here a small class of models and the methods to build them, based on statistical techniques. The most important set of statistical models used derives mathematical relationships between observed variables. The derived mathematical relationships are, themselves, the model. In this field, regression techniques play a central role, so in this chapter we begin by discussing issues associated with the building of linear regression models (Chatterjee & Hadi, 2006). We then extend the discussion to logistic regression and SEM. While we promised to limit the number of equations in this book, we include several equations in this chapter not only because they define the different statistical models of interest, but also because the mathematical representations are used in most papers that adopt this type of model and some familiarity with the equations and formal terminology is valuable when reading and evaluating reports of research that uses modelling techniques.

Simple Regression

The search for a linear relationship between variables is by far the most common approach to statistical modelling. A linear relationship between two variables is simple to understand and to represent on a chart. The chart itself, although a first approximation, is often able to provide useful insights into the phenomenon under study.

The technique is well known and all statistical software packages provide easy to use procedures to work out the necessary calculations. For example, suppose you have collected some data concerning the weekly arrivals of tourists at a destination and the spend for advertising the destination. Provided there is a linear relationship between the two variables, a linear regression should allow you to explain how weekly arrivals are related to spending on advertising and even, under certain conditions, to predict any increases in weekly arrivals that might follow from an increase in spending.

The regression equation

In mathematical terms, the simple linear regression model for the relationship between two variables is expressed as

$$Y = \beta_0 + \beta_1 X + \varepsilon$$

where
- Y is the 'dependent' variable that depends on or can be assumed to be influenced or caused by X, known as the 'independent' variable;
- β_1 is a constant known as the (population) regression coefficient, regression weight or slope of the regression line;
- β_0 is a constant which is the intercept or point at which the regression line meets the Y axis where $X=0$;
- ε is the error that arises when the equation is used to model a real-world relationship that is not perfectly linear.

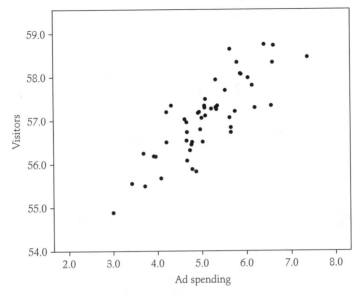

Figure 4.1 Advertising spending and number of visitors

Initial inspection of the data: Is there evidence of a linear relationship?

Before attempting the calculations, as in any other statistical analysis, an understanding of the data is required. For linear regression, a scatter plot of the two variables is drawn (Figure 4.1) to check whether a linear relationship might exist.

A look at a plot of the data is important in order to avoid possible blunders. Figure 4.1 confirms that there is a (roughly) linear relationship between the two variables in this problem, and thus that a linear regression model is likely to be an appropriate representation of it. It also reminds us that there is always some error in a model that expresses the average relationship between variables, and that, in order to evaluate the model, we need to consider how well the model represents the data.

A Solution for Non-Linearity: Transformation

When the underlying relationship between the observed variables is systematic but non-linear, it is often possible to transform one or both of the variables. Typically, the researcher tries several possible transformations, the most common of which is to take the square root, logarithm or inverse of the variable, if necessary after reflecting a variable that is negatively

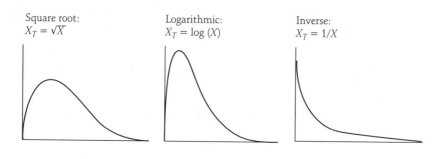

Reflect: $X_R = (\max(X)+1) - X$; then transform

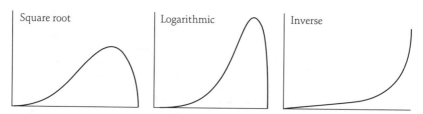

Figure 4.2 Empirical distributions and possible data transformations (suggested transformation for the independent variable is shown)

skewed so that it is positively skewed (Figure 4.2). For example, a power–law relationship, $Y=k \cdot X^\gamma$, can be transformed into: $\log(Y)=\gamma \log(X)+k$, which can be treated with a linear regression method. Obviously, if any variable in the regression equation is transformed, the estimated coefficients must then be retransformed in order to interpret the model using the original units of measurement.

SPSS offers a handy function for exploring the different possibilities for transformation. The Curve Estimation function, which can be found in the Analyse-Regression menu offers the possibility of choosing and comparing the effect on the relationship between the independent variable and the dependent variable of 10 different possible transformations of the independent variable. In addition to statistical measures and tests for the significance of the relationships, a plot is produced to enable a visual comparison of each transformation with the observed relationship between the dependent and the independent variable.

Measuring the quality of the linear regression model

For linear regression, we typically use the coefficient of determination, R^2, to measure model quality. R^2 is the proportion of the variance in Y that is explained by the regression model, and it is therefore often also described as the 'variance explained' and presented as a percentage. Some authors also refer to R^2 as representing the correlation between variables in the model (particularly in simple regression) because the square root of R^2 is, indeed, the correlation coefficient, r. This helps to answer questions about how large R^2 needs to be for us to conclude that the regression model is useful, although there is some controversy on this point, with opinion divided largely along disciplinary lines (Gage, 1978; Hair et al., 2005; Trusty et al., 2004). Social scientists often seek R^2 of 0.5 or more, arguing that if a model cannot explain at least 50% of the variation in the underlying data, it is not very useful. On the other hand, researchers in financial fields might be satisfied with R^2 as low as 0.1, and argue that it is better to be able to explain at least some pattern in relationships than none at all. Other researchers argue that, if r of around 0.3 is considered to be indicative of a strong enough relationship to be of practical significance, then R^2 of 0.09 is sufficient to indicate that a model has some practical value. A close reading of each of these arguments shows that R^2 is evaluated against different criteria in each case, depending on the use to which the researcher plans to put the model, and while each of these points of view can be found in different areas of the tourism literature, we argue that assessment of what is a good R^2 should be based primarily on the use to which the model is put rather than an absolute minimum.

The statistical significance of the regression model

To conclude that the regression model is a suitable representation of the data, we also need to consider its statistical significance, as well as the statistical significance of the parameters that define the intercept (β_0) and the relationship between X and Y (β_1). A statistic related to R^2 is used to test the statistical significance of the regression model as a whole. The test is an F test of the ratio of the variance explained by the regression model to the unexplained ('error') variance. When the F ratio is statistically different from 0, we conclude that the model is statistically significant. Since both R^2 and F share the same numerator, it is clear that the larger the value of R^2, the more likely it is that the regression model is statistically significant. For this reason, some authors refer to the significance of the regression model as the significance of the parameter, R^2.

The statistical significance of the coefficients (β) can be tested with t-tests which compare the estimated value of the coefficient, b, with the error of estimation as represented by the standard error, SE_b. Formally,

$$t = \frac{b}{\mathrm{SE}_b}$$

When the coefficient, b, is sufficiently large relative to the amount of variation, SE_b, about the regression line that it defines, the coefficient is statistically significant. Remember though, that (because the standard error is related to the sample size) even small effects can be statistically significant when the sample size is quite large. While statistical significance is a necessary condition for a meaningful model, it is not sufficient on its own. Both R^2 and the model regression coefficient, β_1, need also to be large enough to describe a meaningful relationship that is of practical value.

Example: A pitfall for the impatient modeller

Computer software will complete the calculations you request and present an apparently perfectly reasonable linear regression model, even when the relationship is not linear. The simplicity of entering data into a software package, selecting a couple of columns and asking for a regression analysis (it can even be done with a desktop spreadsheet such as Microsoft Excel) can lead to meaningless results if care isn't taken to first plot and inspect the data.

In this respect, the famous paper by Anscombe (1973) is probably the best example of what can happen when numerical calculations are performed without plotting and inspecting the data. Anscombe provides four pairs of variables, all of which can be described with the same regression model ($Y=0.5X+3$; $R^2=0.67$), but starting from quite different patterns (Figure 4.3).

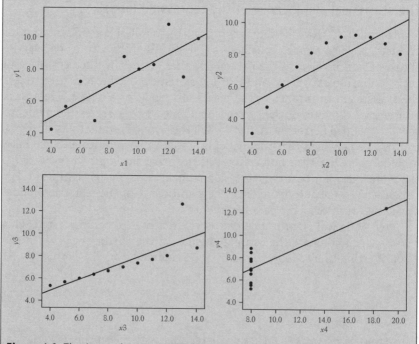

Figure 4.3 The Anscombe quartet (Anscombe, 1973), all regressions have the same parameters

> In Figure 4.3, only the relationships in the two left-hand panels are linear. In the upper left-hand panel, the linear model indicates the direction of the relationship accurately, but there is quite a lot of variation about the modelled regression line. The regression line in the lower left-hand model has been strongly influenced by the second last point; without this value, the slope of the regression line would be flatter, and we would draw a different conclusion about the strength of the relationship between the two variables.

The Anscombe quartet is a confirmation of the fact that a mathematical technique applied to a set of numbers can always generate an answer. The ability to reach a solution does not, however, imply that the relationships described mathematically make any practical sense. A good correlation exists between the number of storks and the number of babies (Matthews, 2000), as good as the correlation between sunspots and financial stock markets (Modis, 2007) or between women's skirt lengths and economic cycles (Fisher, 2008: 194) or between ice-cream sales and drowning deaths (Babbie, 2010). But nobody would really assign a causal effect in these cases.

Assumptions that must be met for a valid linear regression model

As for any other statistical procedure, a simple linear regression has a number of assumptions that need to be verified to ensure that the model is trustworthy. They are

- the observations on which the model is estimated (X_i, Y_i) are sampled randomly;
- the underlying relationship between X and Y is linear;
- ε is a random variable with an expected value=0 (i.e. its mean is 0) – this important assumption means that for any particular X_i, the expected value of Y_i is simply $\beta_0 + \beta_1 X_i$;
- the variance of ε is the same for all values X_i (i.e. ε is homoscedastic, so the variance of Y about the regression line is the same for all values of X);
- ε is normally distributed, and all individual errors, e_i, are independent of one another.

Assessing the Validity of Assumptions

The simplest way to assess the validity of assumptions is to plot the data. A scatter plot such as Figure 4.1 is useful for visualising the relationship between two variables. In addition, all assumptions can be assessed by plotting the error terms, e_i, or 'residuals' that result from using the regression equation to represent the data. A residuals plot shows the residuals (normally the standardised values) on the vertical axis plotted against the independent variable on the horizontal axis. When the residuals are randomly and uniformly dispersed, the assumptions of the linear regression model are met.

Example: Assessing residuals plots

Consider the three examples of linear regression models in Figure 4.4 (the figures use synthetic data sets generated for this example only).

Although not very definite (R^2 is relatively low, as can be seen by the wide dispersion of the observations about the regression line), all three models have statistically significant regression parameters (coefficients and R^2). The residuals plots, however, show us that the assumptions of linear regression do not hold in all three cases. Figures 4.5 through 4.8 show, for each of the three examples, both the histograms and the scatter plots of the standardised residuals.

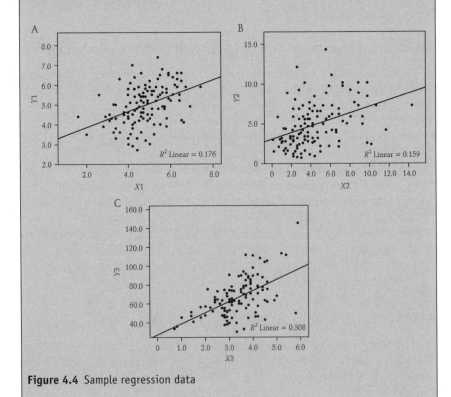

Figure 4.4 Sample regression data

In the case of the first model (Figure 4.5), all residuals seem to satisfy the assumptions. The second model (Figure 4.6) has some problems, however. The left-hand panel clearly shows that the distribution is skewed, and this can also be seen by looking at the scatter plot where the data points gravitate towards the bottom left-hand side of the chart.

In this case, it is possible to transform the dependent variable by taking its square root. The new regression model shows a marked improvement and the distribution of residuals (Figure 4.7) is now in line with the assumptions of the regression model.

In the third case, while the histogram shows that the errors are approximately normally distributed, the scatter plot shows a clear increase in the spread of the points when values of the independent variable increase (Figure 4.8). This is a clear indication of violation of the assumption of homoscedasticity. The variance of the residuals is not constant for all values of X. In such cases, a logarithmic transformation of one or more of the variables might remedy the problem. If not, the

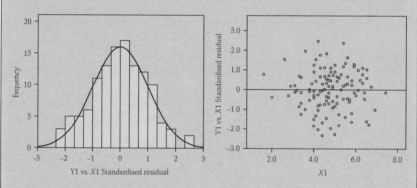

Figure 4.5 Standardised residuals for the regression $Y1$ vs. $X1$

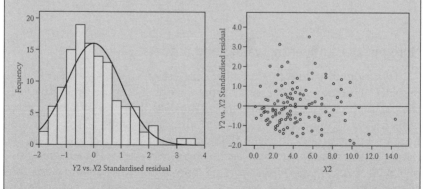

Figure 4.6 Standardised residuals for the regression $Y2$ vs. $X2$

plot suggests that an additional variable, not included in the regression equation, might be systematically affecting values of the dependent variable, Y.

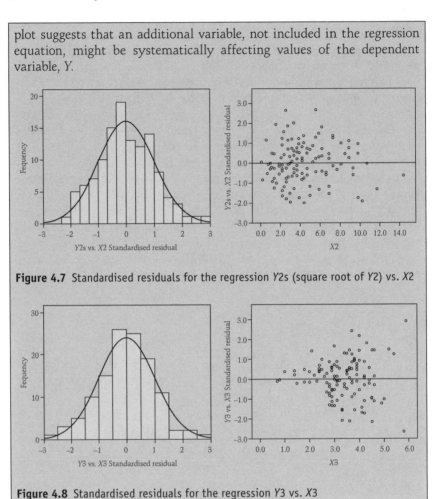

Figure 4.7 Standardised residuals for the regression Y2s (square root of Y2) vs. X2

Figure 4.8 Standardised residuals for the regression Y3 vs. X3

More pitfalls: Influential values and outliers

Two more situations might render a regression analysis problematic: the presence of influential values and the presence of outliers. In both situations, the parameters of the regression model are disturbed. An influential point (which may or may not be an outlier) affects the slope of the regression line, resulting in a coefficient that either over- or under-represents the nature of the relationship between X and Y. An outlier (an extreme value of Y on X, typically defined as a value more than two standard deviations from the mean Y for X) can reduce the coefficient of determination and its significance by increasing the amount of error in the model.

Detecting influential values

For simple regression, influential observations can be observed readily from a scatter plot. Most software packages also generate scores and reports that assist with the identification of influential observations.

An influential observation can be seen in Panel B of Figure 4.4. This value also occurs at the highest value of X. If this value were removed, the slope of the regression line would be quite different and the regression coefficient would be lower. Yet, without knowing the values of Y for other X in this region, it is impossible to know whether the regression equation generated from data that include this influential observation is valid, or rather that the equation generated from data that exclude this value is valid.

Detecting and dealing with outliers

Outliers can usually be detected from the scatter plot of Y on X, but it is also useful to examine the standardised residuals. The following example shows how this is done.

Considering again the example described in Figure 4.1, the relationship between advertising spending and visitors' arrivals can be expressed as

$$\text{Visitors} = 54.85 + 0.823\text{Ad\_Spending}$$

Both β coefficients are significant, and the coefficient of determination is $R^2=0.68$, considered good. Moreover, inspection of the shape of the residuals plots (Figure 4.9) confirms the appropriateness of the linear regression model, but two of the standardised residuals are greater than 2.0. The right-hand panel shows that they occur when Ad_Spending is around 4.9 and 5.8. These individual values can also be seen on close inspection of Figure 4.1.

What action should be taken when an outlier is detected? In some cases, an outlier results from an error in observation or data entry and

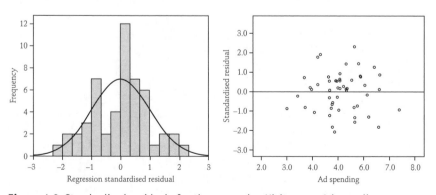

Figure 4.9 Standardised residuals for the regression Visitors vs. Ad spending

can be corrected, or removed from the data set if it is not possible to recover the correct value. Removing an outlier will increase the coefficient of determination because there will be less error in the model, but if the outlier represents a true value in the data set to be modelled, the apparently improved model will lack validity because it does not reflect the true situation. This might occur if the outlier is the result of non-random sampling (e.g. only one observation is available for a valid part of the population). In this situation, the investigator might decide to retain the 'outlier' so that the model comes closer to reflecting the population accurately, but this strategy is still risky because the single outlier might not represent the unrepresented part of the population well. Alternatively, if an outlier (which is confirmed as a true value) occurs at the beginning or end of the data series (the first or last X), it could be removed and the model interpreted as being applicable only when X is restricted to the range that excludes the point at which the outlier occurred.

The extrapolation limitation

Even when a satisfactory regression model has been determined, extreme caution must be used if the researcher wishes to extrapolate the relationship beyond the range of values which have been used to produce the model.

Example: Is it never too hot for tourism?

A mathematical expression can be found to relate the number of tourists arriving at a seaside destination to the average local temperature. This relationship has been observed on many occasions, and temperatures play a central role in the calculation of the tourism climatic index (Mieczkowski, 1985) which has been shown to be a factor in the choice of a destination (Bigano et al., 2006; see also Lise & Tol, 2002).

On the other hand, whatever the linear relationship between arrivals and temperature, we obviously cannot extend this to predict increases (or decreases) in arrivals at a specific destination by much more than a couple of degrees above the maximum (or below the minimum) temperature recorded at the destination.

Say, for example, we produce a linear regression model for tourist arrivals in a city based on temperature measurements in the range 18–30°C, and calculate a regression equation that indicates that, on average, the number of tourist arrivals increases by 0.5% with every degree increase in temperature. Rather obviously, we cannot use this equation to forecast the arrival of more tourists if the temperature rises to 45 or 50°C.

Multiple Regression

In reality, we often need or want to include several independent variables in a regression model. Visitor numbers, for example, usually depend on a number of variables, not just spending on advertising (or temperature and hours of daylight) as suggested by the examples used to illustrate simple regression. All of the issues raised and discussed in relation to simple regression are also relevant for multiple regression, but there are some extensions and specific issues to be considered.

Song *et al.* (2009) list 8 types of variable commonly used in modelling tourism demand, and they list 30 specific independent variables that have been included in econometric models of tourism demand published since 1990. These variables include visitor characteristics such as income and preference; travel-related factors such as cost of travel and prices in the destination country; and economic and environmental factors such as exchange rates and crime rates, as well as marketing expenditure by the destination.

The multiple regression model is an extension to the multiple independent variables of the simple regression model:

$$Y = \beta_0 + \beta_1 X_1 + \beta_2 X_2 + \cdots + \beta_p X_p + \varepsilon$$

for *p* independent variables. The procedure for estimating the model finds the values of the coefficients that minimise the squared differences between the observed and the predicted values of *Y*. (This approach is commonly known as ordinary least squares, or OLS regression.) The assumptions about the error are therefore the same as for the simple regression model, and any independent variables that have a non-linear relationship with *Y* are best transformed before beginning analysis. Residuals plots are used to detect violations of the assumptions of multiple regression, outliers and influential variables in much the same ways as they were used in simple regression.

Modelling categorical variables

Multiple regression models permit modelling of categorical as well as quantitative variables, and both types of variable are often used together in building a model. Qualities of individuals, locations and other objects are represented by 'dummy variables', which are typically coded 1 (presence of the quality) and 0 (absence of the quality). In the case of dichotomous characteristics, it is easy to apply and interpret this coding, e.g. a dichotomous variable, gender, can be created with codes of 1 for males and 0 for females (i.e. not males).

Dummy variables effectively allow you to create a separate equation for each category of interest. While the effect of the quantitative variables in the multiple regression model is the same, the model now also allows the analyst to estimate the effect of being in a specific group, which might be as simple as male vs. female, or as complex as international visitors who are married, female, have a tertiary degree and no children.

Say we collect information about participants in an activity in three categories: local, other national and international. Two dummy variables will be needed: one to represent local (1) vs. not local (0), and one to represent, say, international (1) vs. not international (0). There is no need to create a third dummy variable to represent other national vs. neither local nor international because the dummy coding already permits this distinction: any visitor coded 0 (not local) and 0 (not international) must be 'other national'.

This logic can be extended to as large a number of categories as the data allow, and we always need one less dummy variable than the total number of characteristics because the final category is always defined by being 0 on all the other categories. The 'all 0' category is usually called the 'reference category'.

Assessing the quality of a multiple regression model

The coefficient of determination, R^2, is interpreted in the same way for multiple regression as for simple regression. Some authors refer to this value as the multiple coefficient of determination, but most do not, a practice we will follow. The F test for the significance of the model is conducted in the same way for both simple and multiple regression.

Because R^2 usually increases with the addition of new variables to the regression model, an adjusted R^2 can be used to compare alternative models. The adjustment takes account of the number of variables, p, and the sample size, n, and is calculated as

$$\text{adj } R^2 = 1 - (1 - R^2)\frac{n-1}{n-p-1}$$

It has recently become common to interpret the adjusted R^2 as the (unbiased) variance explained by the regression model, but this is not correct. Furthermore, as Wooldridge (2009) points out in his useful and accessible comparison of R^2 and adjusted R^2, it is R^2 that is tested by the F test, not adjusted R^2. Adjusted R^2 is most useful as a tool to decide whether a simpler model explains the data equally as well as (or almost as well as) a more complex model. This is important because the addition of variables to regression models often has a data collection cost, particularly in the case of attitudinal data collected by survey where survey firms or interviewers are often paid by the length of the survey and respondents are more likely to respond, or respond with less error through lack of attention or fatigue, to shorter surveys.

The statistical significance of each of the regression coefficients (β) is determined using a t-test, as in simple regression, but the interpretation of the regression coefficients is slightly different. Recall that a simple regression model can be interpreted as indicating that, on average, for every unit increase in the value of X, Y increases by the value of the coefficient of the slope (β_1). This logic can be extended, but with caution, to the interpretation of a multiple regression model. To interpret the effect of any single independent variable on Y, we can say that, on average, and *all other things being equal* (or, more precisely, all other independent variables held constant), an increase of one unit in X_p will result in an increase of β_p in Y, but to draw inferences about changes in the value of Y when two or more values of X change, we need first to consider the likelihood that there is some correlation between the independent variables.

The multicollinearity problem

In multiple regression analysis, the correlation between the set of independent variables is called multicollinearity. When multicollinearity is low, we are not unduly concerned (but still take care with the interpretation of the regression coefficients), but high multicollinearity is problematic. At first glance, this might simply seem to be because the use of a regression model based on multicollinear independent variables will bias predictions of Y, but multicollinearity can also cause one or more important variables to have a non-significant regression coefficient, and therefore incorrectly appear to be of no value in explaining or predicting Y. (In some cases, you might even see a significant R^2, but no significant regression coefficient at all.) We therefore need to be able to both detect and remedy multicollinearity. A simple first step is to inspect the correlation matrix for the X variables. Any correlations of 0.7 or above suggest that multicollinearity is a potential problem. The squared multiple correlation (SMC) of each X variable can also be used to identify variables that are multicollinear. Variable by variable inspection of correlation coefficients and SMCs is quite tiresome, though, and most statistical software provides diagnostic tools. A common statistic is the variance inflation factor (VIF), which increases as SMC increases. Multicollinearity is likely to be problematic when VIF is high. A rule of thumb is to suspect that a variable is multicollinear with others when VIF is 10 or greater.

Remedying multicollinearity can be more difficult than detecting it, particularly if there are important reasons for including all independent variables in the regression equation. If one variable has high multicollinearity and the goal of the regression analysis is to explain or predict Y without the need to refer to a specific set of independent variables, one option is to build a simple regression model based on that one variable. This option would be justified on the basis that the selected variable is likely to explain most of the (explainable) variance in Y and a model based on just that variable will be parsimonious, simple to explain and of low cost to use. Another possible remedy, particularly where the researcher is interested in testing the effects of several independent variables, would be to remove the variable on the assumption that it adds little to the understanding of Y beyond the information provided by the independent variables with which it is strongly correlated.

Yet another option is to create one or more 'interaction' variables, typically by multiplying pairs of highly correlated variables. The idea of this approach is that the interaction variable extracts the shared variance from the correlated variables, allowing separate assessment of the contribution to Y of the shared variance (the interaction) and variance that is unique to each of the original variables. While use of an interaction variable can be an attractive practical solution, the result can only be interpreted meaningfully, however, if the interaction has a meaning. Suppose, for example, you are interested in the intentions of (heterosexual) honeymooning couples to return to a destination and you have separate measures of overall satisfaction from males and females, but they are multicollinear. It makes sense to build an interaction term in this case because this will allow you to gauge the effect of shared satisfaction as well as any separate effects of the satisfaction of males and the satisfaction of females.

Choosing a multiple regression model

While an initial model is built on the basis of theory, prior observation or reasoned argument, often – even after dealing with multicollinearity and violations of assumptions – the model contains one or more non-significant coefficients. Should they be removed to produce a final model or not? The answer depends on the purpose of the regression analysis. If the purpose was to test a given model by testing whether certain variables contributed to an explanation of the phenomenon represented by Y, there is no need to remove the non-significant variables from the model: the model has been shown to be poor, or at least to include variables that do not contribute. On the other hand, if the purpose was to build a mathematical model that can be used to explain or predict the phenomenon, a parsimonious model that includes just enough variables for explanation or prediction is often preferred.

Parsimony is often an important consideration. The costs of data collection, and of interpreting and explaining to others the results of a multiple regression analysis that includes many variables, can be quite high. When a model contains several significant variables, it is worth considering whether a more parsimonious model, i.e. a model with fewer X variables, can be used, and whether a model that costs less to build might perform the job required of a model of the phenomenon well enough to be useful. In certain circumstances, such as when it is important to communicate a model to decision makers, a simple model that explains sufficient variance in Y is often more useful than a more complex model that explains a large proportion of the variance in Y.

Several approaches to producing a parsimonious regression model are available. We discuss two of them here: stepwise regression and the all subsets methods. We caution, however, that both methods are quite mechanical. Regardless of the outcome, the theoretical interpretation of the meaning and importance of the different variables should play an important part in their selection for inclusion in the final regression model.

Stepwise Regression

A common approach is to remove non-significant variables one at a time and re-estimate the model. Automated procedures are available to do this 'stepwise removal' (backward stepwise) of non-contributing variables. Automated procedures are also available for forward stepwise construction of a model. Forward stepwise modelling is done by adding at each step the variable that explains most of the (remaining) unexplained variance in Y. Both forward and backward regression can be combined in a (generic) automatic stepwise procedure.

Stepwise methods are easily performed using software packages such as SPSS. Use of automated stepwise procedures carries with it some risk, however, and the literature has strongly debated their usefulness or correctness (Knapp & Sawilowsky, 2001; Miles & Shevlin, 2001; Thompson, 2001; Whittingham et al., 2006). The main problems can be summarised as follows:

- When stepwise procedures are used, it is important to check for multicollinearity to avoid omitting important variables from the model just because the majority of the variance that they might explain has already been explained by variables entered in prior steps.
- The significance of R^2 and the coefficients can be wrong since the p-value calculation depends on the number of variables included in the model. Because all variables are available to the software, stepwise methods can use incorrect degrees of freedom for the set of predictors included in a given model. This inflates the F value (used to decide whether the variable to be evaluated at a given step explains a significant proportion of variance), thus inflating the Type I error rate.
- Moreover, these methods do not necessarily select the best set of independent variables. The series of decisions made (keeping or discarding a variable) is a sequential series and each decision depends on the previous one.
- Finally, the results can be sample specific, so their replication and application with data collected elsewhere or at a later date may be highly problematic.

All Subsets Method

From a computational point of view, the only way to be assured of the results would be to test all possible subsets. In other words, we would need to analyse all possible combinations of sets of predictors in order to determine the best one. This can be quite tedious as the number of regressions to be executed on n variables is 2^n-1, but software packages exist and they can be programmed to do the work.

The simplest statistic available to help with this decision is the adjusted R^2 (another statistic, the Cp statistic, is sometimes used, but it is more complicated to estimate than R^2 and leads to similar, if not identical results in most cases, so will not be discussed here). If adjusted R^2 is compared for each of the competing models (i.e. models with different combinations of dependent variables), the model with the highest adjusted R^2 is the most parsimonious because it contributes the highest proportion of variance for the number of explanatory variables it includes.

Example: Best subsets method for choosing a parsimonious model

In Table 4.1, the models with the highest R^2 all include the variable, $X4$, and R^2 for models that include this variable increases with the number of variables – but the most parsimonious model, as indicated by *adjusted* R^2, is a simple regression that predicts Y on the basis of $X4$ alone.

Table 4.1 Sample comparison of all potential regression models (all subsets) when five independent variables have been tested

Model	R^2	Adj. R^2	Model	R^2	Adj. R^2
X1	0.001	−0.032	X1X2X3	0.023	−0.082
X2	0.010	−0.023	X1X2X4	0.466	0.408
X3	0.009	−0.024	X1X2X5	0.023	−0.081
X4	0.443	0.425	X1X3X4	0.447	0.388
X5	0.009	−0.024	X1X3X5	0.019	−0.086
X1X2	0.012	−0.056	X1X4X5	0.451	0.392
X1X3	0.009	−0.059	X2X3X4	0.460	0.402
X1X4	0.447	0.408	X2X3X5	0.035	−0.069
X1X5	0.010	−0.059	X2X4X5	0.465	0.408
X2X3	0.021	−0.047	X3X4X5	0.450	0.391

Table 4.1 (Continued)

Model	R^2	Adj. R^2	Model	R^2	Adj. R^2
X2X4	0.458	0.421	X1X2X3X4	0.467	0.388
X2X5	0.021	−0.046	X1X2X3X5	0.036	−0.107
X3X4	0.444	0.406	X1X2X4X5	0.472	0.393
X3X5	0.019	−0.048	X1X3X4X5	0.452	0.370
X4X5	0.448	0.410	X2X3X4X5	0.468	0.389
			X1X2X3X4X5	0.473	0.372

Logistic Regression

The regression models examined so far are suitable for metric dependent variables, but what happens when the dependent variable is categorical? This is a common situation, for example, when the goal of building the model is to explain or predict intentions to engage in a behaviour or return to a destination. In these cases, a linear regression model is not suitable. Instead, what is modelled is the probability of being in one category rather than in another. This S-shaped relationship looks something like Figure 4.10 for a single predictor variable (the exact nature of the S shape varies with the probability of classification in the category of interest for each value of the

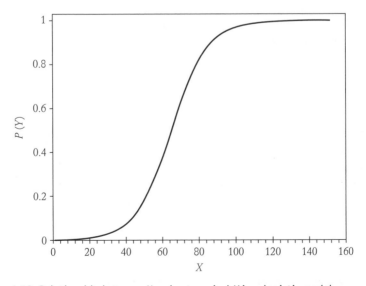

Figure 4.10 Relationship between *X* and categorical *Y* in a logistic model

X variable). This is a logistic distribution, and the regression models created when the dependent variable (often called the 'response' variable in logistic regression) is categorical are therefore known as logistic regression models.

The logistic regression model

Logistic regression models are set up in much the same way as linear regression models. There may be a single or multiple predictor variables, and there may be dummy variables representing qualities, quantitative variables or a combination of the two types of variable. The difference is in the representation of the dependent variable in probabilistic terms, as the logit or log odds of a case being in one category rather than another, formally:

$$\log_e\left[\frac{P(Y=1|x_1,x_2,...,x_p)}{1-P(Y=1|x_1,x_2,...,x_p)}\right]=\log_e\left[\frac{P}{1-P}\right]=\beta_0+\beta_1x_1+\beta_2x_2+...+\beta_px_p+\varepsilon$$

Note that the right-hand side of this equation (model) is the same for both multiple regression and logistic regression. The significance of the logistic regression coefficients is measured by a test statistic, usually a Wald statistic, although other tests are available and may be preferred (Agresti, 2002).

The notion of log odds can be better understood by focusing on the odds ratio (the expression in brackets in the left-hand side of the equation). In general, odds ratios estimate the odds that an event will occur (e.g. that a case will be classified in a selected category) relative to the odds that the event does not occur (e.g. the probability that a case will not be classified into the selected category):

$$\text{Odds}=\frac{P(Y=1|x_1,x_2,...,x_p)}{1-P(Y=1|x_1,x_2,...,x_p)}$$

Logistic regression models exist for binary response variables (e.g. intention to return, coded into two categories: yes and no) or response variables with more than one category (e.g. intention to return coded into three categories: yes, unsure, no). The latter category of models is known as multinomial logistic regression. Binary logistic models are simpler because $1-P(Y=1)=P(Y=0)$, and the odds ratio can be simplified:

$$\text{Odds}=\frac{P(Y=1|x_1,x_2,...,x_p)}{1-P(Y=1|x_1,x_2,...,x_p)}=\frac{P(Y=1|x_1,x_2,...,x_p)}{P(Y=0|x_1,x_2,...,x_p)}$$

When there are more than two response categories, $1-P(Y=1)$ is $P(Y=$all other response categories) and two or more comparisons are needed, technically speaking, the ratio of interest is a relative risk ratio rather than an odds ratio, but we will use odds ratio as a shorthand for both types of ratio in this chapter. In terms of deciding how many comparisons are needed, there is an analogy here with the construction of dummy variables: there will be one fewer comparison required than the number of categories of Y, with one category nominated the reference category. Selection of the reference category is, empirically, arbitrary, but it is a good idea to select a reference category that helps with interpretation: recall that the logistic regression model predicts the log odds of being in one category rather than another, so pick the reference category as the category most easily considered 'the other'.

Assumptions of logistic regression

Logistic regression makes fewer assumptions of the data than linear regression. In particular, the variables do not need to be normally distributed and errors do not need to be homoscedastic. While a linear relationship between each independent variable and the dependent variable is not assumed, there does need to be a linear relationship between each independent variable and the logit of the dependent variable – an easier requirement to meet, particularly when the independent variable is a dummy variable with two categories. Indeed, some data sets that prove intractable for linear regression can be transformed into sets of categorical variables and modelled using logistic regression.

Interpreting and reporting the results of logistic regression analyses

The main difficulty that arises in logistic regression is the interpretation of the results. Thrane (2004) discusses the problems that arise in tourism research when only regression coefficients are reported for logistic regression. The problem with relying on the regression coefficient is that it is difficult to interpret; for example, the regression coefficient of a quantitative independent variable in a logistic regression model is interpreted as the expected change in the log odds of being in the category of interest (i.e. $Y=1$) for every unit change in the independent variable.

While Thrane (2004) provides several suggestions for more meaningful reporting of the results of logistic regression, here, we emphasise what has become a common approach: the reporting and interpretation of the odds ratio. Fortunately, the output of logistic regression analyses in almost all software programs now includes odds ratios (which may be called relative risk ratios for multinomial models) as well as regression coefficients. For binomial models, the odds ratio can be readily interpreted as the change in the probability of being in the category of interest rather than in the reference category for every unit increase in the dependent variable: an odds ratio above 1 indicates that the probability of being in the category of interest will increase by the value of the odds ratio, while an odds ratio below 1 indicates that the probability of being in the category of interest will decrease by the inverse of the odds ratio (i.e. 1/odds). An odds ratio of 1 indicates that there is no change, i.e. that the independent variable does not contribute to the model. Similarly, the odds ratio for an independent variable entered into the model as a dummy variable is interpreted as the change in the odds of a case being in the category of interest when it is in the category measured by the dummy variable. For multinomial models, the logic is the same, but interpretation is always the odds (or relative risk) of being in the category of interest rather than any of the other categories.

Example: Interpreting the results of binary logistic regression analysis

Consider the SPSS output from a logistic regression of three variables on intention to return to a destination coded 1 for yes, intends to return, and 0 (reference category) for no, does not intend to return, presented in Table 4.2.

The B column in Table 4.2 contains the regression coefficient. SPSS uses a Wald statistic to test the statistical significance of each coefficient, and here we can see that each coefficient is statistically significant (the Sig. column). Exp(B) is the odds ratio. Attitudes is a quantitative variable (measured on a five-point scale), so this value can be interpreted as saying that the odds that a visitor will intend to return (rather than intend not to return) increases, on average, by 2.55 for every one point increase in attitudes to the experience (holding values of the other variables equal). HolidayLeave is a dummy variable indicating whether the visitor receives paid holiday leave (1) or not (0). The odds ratio for holiday leave indicates that visitors who receive paid holiday leave are 1.143 times more likely to say that they intend to return than that they do not.

Table 4.2 Results table for intention to return model, multinomial logistic regression with *does not intend to return* as the reference category

Independent variable	B	SE	Wald	df	Sig.	Ex(B)
Attitudes	0.937	0.050	348.467	1	0.000	2.551
PartnerNorm	0.661	0.021	966.268	1	0.000	1.938
HolidayLeave	0.133	0.029	21.220	1	0.000	1.143
Constant	6.836	0.185	1370.301	1	0.000	930.518

Often, it can be useful to plot the results. See Thrane (2004) for suggestions on how this might be done.

With multinomial logistic regression, significance tests are provided for both the overall contribution of each variable to the model and the contribution of the variable to membership of each category relative to the reference category. To be able to compare all categories, most software packages require you to run the model twice, changing the reference category in the second run to provide comparisons between the formerly omitted reference category and the remaining categories.

Evaluating the quality of a logistic regression model

As with other regression models, the quality of a logistic regression model is evaluated – at least statistically; it, of course, also has to make sense in the real world – in terms of the statistical significance of the model coefficients and its ability to explain the data. We have already discussed the significance of the model coefficients. Here, we concentrate on fit.

A fit statistic which compares category membership as predicted by the logistic regression equation to the observed category of membership is used to test the overall statistical significance of a logistic regression model. If maximum likelihood (ML) modelling has been used, the -2 log-likelihood is (also) reported. A deviance statistic called 'pseudo R^2' is usually reported and, although there are several different variants and the relationship to R^2 is not exact, this statistic is often interpreted in the same way as R^2. We caution you not to rely on the deviance statistic alone, however. A good logistic regression model will be able to classify cases, with reasonable accuracy, into the categories of the response variable, but it is possible to obtain satisfactory R^2 (and significant coefficients) even when classification is poor.

Example: A classification table for destination return intentions

Table 4.3 shows the classification table for a logistic regression for the intention to return model that appears in Table 4.2 (the output is produced by SPSS).

In this case, the destination managers wanted to be able to increase the number of visitors who intended to return, so they needed to be able to connect aspects of visitors' experience (the independent variables in the model) to their intention; however, although the model classifies a high proportion of cases (85.4%) accurately, has a satisfactory pseudo R^2 (0.43, not shown in the table) and is statistically significant, it fails to distinguish people who intend to return from those who do not. This could be an indication of asymmetry in explanations: different aspects of their experience might be influential for those visitors who say they want to return to the destination and those who say they do not want to return (Bloor, 1976; Shapin & Schaffer, 1989).

Table 4.3 Poor classification in an otherwise good logistic regression model

Observed		Predicted		
		Intention		
		0 no	1 yes	Percentage correct
Intention	0 no	701	1	99.9
	1 yes	119	0	0
	Overall percentage			85.4

Logistic models are often used for modelling tourism demand. A detailed technical treatment of different approaches is provided in Song *et al.* (2009). Most software packages offer two types of procedure for logistic regression modelling. For example, interactive SPSS offers both binary logistic and multinomial logistic regression from the Regression menu, but also offers logit regression under the Log-linear menu. The functions found under the Regression menu are presented in a way that is well known to analysts who are familiar with OLS regression models. The functions available from the Log-linear menu permit more complex multinomial models to be constructed for situations in which both the dependent and independent variables are categorical (quantitative variables may be included as covariates), and provide different output options, but generally require deeper knowledge of the different approaches to logistic regression modelling to be used effectively.

Path Modelling

So far, we have presented classes of models that are represented by a single equation, but many situations are better modelled by multiple equations. One such situation arises when the response or outcome of interest is the result of a chain of situations or influences. (This type of model is often called a process model, particularly when the chain involves an input, an operation or intervention that can be measured and an output.) Although a separate set of regression models could be built for each successive dependent variable in the chain in a form of hierarchical regression, such models can be cumbersome to construct. Another approach is to compute all relationships simultaneously. This approach is often described, generically, as path modelling.

In tourism, path modelling is commonly used to model intentions to visit or return to a destination (e.g. Cole & Illum, 2006). It can be used to test the hypotheses embedded in a single model or to compare different models, as illustrated in the following example.

Example: Path modelling of intention to return

Intention to return to a destination or event is influenced by satisfaction with previous experiences associated with that intention or event, but different studies model the relationships between these variables in different ways.

For example, intention to return might be modelled as a function of satisfaction with the destination along with the individual characteristics of the visitor, while satisfaction might be modelled as a function of the characteristics of the destination itself and the experiences that the visitor had while there. Or, perhaps the individual characteristics of the visitor directly affect his/her satisfaction with the destination rather than intention, or perhaps individual characteristics directly affect both satisfaction and intention.

All three potential models are presented in a simplified form in path diagrams in Figure 4.11.

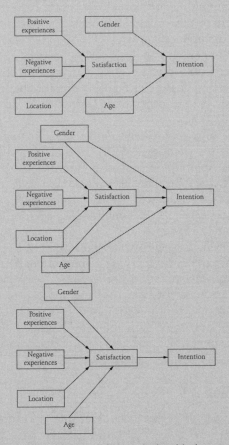

Figure 4.11 Three potential models of the relationship between experience at a destination, personal characteristics, satisfaction and intention to return

Although path modelling dates back to the work of the geneticist, Sewall Wright, in the early 20th century (Denis & Legerski, 2006), two approaches currently dominate the social science (and tourism) literature. Both approaches begin with a hypothesised model of the relationships between variables; typically, the model is represented as a graphical path model rather than a set of equations. The approach, traditionally called structural equation modelling, seeks an optimum fit, usually through ML or Bayesian estimation, between the hypothesised model and the data as represented in a matrix of covariances (or correlations) between observed variables (Jöreskog, 1967; Jöreskog et al., 2016; Jöreskog & Sörbom, 1976). The second approach, traditionally known as partial least squares (PLS) modelling, models the paths as a series of OLS regression equations, seeking to maximise the explained variance in each dependent variable (Wold et al., 1983, 1987, 2001).

Both approaches allow researchers not only to estimate the path model through simultaneous equations, but also to simultaneously estimate multivariate measurement models for one or more variables. Again, different techniques are used. PLS builds measurement models using principal components analysis (PCA) which, as we pointed out in Chapter 3, does not consider error variance in observed variables, and thus is not well indicated for analysis of data obtained from human participants. SEM, on the other hand, specifically takes measurement error into account.

A number of important recent works describe both approaches as 'SEM', distinguishing traditional SEM, described as 'covariance-based SEM' or 'CB-SEM' from PLS, described as 'variance-based SEM' (Reinartz et al., 2009; Ringle et al., 2012) or 'PLS-SEM' (Hair et al., 2011, 2016). This nomenclature has two advantages. Firstly, it highlights the fact that both techniques are approaches to the simultaneous solution of a model with multiple paths (and, therefore, distinct from hierarchical regression). Secondly, when distinguishing covariance-based SEM from variance-based SEM, it signals that the techniques are computationally different. On the other hand, this nomenclature does not recognise the important difference in measurement methods between the two approaches, and the impact that this difference has on the estimation of the discriminant validity and statistical significance of path models. To underline the differences between the two approaches, we will retain the traditional distinction between SEM and PLS in this chapter.

Comparing SEM and PLS

Because they use different techniques to measure variables and estimate the paths in a model, SEM and PLS are often considered to be competing approaches to path modelling. All other things being equal, it would be possible to recommend PLS for simple models that do not use data from human subjects and SEM for models that require simultaneous estimation of measurement and path models when data are obtained from human subjects. Of course, it is not as simple as that. Indeed, there is a great deal of controversy over considerations for choosing to use SEM or PLS for path modelling (Fornell & Bookstein, 1982; Hair et al., 2011; Reinartz et al., 2009). Proponents of PLS suggest several conditions under which it can be preferred over SEM, but developments in both the features available in SEM software and understanding of PLS mean that not all of them still apply. Of particular importance for understanding the strengths and weaknesses of PLS is the table provided by Henseler et al. (2016: 14 – Table II), which compares 'traditional' heuristic reasons for using PLS with a 'modern' understanding of whether or not those heuristics apply. For example, Henseler et al. (2016: 14) point out that the claim that PLS does not assume normality is flawed, and that 'PLS does not differ from other SEM techniques' in 'the assumptions made for the estimation of parameters'. In fact, PLS works with non-normal data because it takes many successive samples from the data in a process called bootstrapping; consistent with the central limit theorem, the distribution of the means of a large number of samples taken from the same data set will be normally distributed around the grand mean (the mean of the means).

The ability of PLS to estimate paths for non-normal variables offered an advantage over traditional SEM when bootstrapping was not available for SEM, but now that SEM software such as AMOS and MPlus provide bootstrapping, this advantage no longer exists. Furthermore, SEM software allows the analyst to choose an approach to bootstrapping, reports bootstrapped distributions for each variable in the model and (in MPlus) robust fit statistics that permit tests of fit to data that is not multivariate normal, or (in AMOS) can test for statistical differences between the bootstrapped and unbootstrapped models. These features offer an advantage (at least for the moment) for the use of SEM rather than PLS for non-normal data, if the other requirements for SEM are met.

Henseler et al. (2016) also point out that sample requirements for valid and reliable PLS and SEM are no different. In both cases, the sample needs to be representative of the population and large enough to ensure statistical tests have sufficient power. At the same time, rules of thumb for the minimum sample needed for valid and reliable SEM have been relaxed in favour of the assessment of validity, reliability and power.

Its use of bootstrapping also led to a preference for PLS when models contained categorical data, but now that SEM software is available to model categorical data, PLS need no longer be preferred over SEM for categorical data. Again, modern SEM software offers a number of features for categorical data that are not currently available in PLS (Asparouhov, 2005; Byrne, 2011; Curran et al., 1996; Jöreskog et al., 2016; van de Schoot et al., 2012). In addition to bootstrapping, MPlus and AMOS offer the ability to analyse non-continuous data and Bayesian modelling.

We therefore recommend that analysts and researchers consider the modern understanding of PLS alongside up-to-date developments in SEM before they choose PLS in order to overcome data limitations. Finally, we caution against the adoption of PLS in order to 'get better results' (i.e. statistical significance), an explanation we hear surprisingly frequently from inexperienced researchers. PLS is more likely to report statistical significance than SEM because of the methods of estimation that it uses – but this is not a reason to choose PLS. PLS should be chosen when the statistical approach to path modelling that it offers is appropriate for the problem and hypotheses under investigation.

This rest of this section will focus on (covariance-based) SEM. We refer readers to the works of Hair, Ringle, Renseler and others, cited above, for details of how to conduct and interpret analyses conducted with PLS.

The language of covariance-based structural equation modelling

SEM has quite a long history, but like many of the most useful mathematical modelling techniques available today, it gained widespread acceptance only after the introduction of computer software that allowed analysts to concentrate on building the model more than conducting the calculations. (The software was LISREL, developed by Jöreskog and Sorbom [1976, 1993].) Works about SEM range from thoughtful, but rather complex, evaluative books such as Hayduck (1996) and papers published in the excellent *Structural Equation Modeling* journal to works that combine rigor with straightforward descriptions of benefits and methods (e.g. Byrne, 2009) and works that are somewhere in between (e.g. Kaplan, 2009). Useful information about SEM in general and the different types of models that can be built using SEM methods is also available in the manuals that accompany the major software packages for SEM; several of these are listed in the Appendix. All these works are useful, and while we introduce most of the major elements of SEM and some of the pitfalls and controversies here, we recommend you read further when you apply this approach in your own work.

While you do not have to be an expert in matrix algebra to use SEM, its language is the language of matrixes and an understanding of the meaning of some of the key terms helps to evaluate and interpret the results, so we introduce some key elements here, primarily using LISREL notation, but also referring to equivalent terms used in other SEM software. The terms *independent variable* and *dependent variable*, while sometimes used in setting up hypotheses and interpreting SEM, are more formally replaced by the terms *endogenous* variable and *exogenous* variable. Each model has a different set of endogenous (or x) variables (the variables represented here on the left-hand side of the model which act only as independent variables, hypothesised to affect other variables in the model). The exogenous (or y)

variables are variables that are hypothesised to be affected by one or more variables (which themselves may be either endogenous or exogenous). In the first model in Figure 4.11, for example, satisfaction is an exogenous variable that is affected by three endogenous variables: positive experience, negative experience and location. Satisfaction, in turn, affects another exogenous variable, intention, which is also the final outcome variable in our model.

The system of equations that defines a structural model can be written in a form that emphasises the similarity of SEM to multiple regression modelling:

$$y = \alpha + \mathbf{B}y + \Gamma x + \varsigma$$

where

- y is a vector of p endogenous (dependent) variables;
- x is a vector of q exogenous (independent) variables;
- $\mathbf{B}$ (beta) is a matrix of relationships (regression coefficients) between endogenous variables;
- Γ (gamma) is a matrix of relationships (regression coefficients) between endogenous and exogenous variables;
- ς (zeta) is a vector of random disturbances (also known as errors or residuals).

Two additional matrixes are important for the estimation of structural models:

- Ψ (psi) is the covariance matrix for errors (i.e. covariance of ς);
- Φ (phi) is the covariance matrix of the exogenous (x) variables.

$\mathbf{B}$ and Γ describe the structural model (with error Ψ). When a model is specified, relationships that do not exist are specified to be 0, otherwise they might be *fixed* (or 'constrained') by the researcher to a certain value or left *free* to be estimated as parameters of the model. For example, the relationship between satisfaction and intention in all of our models will be allowed free to vary (and represented as non-0 in the $\mathbf{B}$ matrix). Similarly, the relationship between location and intention will be represented by a parameter in the Γ matrix. Errors can also be fixed or left free to vary in the Ψ matrix. (Note that the diagonal of B is fixed to 0, so that no y variable is incorrectly modelled as having an effect on itself.)

Specifying a structural equation model

Fortunately, you do not have to specify the relationships and fixed values in matrix form to use SEM. All SEM software allows the investigator to specify each relationship of interest using a simple set of linear equations similar to those used in multiple regression. Most modern SEM software also permits relationships to be specified by drawing a path diagram.

Basic operations of SEM

SEM models are constructed by fitting a model of covariances (usually called Σ or sigma) between the variables in the model using the observed covariances (usually called S). ML estimates are used in almost all situations. The result, for structural models such as those in Figure 4.11, is a set of values for the parameters defined by the **B**, Γ and Ψ matrixes. The values in **B** and Γ are interpreted in the same way as regression coefficients, and the statistical significance of each coefficient can be tested with a t-test.

Measuring the fit of a structural equation model

In addition to the statistical significance of the parameter weights, the quality of a structural equation model is evaluated primarily on the basis of the fit (or discrepancy in fit) between the modelled and the observed covariance matrix. Goodness of fit indexes are provided by all SEM software. Although many fit indexes are reported, there is no need to use all of them. Some have been superseded by others over time, while others are applicable only in specific situations.

SEM fit indexes are based on some estimate of the discrepancy between the hypothesised model, which we will call model h, and a null model in which no relationships are specified and thus all parameters except the variances of the variables (i.e. all regression coefficients) are 0 (we will call this model 0). We summarise the most widely used modern fit indexes in Table 4.4, where we distinguish between three different types of fit index: absolute fit indexes, which do not take the number of parameters of the model into account; comparative (or incremental) fit measures, which can be used to compare alternative models; and parsimony (or relative) fit indexes, which adjust for the number of parameters in the model. It is sufficient to review and report one of each type of fit index, in addition to χ^2, degrees of freedom and the p-value of the χ^2 test. A measure of estimation error, either root mean square residual (RMSR) or root mean square error of approximation (RMSEA), is often reported. (We have excluded two early fit indexes, the goodness of fit index [GFI] and the adjusted goodness of fit index [AGFI], from this list because they are now considered too simplistic, and are rarely referred to in modern texts. Along with other authors, we do not recommend their use [see Sharma *et al.*, 2005].)

Although all fit indexes are based on errors derived from comparisons of parameters rather than errors in estimating the scores of individual cases, sample size still affects estimates of chi-square, which is likely to be non-significant with samples of 250 or more. Table 4.4 therefore

Table 4.4 Fit indexes commonly used in structural equation modelling

Category of fit index	Fit index	Formula	Rule of thumb
Absolute fit measures	χ^2	$(n-1)F(S;\Sigma(\theta_h))$ where $F(\mathbf{S};\Sigma(\theta_h))$ is the model fit function (see Jöreskog and Sorbom [1993] for detail of how fit functions are determined). In simple terms, χ^2 can be thought of as $(n-1)(S-\Sigma)$	*Not* statistically significant where $n<250$ and $m\geq30$, otherwise, not reliable
	Root mean square residual (RMSR)	Average residual covariance, usually expressed as average residual correlation (sometimes used in the *standardised* version: SRMSR) to aid evaluation	<0.08
	Root mean square error of approximation (RMSEA)	$\text{RMSEA} = \sqrt{\dfrac{\max(\chi_h^2 - df_h, 0)/n}{df_h}}$ where $(\chi_h^2 - df_h, 0)$ is the maximum of $(\chi_h^2 - df_h)$ and 0	<0.08; <0.07 with $n>250$
Incremental fit measures	Tucker–Lewis index (also known as the non-normed fit index, NNFI)[a]	$\text{TLI} = \dfrac{\left(\chi_r^2/df_r\right) - \left(\chi_h^2/df_h\right)}{\left(\chi_r^2/df_r\right) - 1}$ where r is the reference model to which h is compared	>0.92 for $m\geq30$; >0.95 for $12\leq m<30$; >0.97 for $m<12$
	Comparative fit index[a]	$\text{CFI} = \dfrac{\left(\chi_r^2 - df_r\right) - \left(\chi_h^2 - df_h\right)}{\chi_r^2 - df_r}$	>0.92 for $m\geq30$; >0.95 for 12 $m<30$; >0.97 for $m\leq12$
	Normed fit index	$\text{NFI} = \dfrac{\chi_r^2 - \chi_h^2}{\chi_r^2}$	>0.9
	Akaike information criterion	$\text{AIC}=\chi^2+m(m-1)-2df$	When comparing two models, the one with a smaller AIC is preferred

(Continued)

Table 4.4 (Continued)

Category of fit index	Fit index	Formula	Rule of thumb
	Bayesian information criterion	$BIC = \chi^2 + [m(m-1)/2 - df]ln(n)$	When comparing two models, the one with a smaller BIC is preferred
	Other information criteria (IC)	Other information criteria, which use different penalties for the estimated number of parameters, are available from software packages	When comparing two models, the one with smaller IC is preferred
Parsimony fit measures	Normed χ^2	χ^2/df	$<5^b$
	Parsimonious normed fit index	$PNFI = \dfrac{df_h}{df_0} \cdot NFI$	Differences of 0.06–0.09

Note: h=hypothesised model; 0=null model; r=reference model; m=number of observed variables.

[a] In the special case where r=0, these indexes act as parsimony fit indexes.

[b] Rules of thumb for acceptable normed χ^2 range from <5, as originally proposed by Wheaton et al. (1977) to <2, a very stringent criterion for 'good' fit attributed to Arbuckle (2003) in the AMOS User's Guide and subsequently adopted by several textbooks (it is relaxed to between <3 and <2 in the 2016 AMOS 23 help file entry, CMIN/DF).

includes different rules of thumb for some indexes, derived from the helpful summary provided by Hair *et al.* (2010) to which we refer the reader for a straightforward critical review of the strengths and weaknesses of each index. It is also worth consulting the useful and authoritative website, Measuring Model Fit, maintained by David Kenny (http://davidakenny. net/cm/fit.htm). More stringent criteria than those listed here may be warranted in models with small samples or a small number of observed variables, or both. Finally, it is useful to know that not all fit indexes are reported when the data file contains missing data. Although SEM packages estimate missing values, this process reduces variances and covariances, which in turn biases fit.

Assumptions of SEM and associated issues in estimation

As the equation for the model suggests, SEM is a linear modelling technique, and the issues associated with distributions that have been discussed for regression models also apply to SEM. Metric variables with high kurtosis can create problems and may need to be transformed, and high multicollinearity can result in a singular matrix and prevent a solution being generated. (Singularity is a common cause of the 'matrix not positive definite' message that often causes headaches for users of SEM.) Both metric and categorical variables can be included in an SEM model, although methods for categorical variables are not as simple to use as methods for metric variables.

Only models that are 'identified' can be estimated. Identification means that there is a unique solution to the specified system of equations, and this will occur only if there are as many pieces of available information (observed variances and covariances) as parameters to be estimated. While identification is necessary for estimation, it is insufficient for hypothesis testing, which requires one or more degrees of freedom. The goal is therefore to specify a model that is over-identified. Note that identification is primarily concerned with the specification of the model to be estimated, rather than the sample size.

Degrees of freedom for a structural equation model are calculated as

$$df = \frac{1}{2}\left[(p+q)(p+q+1)\right] - t$$

where
- p is the number of observed exogenous variances and covariances;
- q is the number of observed endogenous variances and covariances;
- t is the number of parameters to be estimated in the model.

Measurement models and structural models

The value of SEM comes not only from its ability to model paths of structural relationships between concepts, but also from its ability to simultaneously model measurement (factor) models with structural models. In fact, SEM can be used for measurement modelling alone, in which case it is said to be used for confirmatory factor analysis (CFA; see Brown, 2006). We will consider the measurement model first, before combining the measurement and structural models.

Measurement Models

Measurement models are represented by two systems of equations, one for the exogenous latent variables in the model and the other for any endogenous latent variables that are specified. For the endogenous variables, x, the measurement model is

$$x = \Lambda_x \xi + \delta$$

where
- ξ (xi) is a vector of latent exogenous (independent) variables;
- δ (delta) is a vector of measurement errors for x.

For the exogenous variables, y, the measurement model is

$$y = \Lambda_y \eta + \varepsilon$$

where

- η (eta) is a vector of latent endogenous (dependent) variables;
- ε (epsilon) is a vector of measurement errors for y.

Additional matrixes needed to represent measurement models are
- Λ_y (lambda y), the matrix of regression coefficients λ_y for observed variables predicted by latent exogenous variables;
- L_x (lambda x), the matrix of regression coefficients λ_x for observed variables predicted by latent endogenous variables;
- Θ_ε (theta epsilon), the matrix of error covariances associated with the prediction of the observed variables by the latent endogenous variables;
- Θ_δ (theta delta), the matrix of error covariances associated with the prediction of the observed variables by the latent exogenous variables.

Example: Specifying the measurement model

While, in Figure 4.11, we drew the variables, positive experiences and negative experiences, as observed variables (using, as customary in SEM, a square box to represent an observed variable), we could obtain a more complete indication of the quality of the experiences that visitors had if we constructed a multi-item scale to measure these two concepts. In Figure 4.12, positive experiences and negative experiences are represented as latent variables (ellipses), each of which is reflected by four items which the investigator has extracted from other studies of visitor intentions. Both variables are modelled as endogenous latent variables, and they are correlated with one another. ζ are nominated $e1$ to $e8$, and the 1 on the arrow connecting each ζ to the observed variable both identifies the relationship and sets the scale for the measurement of ζ to that of the variable.

In order to be able to estimate the measurement model, we also need to identify each latent variable. This can be done by fixing one parameter associated with the variable. The value to which the parameter is fixed is arbitrary, but the general rule is to fix the regression weight for the observed variable expected to have the strongest relationship with the latent variable to 1 in order also to set an easily interpreted scale.

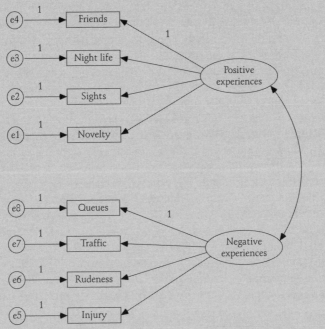

Figure 4.12 Simplified measurement model for the correlated latent variables, positive experiences and negative experiences

Note in Figure 4.12 that the arrows between each observed variable and the respective latent variable point from the latent variable to the observed variable and not the other way around. This is because we hypothesise that the latent variable exists and the observed variables reflect or represent that latent variable. The coefficients will provide an indication of how well this hypothesised measurement model represents each latent variable. Low and non-significant coefficients indicate variables that do not represent the concept well. (It is also possible to model observed variables as 'indicator' variables, in which case the hypothesis is that the observed variables cause or define the latent variable. We will not consider this type of measurement model here, although it can be useful in situations where the latent variable is an index constructed from a set of observed variables.) Effectively, Figure 4.12 presents a confirmatory factor model as a simple structure in which we hypothesise that the eight observed variables form two correlated factors, and that friends, night life, sights and novelty will have non-0 loadings on positive experiences and 0 loadings on negative experiences, and queues, traffic, rudeness and injury will have non-0 loadings on negative experiences and 0 loadings on positive experiences.

A number of criteria are used to evaluate a measurement model. Firstly, all estimates should make sense. There should be no negative error variances ('Heywood cases') or standardised coefficients greater than 1.00. In these situations, the distributions of the observed variables should be re-examined, along with their correlation with other variables in the model to identify any obvious sources of error or difficulty. It is possible to fix the parameters to acceptable values (e.g. 0.005 for Heywood cases) but this approach might hide an underlying problem, even if it resolves the immediate difficulty. All coefficients (λ_x and λ_y) should be statistically significant, and a rule of thumb is that the standardised coefficients should be 0.7 or more.

In addition to statistically significant coefficients, a good measurement model, like any other factor model, must explain sufficient variance in the observed variables ('communality' in factor analysis terms) and satisfy criteria for reliability. The variance explained for each observed variable is reported by most software packages, usually as 'R-squared', as is the squared standardised coefficient. A rule of thumb is that the variance in each observed variable explained by a latent variable should be at least 0.5. It is common to report an indicator of total variance extracted, calculated as

$$\text{Variance extracted} = \frac{\left(\sum \text{standardised } \lambda^2\right)}{\left(\sum \text{standardised } \lambda^2\right) + \sum \varepsilon}$$

Cronbach's alpha is often reported for each latent variable, but a reliability measure that is more specific to SEM is

$$\text{Construct reliability} = \frac{\left(\sum \text{standardised } \lambda\right)^2}{\left(\sum \text{standardised } \lambda\right)^2 + \sum \varepsilon}$$

Finally, the quality of the measurement model (for each latent variable, or for all latent variables together) can be measured using the same set of fit indexes that is available for structural models.

Because an SEM measurement model is a confirmatory factor model, purists might say that, if problems are identified with measurement, they should be accepted and modelling should proceed since, in any case, the estimation of the structural model takes measurement error into account. In practice, SEM modellers usually fine-tune problematic measurement models before proceeding, but extreme care needs to be taken to ensure that any changes made are consistent with theory or what can reasonably be considered feasible. Any modifications that affect hypothesis tests are to be avoided. The types of modification that are most often justified are removal of observed variables that cause problems in reaching a solution, and removal of observed variables that have low loadings and therefore low variance explained. In both cases, the assumption is that there is an error in specification, definition or measurement that means that the removed variable(s) does not satisfactorily reflect the concept represented by the latent variable. This is justifiable if sufficient observed variables remain to represent the latent variable adequately (three observed variables are required per latent variable to provide sufficient degrees of freedom for the estimation of trustworthy fit indexes, but a latent variable can be modelled with only one observed variable, if necessary).

Most SEM software provides modification indexes (MI) that can be used to detect problems with both measurement models and structural models. Often, the MI suggest that, if the error terms for two observed variables in the measurement model (these variables might form part of the measurement model for one latent variable or for two different ones) were permitted to be correlated, the model would be a better fit to the data. Allowing such a correlation may result in over-fitting of the model and reduce the ability to generalise to the population, so we strongly advise against it. We prefer to inspect any pairs of variables with correlated error terms for conceptual similarity and other problems, and to remove problem variables if both feasible and necessary.

The Structural Model

After confirming (and, if necessary, refining) the measurement model, the structural model can be estimated. Except in specific circumstance, the measurement model and the structural model are estimated concurrently. We show how a structural model is built concurrently with a measurement model in the following example, which uses AMOS software.

Example: A complete structural equation model

Figure 4.13 shows a structural equation model that combines our measurement model for experiences with the structural model of relationships shown in the middle panel of Figure 4.10.

The coefficients are standardised for display. There were 90 observed covariances and variances and 38 parameters to estimate, leaving 52 degrees of freedom, so the model was over-identified, as required for hypothesis testing. All coefficients in the model, except the coefficient for the relationship between gender and satisfaction, are statistically significant.

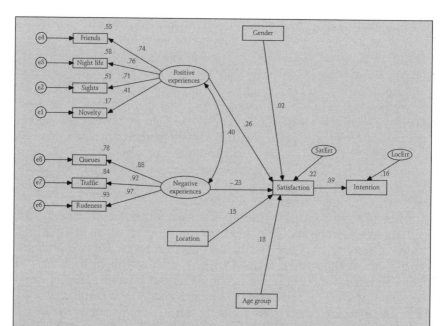

Figure 4.13 Structural equation model for the example: The measurement model and the structural model are estimated together (standardised coefficients)

Looking first at the measurement model, we see that *injuries* no longer forms part of the measurement model for Negative Experiences. That is because too few respondents experienced or observed injuries to be able to rate their experience on this variable and the large number of missing values prevented model estimation. The reduced measurement model for Negative Experiences was satisfactory, however, without *injuries*. We can see this from both the coefficients (on the arrows) and the R^2 for each observed variable (at the top right-hand corner of the observed variable). We have retained *novelty* in the measurement model for Positive Experiences, even though it appears to reflect them weakly.

In this example, *novelty* is conceptually an important element of the positive experience and, in the absence of any technical explanations of its low loading, we accept that this might be a sample-specific problem. The other variables are all satisfactory. This leaves Positive Experiences with variance extracted and construct reliability a little below the rule of thumb values (not shown), but we accept that (at least for now).

For interest, we report the equations that define the (unstandardised) measurement model (Figure 4.13) for Negative Experiences. The second term in each equation is the error variance, and the R^2 is taken from the standardised measurement model (Figure 4.14).

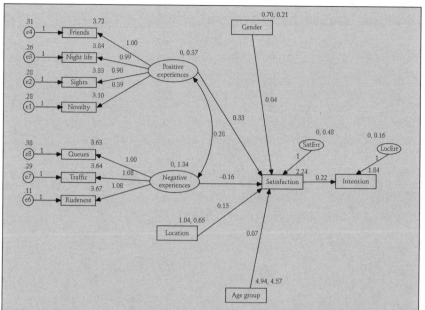

Figure 4.14 Structural equation model for the example (unstandardised coefficients)

$$\text{Queues} = 1.00 \text{ Negative\_Experiences} + 0.38, \ R^2 = 0.78$$

$$\text{Traffic} = 1.08 \text{ Negative\_Experiences} + 0.29, \ R^2 = 0.84$$

$$\text{Rudeness} = 1.08 \text{ Negative\_Experiences} + 0.11, \ R^2 = 0.97$$

The set of equations that expresses the structural relationships in the model is

$$\text{Intention} = 0.22 \text{ Satisfaction} + 0.16, \ R^2 = 0.16$$

$$\text{Satisfaction} = 0.33 \text{ Positive\_Experiences} - 0.16 \text{ Negative\_Experiences}$$
$$+ \ 0.04 \text{ Gender} + 0.07 \text{ Location} + 0.48, \ R^2 = 0.22$$

Different software packages report the results of an SEM analysis in different ways, and even when coefficients are mapped to a path diagram, some details must be read from the text output. When an SEM contains more than one exogenous variable, useful additional information can be obtained from the estimated total effects of each variable in the model on the outcome variable (intention, in our example). Total effects (both standardised and unstandardised) can be requested in all SEM software.

Example: Total, direct and indirect effects

An AMOS table of total effects for our example is provided in Table 4.5. We use standardised effects to enable comparison of the relative effect of each variable in the model.

The first eight lines provide information about the measurement model and the direct effects of the endogenous variables on satisfaction (the same information that we can read from the path diagram or text report of standardised coefficients), but the last line reports the total effects of all variables in the structural model on intention. Here, we can see that satisfaction has the strongest total effect, but we can also see the effect on intention of variables that affect (or 'act through') satisfaction.

Positive and negative experiences have a similar effect, but in opposite directions; age and location both have a slightly smaller effect. We have already seen that the direct effect of gender on satisfaction is non-significant, so its small indirect effect on intention through satisfaction is not of interest.

A description of a structural equation model is incomplete without a report of the fit of this model. For our example, we report the chi-square – even though we know that with a large sample it is likely to be non-significant – because this is the common practice in reporting the results of SEM analyses. We also report the RMSEA as an absolute index that is robust to sample size, and the CFI, which we use as a parsimony index in this case. Chi-square is high and significant: 18.199 (with $df=52$), $p<0.001$. RMSEA is 0.08, which is satisfactory for a model this size, and CFI is 0.84, which is below the recommended value of 0.92 for a model this size.

Table 4.5 Table of standardised total effects, as presented in AMOS

	Positive_ Experiences	Negative_ Experiences	Gender	Age	Location	Satisfaction
Friends	0.74	0.00	0.00	0.00	0.00	0.00
Night life	0.76	0.00	0.00	0.00	0.00	0.00
Sights	0.71	0.00	0.00	0.00	0.00	0.00
Novelty	0.41	0.00	0.00	0.00	0.00	0.00
Queues	0.00	0.88	0.00	0.00	0.00	0.00
Traffic	0.00	0.92	0.00	0.00	0.00	0.00
Rudeness	0.00	0.97	0.00	0.00	0.00	0.00
Satisfaction	0.26	0.23	0.02	0.18	0.15	0.00
Intention	0.10	−0.09	0.01	0.07	0.06	0.39

Completing a structural equation model in practice

As in regression modelling, once a structural equation model has been built and the measurement model, structural effects and model fit have been evaluated, the modeller needs to decide what is to be the next step, and again, the next step depends on the purpose for which the model was built. If the purpose was testing whether the hypothesised relationships provided a good model to explain the outcome variable, no more work needs to be done. If the purpose was, on the other hand, to find a good model to predict the outcome variable, then more work may be needed. To move ahead, it is important to understand whether any shortcomings in the model reflect conceptual issues, specification issues (including measurement issues), empirical issues or a combination of these issues. Conceptual issues might include the inclusion of endogenous variables that are not realistically related to the exogenous variable(s) of interest, or the exclusion of variables that would improve the quality of the model. Specification issues include the specification of both the measurement and the structural models. Empirical issues include data quality, but also require attention to the possibility that the results obtained in an analysis are sample specific.

In some circumstances, the modeller might attempt to fit an alternative model using the available data. (This should not, however, be done just to obtain satisfactory values on the fit indexes, a motivation that is most likely to result in a model that cannot be generalised beyond the sample used to develop it.) Most SEM software allows alternative models to be compared in a single analysis. The alternative models are proposed and compared using all measures of quality: conceptual validity, significant coefficients, R^2 and fit indexes. To compare models, incremental (comparative) fit indexes are examined, and any model that has clearly a superior fit is marked as a suitable model for future analyses. Note here that we say 'for future analyses'; there is a strong risk of over-fitting when a potentially superior model is identified in this way, and the only way to confirm that it is, in fact, superior, is to gather new data and run the SEM again.

Example: Options available to the destination intention modeller

The model presented in Figure 4.13 is imperfect (gender did not have an effect as expected; novelty was not a relevant positive experience for this sample; and only small proportions of the variance in satisfaction and intention are explained); however, it also has several satisfactory elements: confirmation of some of the proposed elements of the measurement of experiences at the destination; confirmation that both positive and negative experiences have an effect on satisfaction, and through satisfaction on intention; and an indication that satisfaction (and thus, intention) differs with the visitor's home location and age. Let us assume that the modeller's goal was to identify a parsimonious and realistic model of effects on satisfaction and intention to return. In this case, he/she might reconsider the inclusion of gender in the model and decide that there is no reason to expect that the destination would appeal more to either males or females; he/she might therefore respecify the model without gender. This would probably improve the fit statistics, but it would not improve the ability to explain either satisfaction or intention. On the other hand, in Figure 4.10, we saw several alternative specifications of the relationships between the variables in this model; is one of the other specifications, or yet another likely to provide a better model? While *post hoc* respecification risks the development of a model that is sample specific, in this case, it would be quite legitimate for the modeller to compare the three alternative models proposed prior to building the mathematical model.

Dealing with small samples

Small samples (less than 250, depending on the complexity of the model) can cause problems when both measurement and structural models are estimated simultaneously. One possible remedy is to simplify the structural equation model by using 'composite variables' to represent each of the latent variables. The measurement model is thus removed from the structural model, leaving fewer parameters to be estimated. Composite variables might be calculated, for example, by taking the mean of the values that load most highly on each variable in a classical exploratory factor analysis – an imperfect solution, but sometimes the only one available. When composite variables are used, measurement error can (and should) still be included in the specification of the structural model. Methods for estimating error variance when using composite variables are described by McGill *et al.* (2003) and Holmes-Smith and Rowe (1994).

Mediation and Moderation in Model Building

One issue that causes confusion in model specification is how to describe and test the nature of the relationship between variables when a variable has an indirect effect on another or mediates or moderates the effect of an independent variable on a dependent variable. Mediation occurs when, although a direct effect of X on Y can be observed, the effect can be explained (in whole or in part) by another 'mediating' variable. Moderation occurs when the effect of X on Y varies according to certain conditions.

Example: Differentiating between an indirect effect and mediation

The difference between mediation and an indirect effect appears subtle, but important. A path model can be built as a series of direct effects ($X1$ to $X2$, $X2$ to $X3$, $X3$ to Y), without the need to develop hypotheses of direct effects between X (the endogenous variable in SEM) and the exogenous independent variable, Y.

The model shown in Figure 4.14 and Table 4.4 is of this type. The researcher is interested in the path or chain of effects, from positive and negative experiences to satisfaction, and from satisfaction to intention to return, with no hypotheses about mediation. There is therefore no need to test for mediation. The size of the indirect effects can be tested by examining each intermediate path and the total effect of each X variable on Y (Table 4.4). (Testing the statistical significance of an indirect effect is not, however, straightforward, suffering from the difficulty of estimating the standard error of an effect that travels through paths of correlated variables. We discuss approaches to dealing with this difficulty with hypothesis testing for mediation.)

A hypothesis of mediation begins with a hypothesis or observation that X has a direct effect on Y. For example, rather than building up a sequence of effects in a path model of the kind shown in Figure 4.14, the analyst could have begun by hypothesising that experience quality has an effect on intention to return, as shown in Figure 4.15.

The analyst wants to go beyond this simple relationship to test whether a cognitive or psychological mechanism underlies, or can explain, the relationship between experience quality and intention to return. He/she believes that experience quality affects intention to return by affecting satisfaction, as illustrated in Figure 4.16. Although this effect is

Figure 4.15 Hypothesised direct effect of experience quality on intention to return

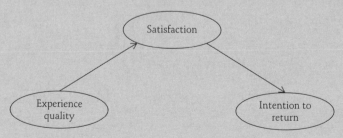

Figure 4.16 Hypothesised mediating effect of satisfaction between experience quality and intention to return

modelled in the same way as a path model, the hypothesis is a hypothesis of mediation *between* two variables (experience quality and intention to return) rather than a hypothesis of indirect effect (experience quality affects satisfaction, which *in turn* affects intention to return).

Mediation

The influence of a variable, X, on a variable, Y, might be wholly or partially mediated by the intervening variable. In Figure 4.16, we modelled intention to return as fully mediated by experience quality. Partial mediation occurs when the mediating variable accounts for only a portion of the effect of X on Y, as illustrated in Figure 4.17.

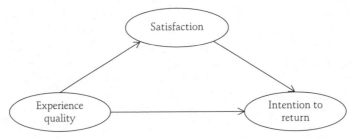

Figure 4.17 Hypothesised partial mediation of satisfaction between experience quality and intention to return

Example: Partial mediation

A hypothesis of partial mediation between experience quality and intention to return is modelled as shown in Figure 4.17: experience quality is hypothesised to have an effect on intention to return in two ways (i.e. through two paths): a direct effect on intention to return and a mediated effect through satisfaction.

Example: The mediating role of satisfaction between service quality and intention

Cole and Illum (2006) used SEM to test relationships between performance quality at a community fair, experience quality, satisfaction and intention to tell others about the fair and to return.

The model in Figure 4.18 (adapted from Cole and Illum's [2006: 168] – Figures 1 and 2) shows how overall satisfaction partially mediated

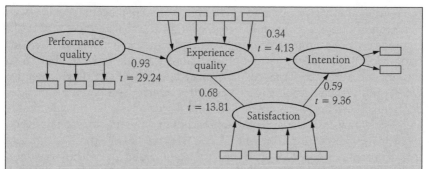

Figure 4.18 Path model showing satisfaction as partially mediating the effect of experience quality on intention as well as an indirect effect from performance quality to satisfaction and intention (standardised path coefficients and the *t*-value are shown on each structural path; square boxes indicate the number of observed variables used to measure each of the latent variables; adapted from Cole & Illum, 2006)

the effect of experience quality on intentions. Performance quality had an indirect effect on satisfaction and intention through its effect on experience quality.

Testing for the existence, nature and extent of a mediating effect is not straightforward. Although mean effects can be estimated reliably in SEM, estimation of the standard error of the mediation path (the path from experience quality to intention to return, in Figures 4.16 and 4.17) is confounded by correlation (covariance) between the independent variables in the chain of effects. The higher the correlation, the lower the standard error of the chain of effects and the higher the probability of incorrectly deciding that a significant effect exists when it does not (Type I error). This problem is compounded in models with multiple mediated paths (e.g. from multiple independent variables through a single mediator, or from a single independent variable through multiple mediators, or multiple independent variables through multiple mediators).

Three main approaches are available for testing hypotheses of mediation: use of an interaction term; a four-step procedure which accounts for the common variance in regression models (made popular by Baron & Kenny [1986] as the Sobel test following Sobel [1982], and MacKinnon [2008]); and comparison of the fit of alternative models in SEM. There is some controversy about which approach is 'best'. Generally, researchers with a strong background in regression and econometric methods prefer the four-step procedure, while researchers with a strong background in behavioural research and SEM prefer the SEM approach.

Several alternative approaches to the four-step procedure exist with MacKinnon's approach preferred to the original Sobel test because it (in common with other more recent approaches) estimates an 'unbiased' standard error, adopting an asymmetric, rather than a normal error distribution to account for correlated variance. This procedure is well described in several works, and we refer readers to Hayes (2013) which describes and compares different procedures, and provides research-based advice on the advantages and disadvantages of the different approaches in different situations. Several software packages, including PROCESS (Hayes, 2013) and PRODCLIN (MacKinnon *et al.*, 2007), can be run stand-alone or within common statistical packages such as SPSS and SAS (Preacher & Hayes, 2004). A number of calculators for the Sobel test are available on the internet, notably the web page maintained by Preacher and Leonardelli at http://quantpsy.org/sobel/sobel.htm, which also offers valuable advice on the data requirements for a Sobel test, and the circumstances under which the results of a Sobel test are similar to those of other four-step procedural approaches.

SEM offers a simpler procedure. (It is also possible that it is more reliable, particularly in cases of multiple mediation, although research is still needed to test this assertion. The relative strengths and weaknesses of SEM and the four-step approach are discussed well by Kelloway [2013], who refers to recent advances in SEM, and MacKinnon [2008].) SEM can be used to compare several alternative, 'nested' models in a single run. Figures 4.14 through 4.16 are nested models: Figure 4.14 shows a single direct path, with only one effect to be estimated; Figure 4.15 has one hypothesised path with two direct effects; Figure 4.16 is the most constrained model with two hypothesised paths, including the mediated path which requires estimation of two direct effects. Mediation is tested by comparing the fit statistics for each model. Higher comparative and parsimonious fit measures suggest that one model has a better fit than the others. Importantly, a statistical test is available: a statistically significant change in chi-square between the less constrained and the more constrained model indicates that the more constrained model is a significant improvement on the less constrained model, and that mediation (or partial mediation) exists.

Moderation

Example: Moderation in the theory of planned behaviour

A theory-based approach to the 'intention to return' examples we have used in this chapter might adopt the theory of planned behaviour (TPB, Ajzen, 1991) which proposes that, when people take actions about which they have given some thought, behaviour (e.g. return to a destination) follows the formation of intention, and intention in turn is influenced by attitudes to the behaviour (would returning be good or bad for me?), subjective norms (what do other people who are important to me want me to do? what would *they* do?) and perceived control (e.g. do I have enough time and money to return?).

But behaviour does not always follow the formation of intention; even when a person wants to return to a destination, he/she might be prevented from doing so by a number of intervening events or conditions, such as lack of leave, costs that are beyond his/her means or volcanic ash clouds that prevent travel on the planned dates. These effects are illustrated in Figure 4.19.

Intention is modelled as mediating the effects of attitude, subjective norm and perceived control on actual return, while external events are modelled as moderating the effect of intention on actual return.

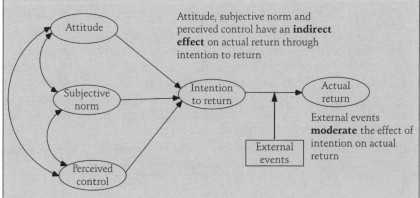

Figure 4.19 TPB model of return to destination, showing mediation and moderation

Both regression and SEM offer techniques for testing moderation. The classical approach in regression analysis is to define one or more dummy variables to represent a categorical moderator. (See the discussion of dummy variables in regression, earlier in this chapter, for more detail of how to define dummy variables.)

The most common way to test for moderation in SEM is through multi-group analysis. If the moderating variable is a categorical variable with a limited number of categories (geographic location, classified as north, centre, south), each level is treated as a group and, providing each group has a sufficiently large sample size, multi-group analysis is run without data transformation. If the moderator is measured on a metric scale, or an ordinal scale with quite a large number of categories, it must be transformed to a categorical variable. When transforming a metric mediator into categorical groups for multi-group analysis, care has to be taken to meet sample size requirements while, at the same time, setting cut-points that are consistent with the hypothesised moderation effect.

> ## Example: Coding for age as a moderating variable
>
> Tourist evaluation of outdoor activities varies by age as well as by type of activity. In this example, a beach paragliding rental operator examined the effects of several variables on customer evaluation of their experience. Among other things, the firm wanted to test their staff's belief that older customers were less likely than younger customers to make a repeat booking, regardless of the customer's evaluation of the firm and his/her paragliding experience.
>
> The firm's database included the date of birth of all customers, so exact age could be calculated as a metric variable. Because the goal was to compare older to younger customers, it was possible to conduct multi-group SEM with age as a moderator of the relationship between overall evaluation and intention to make a repeat booking. Data were available for 500 customers who had registered during the first month of the summer season. To avoid small groups, the firm's analyst decided that she would divide the customers into no more than two groups.
>
> To determine the cut-point, she plotted the distribution of customer age and found that most customers were aged between 18 and 25. After checking with the firm's owner, she established 25 as the upper limit for the 'younger' customer group. All customers aged 26 or older were classified as 'older' customers. There were 330 younger customers and 170 older customers. Although the number of older customers was a small sample for SEM, she decided to retain the split at 25 years after testing that it was sufficient by running a trial multi-group SEM.

Procedures for running a multi-group analysis are described in the next section with procedures for using SEM for modelling multilevel effects.

Multilevel Modelling

Another important aspect of modelling, to which increasing attention is being paid, is the potential for misspecifying models and inflating effect sizes when models include elements that are drawn from different levels of analysis. For example, if data are being collected from staff at several hotels in order to study the relationship between employee satisfaction and turnover in the hotel industry, any model that is built should account for the fact that aspects of the management of each hotel will mean that the staff at each hotel will share common perceptions of satisfaction and turnover. There will be pools of common variance in the data that reflect hotel-level variance, in addition to variance among individuals that is not associated with a specific hotel. Whether the investigator is interested in the relationship between satisfaction and turnover across different hotels, or among individual workers in the industry, or both, a correctly specified model needs to take sources of variance at both levels into account. Techniques for multilevel modelling are described in Hox (2010), Snijders and Bosker (1999) and other works.

Hierarchically structured data

Data are often hierarchically structured, in the sense that data gathered to measure the phenomenon of interest (Level 1 data) might be gathered or nested in groups or clusters (Level 2 data), which themselves might be nested in groups (Level 3 data) and so on. The higher-level groups might be tour groups, organisations, classrooms, raters in tests of inter-rater correlation, geographical regions or any other group form which data about individual cases (individual travellers, employees, trainees, rating, performance data, etc.) might be obtained.

Hierarchical data are common in studies where data are collected from or about individuals by approaching the organisations in which they work. Unless only one individual is sampled from each organisation, systematic effects associated with organisational differences need to be accounted for before accurate estimations of effects due to individuals can be obtained. Studies that seek to understand individual factors associated with employee commitment to his/her organisation and intention to stay in the hospitality industry can be significantly confounded by higher-level organisational effects. In more formal terms, multilevel data violate the assumptions of independence that underlie most statistical tests: Level 1 data gathered from Level 2 sources dependent on Level 2 conditions which depend on Level 3 conditions and so on.

Example: Best subsets method for choosing a parsimonious model

Performance data are often hierarchically structured. For example, assessment of the performance of the concierge service in a large hotel chain uses customer satisfaction reports to assess service quality – but each concierge service is located within a specific hotel and each hotel is one of several in a specific region. How much of the variance in team performance scores across the hotel chain is due to actual differences in team performance, rather than the characteristics of the hotel (management style, organisational culture, physical condition, etc.) or region (regional management practices, economic situation, sociocultural norms, etc.) in which they work? Comparison of service quality provided by the team (Level 1 effects) should take account of hotel characteristics

(Level 2 effects) and regional characteristics (Level 3 effects). The three-level hierarchy defined by these different sources of data is illustrated in Figure 4.20.

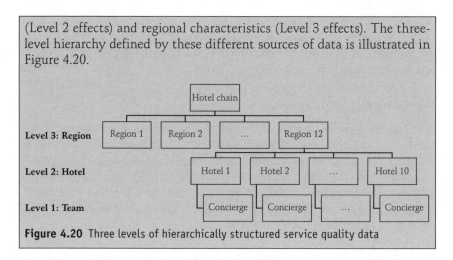

Figure 4.20 Three levels of hierarchically structured service quality data

Testing for multilevel effects

The strength of multilevel effects for a variable can be measured by the intra-class correlation (ICC) coefficient. In a data set with two levels, the ICC compares the similarity of scores obtained from Level 1 cases within the Level 2 groups to the similarity between Level 1 cases assuming no grouping exists. (Readers familiar with analysis of variance [ANOVA] will see that Level 2 could be interpreted as a factor and Level 1 scores as the dependent variable in an ANOVA model where Level 1 similarity is measured as the variance between cases and Level 2 similarity is measured as the variance of cases within groups. In fact, the ICC goes back to Ronald Fisher and the invention of ANOVA.) The ICC, which ranges from 0 to 1, is interpreted in multilevel modelling as the percentage of variance observed in one level that is, in fact, due to a higher level. In a two-level model, for example, it is an index of the dependence of Level 1 scores on Level 2.

There are several different types of ICC, but the most commonly used to test multilevel effects is the one-way ICC. The formula for this simple ICC is given by

$$\rho = \frac{\sigma_l^2}{\sigma_l^2 + \sigma_e^2}$$

where σ_l^2 is between group variance and σ_e^2 is the (error) variance that cannot be explained by grouping. This ICC also allows for a simple interpretation: the proportion of total variance explained by the (Level 2) grouping. Because it is a ratio of variances, its statistical significance can be tested using the F distribution.

Example: Calculating the ICC in SPSS

Sam wants to examine the relationship between organisational commitment (OC) and intention to continue to work for the organisation in the hotel industry. He collected data on OC and intention to stay from 574 employees in three hotels. His first analytical task is to check if the fact that the employees are grouped in hotels will affect his estimate of the effect of OC on intention to stay. SPSS provides a simple method to estimate ICC for testing inter-rater reliability, but this method is unsuitable for estimating multilevel ICC. Instead, Sam chooses the Variance Components procedure from the General Linear Model menu. He enters a marker variable for Intention to Stay as the dependent variable and Hotel as a random effect (because, as we note below, he has sampled employees from only three hotels, rather than the population of hotels), then clicks Options and selects Maximum Likelihood from the Methods options because his subsequent model will use Maximum Likelihood estimation. The syntax looks like this:

VARCOMP IntStayMarker BY Hotel
/RANDOM=Hotel
/METHOD=ML
/CRITERIA=ITERATE(50)
/CRITERIA=CONVERGE(1.0E-8)
/DESIGN=Hotel
/INTERCEPT=INCLUDE.

When he runs the procedure, Sam receives a report on the amount of variance explained by each source, as shown in Table 4.6.

Using the formula for correlation of the one-way ICC, he determines that grouping by hotel (Level 2) accounts for 19.6% of the variance in employees' (Level 1) intention to stay as measured by the IntStayMarker variable. He concludes that a substantial portion of the variance in the dependent variable for his study is due to Level 2 hotel effects, which he must extract from his model so he can see the effects that are due to individual differences between employees' commitment to the organisation. As a side effect, he has also learned that the hotel of employment has a substantial influence on intention to stay.

Table 4.6 Variance estimates obtained from the SPSS Variance Components procedure

Component	Estimate
Var(Hotel)	0.163
Var(Error)	0.667

Note: Dependent variable: IntStayMarker.

Modelling multilevel effects

Multilevel models seek to partition the effects of a set of independent variables at different levels on a dependent variable. The purpose varies from seeking an unbiased estimate of the Level 1 effects to estimating effects at all levels, depending on the researcher's needs.

A decision to be made when modelling multilevel effects is whether the effects of the independent variables are fixed or random. When all groups in the population are represented in the data set, the group effect is fixed. If the groups represent only a subset or sample of the population of groups, they are treated as random (as in randomly sampled from the population – even if, in practice, they are selectively chosen by the researcher).

Most software packages also distinguish between factors and covariates in a multilevel model. Categorical variables (grouping variables) are entered as factors (with a similar meaning to factors in ANOVA) while continuous variables are entered as covariates (regardless of the role they might play in the model, i.e. covariate, independent predictor or control variable).

Multilevel Regression Models

General linear modelling (GLM) in the most widely used software packages (including SPSS, Stata, MPlus and R) permits a variety of multilevel regression models to be built, including linear, binomial and polynomial. Different estimation methods are available, although the most commonly used is ML.

The models estimate a nested set of equations in which the variance explained by each higher level is modelled as an error term in each lower-level equation. In a three-level model with a single independent variable at each level:

$$\text{Level 1:} \quad y_i = x_i + \mu_{i2} + \varepsilon_i$$
$$\text{Level 2:} \quad \mu_{i2} = k_{i2} + v_{i3} + \varepsilon_{i2}$$
$$\text{Level 3:} \quad v_{i3} = k_{i3} + v_{i3} + \varepsilon_{i3}$$

Models are built hierarchically to permit the estimation of the amount of variance explained at each level. The differences between variance explained at each level provide an indication of the importance of the higher-level grouping. At the same time, because variance is extracted from the higher-level independent variables as the lower-level variables are estimated, 'true' estimates of the lower-level effects can be obtained. Because multilevel grouping of cases reduces the standard error of coefficients, GLM functions also offer robust estimates, which should be selected if the purpose of the study is to test and/or compare effect sizes.

Multilevel regression models permit more than the estimation of the effect due to the existence of a higher level. They also allow the higher-level factor to be defined by one or more variables, increasing the researcher's ability to explain how higher-level factors influence lower-level variables. A good example is the estimation of the effect of regional socio-economic conditions on an individual or organisational issue of interest. Provided data are available from a large enough number of regions to obtain reliable results (often considered to be 20 or more, but see Meuleman and Billiet [2009]), economic variables such as the average wage and social variables such as the unemployment rate can be included in the multilevel regression equation (at Level 2 or above).

Example: Differences in the turnover of staff paid locally or expatriate wages in developing countries

Stuart Carr and colleagues (Carr et al., 2010) investigated the effects of wages on turnover among 1290 employees of 202 organisations in six developing countries across the Pacific Islands, Africa and Asia. To uncover the effect of wage on employee turnover, they needed to first account for organisational- and country-level effects. The effects of interest can be modelled in the following equations (we have simplified the actual model to highlight the different levels).

Carr et al. calculated ICCs of 0.12 ($p<0.001$) for the organisational effect and 0.01 (non-significant) for the country effect on turnover. Because the country effect was non-significant (albeit with low power because of the small number of countries in the study), Carr et al. built a two-level model to estimate organisational (Level 2) and individual (Level 1) effects only.

Selected results are shown in Table 4.7. The random effects in the table show that organisational-level effects accounted for 7% of variance

Table 4.7 Extract from results of two-level modelling of the effect of wage comparison on turnover intention in 202 organisations

Fixed effects	Coefficient (SE)
Intercept	3.12*** (0.39)
Job satisfaction/engagement	−0.70*** (0.0)
Wage comparison	0.18*** (0.04)
...	
Random effects	Variance (SE)
Organisational-level variance	0.07* (0.03)
Individual-level variance	0.57*** (0.03)

* significant at $p < 0.05$; *** significant at $p < 0.001$

Source: Extracted from Carr et al. (2010).

in turnover, while the individual effects of interest accounted for 57%. Of the two fixed effects we have included in this extract, job satisfaction had a strong, negative effect on turnover ($b=-0.70$, SE$=0.05$, $p<0.001$) while wage comparison (conscious comparison of one's own wage with that of others, measured using the same response scale as job satisfaction) had a positive but weaker effect ($b=0.18$, SE$=0.05$, $p<0.001$).

Multi-Group Analysis in Structural Equation Modelling

Group-level effects can be modelled separately in SEM. This is useful when seeking to explain how different paths act differently for different groups. Like other multilevel models, the higher-level group might be an artefact of the data collection procedure for the study (such as organisation) or a grouping variable that represents different conditions that might be observed in different natural categories (such as geographic regions).

For multi-group analysis, SEM software asks the user to define the groups in the data (e.g. regions grouped as north, south, centre). In the simplest type of multi-group model, all groups are assumed to have the same paths, but certain parameters are expected to vary. The user selects which parameters to fix (typically, measurement weights to ensure that each latent construct is measured the same way for each group) and which to leave free (typically structural path coefficients).

The existence of multilevel effects is determined by differences in fit statistics between the 'unconstrained' model (i.e. the model without taking group membership into account) and the multi-group model. A significant change in the fit statistics indicates that multilevel effects exist. The nature of the multilevel effects, if path coefficients are left free, can be seen in differences in the coefficients between pairs of groups.

Example: Comparing regional differences in the effect of wage comparison on turnover of staff paid locally or expatriate wages

What if Carr *et al.* (2010) wanted to examine possible differences in the relative effects of wage comparison and job satisfaction on turnover in the different regions that they studied? One way to do this, with a small number of regions, is to run multi-group SEM where each region is treated as a group.

The nature of the potential differences between groups first needs to be considered (and hypotheses developed, if appropriate). In this case, we assume metric indifference in terms of measurement weights, but hypothesise that metric intercepts and path coefficients vary for each region.

Figure 4.21 shows the full range of restrictions that can be placed on multi-group measurement models in the form provided by the AMOS multi-group modelling tool. We will adopt the least restrictive approach, assuming that each latent variable can be measured in the same way, i.e. using the same variables which each carry the same weight, in each region. We do not restrict measurement intercepts because we expect the base level of each variable to vary across regions, and for a similar reason, we do not restrict structural intercepts. Our hypothesis tests require that structural weights vary across regions. Additionally, we do not restrict structural means and covariances because we expect differences across regions. Thus, although eight different models would be generated in a test of complete indifference (equality) across groups, we need to generate only one model, a model restricting measurement weights. A simple model with these restrictions is shown in Figure 4.22.

The statistical significance of the difference between groups can be tested by comparing the difference in chi-square between the fixed measurement (constrained) model and the unconstrained model. In this case, the p-value of the difference is below 0.001, indicating that improved fit is obtained when the measurement weights for each of the three groups are constrained to be equal. Table 4.8 uses parsimony fit indexes to provide more information about the improvement in fit,

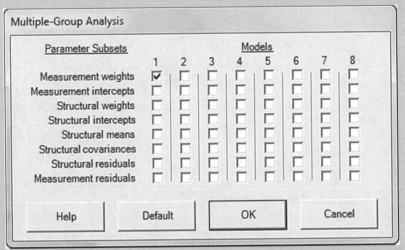

Figure 4.21 Options available for restricting multi-group models (Source: IBM SPSS AMOS 23)

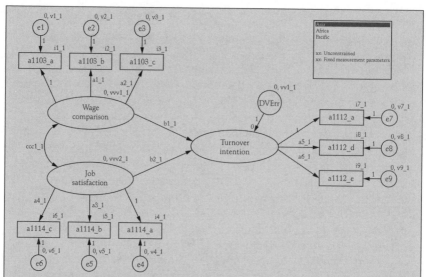

Figure 4.22 A simplified model of effects on turnover intention, showing parameters established for Group 1 in a multi-group analysis. Constrained parameters keep the suffix _1 for all groups, while the suffix for unconstrained parameters takes on the group number. Inset window shows that three groups have been defined (Asia, Africa, Pacific) and two models will be estimated (completely unconstrained and constrained for equal measurement weights) (Model illustrated using IBM SPSS AMOS 23.)

Table 4.8 Parsimony fit indexes showing that the fixed measurement parameter model is more parsimonious than the unconstrained multi-group model

Model	Parsimony fit indexes		
	PRATIO	PNFI	PCFI
Unconstrained	0.53	0.52	0.53
Fixed measurement parameters	0.62	0.60	0.61

showing that the constrained model provides a more parsimonious fit to the data than the unconstrained multi-group model.

Once the measurement assumptions are confirmed satisfied, the structural effects can be compared, as shown in Table 4.9. At α=0.05, job satisfaction is significant for all regions, but wage comparison is significant only for Asia. (Note that this is an illustrative example, not using Carr *et al.*'s actual data or results.) The labels in the table are the AMOS path coefficient labels. When requested in the Output options, AMOS provides a table of Pairwise Parameter Comparisons which enables each pair of parameters to be compared. The Pairwise Parameter Comparisons table reports the 'critical ratio' (effect/standard error) of the difference between every pair of parameters, e.g. between b1_1

Table 4.9 Comparison of path coefficients for three regions

	Asia				Africa				Pacific			
Effect	b	SE	p	Label	b	SE	p	Label	b	SE	p	Label
Job Satisfaction	0.14	0.04	***	b1_1	0.21	0.04	***	b1_2	0.1	0.03	***	b1_3
Wage Comparison	0.08	0.04	0.04	b2_1	0.08	0.04	0.07	b2_2	0.06	0.04	0.08	b2_3

Note: Coefficients derived from measurement constrained model.

and b2_1, and between b2_1 and b3_1. Applying the threshold critical value of 1.96 for a non-directional t-test with $\alpha=0.05$, we could find no significant regional differences between the effects of job satisfaction or wage comparison (i.e. no critical value is 1.96 or above).

The same approach can be taken when comparing effects for hypothetically different groups in a population. For example, a model could be created to compare the relative effects of the independent variables on turnover intention for employees paid a local salary and expatriate employees paid as they would be paid in their home country. In this case, two groups would be defined – local and expatriate – and the analysis would proceed in the same way as the regional comparison.

Common Method Variance: A Special Case of Multilevel Variance

Self-report measures, i.e. responses obtained by asking people to answer questions, typically as survey responses, are subject to more error than measures obtained by direct observation (e.g. financial accounts, system logs). Errors can arise from both the respondents themselves and the instruments used to gather responses. If these systematic errors are not taken into account, the observed relationships between variables can be either inflated or attenuated (appear higher or lower than the 'true' relationship in the sample) (Williams & Brown, 1994). Several of the sources of error included in Table 4.10 are of this kind. Table 4.10 extends the potential sources of error in self-report measures to provide more detail of sources of individual response bias and method bias. More information is available from Furnham (1986).

Figure 4.23 partitions the variance in a hypothetical variable with a standardised regression or factor coefficient (β or λ) of 0.7, the recommended minimum for reliable measurement. Panel A assumes no systematic measurement error while Panel B illustrates how true construct variance is reduced to below 49% (0.7 squared) of total variance when systematic error variance is accounted for.

Table 4.10 Sources of error variance in self-report variables

Source category	Source of error variance
Response bias	Mood state – feeling positive or negative at the time survey responses are provided.
	Positive or negative affectivity – a personality trait or predisposition to be positive or negative about life in general.
	Response tendency – tendency to avoid use of the extremes or to use only the extremes or the central value on a scale.
	Dissimulation – faking responses.
	Social desirability – exaggerating or falsely providing answers that put the respondent, group or object being evaluated in a positive light.
Method bias	Response scale limits the responses that can be provided.
	All items for all constructs are measured using the same response scale.
	Questions are asked or item sets introduced in a way that can bias responses.
	Order in which questions are asked or items are presented to the respondent.
	Use (or not) of reverse coded items.
Random error	Error that cannot be explained by any systematic characteristic of the data or omission of a variable from the model. Random error demonstrates random distribution on residual analysis.

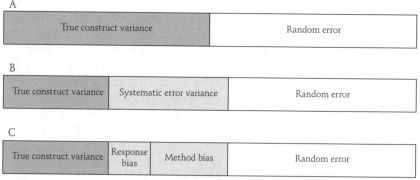

Figure 4.23 Sources of error variance in a hypothetical variable. Panel A assumes all explained variance is true construct variance. Panel B takes account of hypothetical systematic error variance. Panel C partitions systematic error variance into response bias and method bias

Accurate measures and tests of relationships rely on identification and accounting for sources of systematic error. In Chapter 1, we discussed methods for identifying and accounting for response bias. These methods relied on identification of patterns in individuals' responses. Because error associated with data collection methods is common across the sample, a different approach is taken to identification of the common method bias. Although different techniques are available, they all attempt to measure the amount of variance in the sample that is associated with the common method. This variance is known as common method variance (CMV).

The effects of CMV

Although it is often assumed that CMV incorrectly inflates relationships and results in incorrect conclusions that effects exist when they do not (Podsakoff & Organ, 1986), the effect of CMV on effect sizes is actually quite complex. While weak effects might appear stronger than they would if measures were unbiased, strong affects can also appear weaker (Williams & Brown, 1994).

Techniques for identification and remediation of CMV

The simplest approach to the identification of CMV is to examine the correlations between all observed variables in a study. Because not all variables are theoretically correlated with one another, there is evidence of CMV if all correlations are above 0. The second lowest correlation is considered the best indication of CMV. (The second lowest correlation is used on the assumption that there will be some randomness in observed correlations and the lowest observed correlation is likely to underestimate the CMV.) This approach is prone to exaggeration of CMV across a set of analyses.

Example: Estimation of common method variance in measuring hotel service quality

In a set of data gathered to measure different aspects of hotel service quality, questions are also asked about satisfaction with shopping outlets near the hotel. Respondents are assumed to answer both sets of questions independently, so if the second lowest correlation is 0.32, the error variance associated with CMV in this data set is 0.32 squared, i.e. a not insubstantial 10.2%. While this technique is believed to provide a good approximation of CMV, it leaves remediation largely in the interpretation of results, e.g. if concierge service quality is found to explain 15% of the variance in hotel quality, the researcher might assume that the correct explanatory effect is only 5%.

SEM offers an approach that both measures CMV and remediates it in one step. To do this, a CMV factor is added to the measurement model and all observed items are modelled as reflecting the common factor. Several approaches are discussed in the literature. We illustrate the simplest, which assumes that method bias is equal across the entire data set. (Other approaches attempt to account for differences in CMV associated with different response scales or other differences in method.) An excellent survey of sources of common method bias and potential remediation can be found in works by Podsakoff *et al.* (2003, 2012).

Example: Accounting for common method variance in measurement of attitude and perceived control using SEM

Studies of traveller satisfaction with a location often use short questionnaires in which travellers are asked to rate their satisfaction (typically on a four- or five-point response scale) with a number of aspects of their accommodation, facilities, attractions, etc. These surveys often suffer from high CMV. Indeed, it can be so high that it is difficult to determine which components are most strongly associated with satisfaction or dissatisfaction with traveller experience in the location.

Figure 4.24 shows how CMV is estimated and taken into account in a study of satisfaction with three components: accommodation; local attractions and local infrastructure; and non-hotel facilities. The measurement model for Accommodation and Local Attractions is constructed in the normal way. Items H1 to H4 measure satisfaction with different aspects of accommodation; items A1 to A3 measure satisfaction with attractions; and items F1 to F4 measure satisfaction with facilities. All items are measured on the same five-point scale, so CMV is expected. The CMV factor is constructed as a latent variable, measured by the common variance in all items (A1 to F4). Note that each item retains its specific error variance ($e10$ to $e34$). We fix the variance of the CMV factor to 1, allowing all CMV path coefficients to vary.

After the model is run for a survey conducted by the tourism authorities in a remote region (Figure 4.25), CMV is found to affect the measurement of satisfaction with local facilities, but not the other factors: the CMV loadings are high enough to reduce loadings on three of the four Local Facilities items, but have little or no effect on loadings on Local Attractions and Accommodation. The measurement model for Local Facilities, which was not good before the addition of CMV, is now unsatisfactory. Remedies include removing the two Local Facilities items with low loadings after CMV adjustment and removing the Local Facilities latent variable from the model. Removing the Local Facilities variable would remove important information from the study and should be rejected in this case. If items affected by CMV are retained, the CMV latent should also be retained for both measurement modelling and structural modelling.

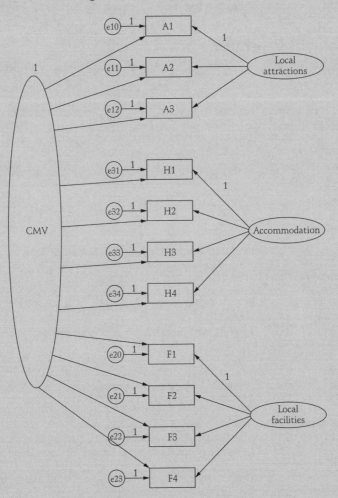

Figure 4.24 AMOS measurement model with common variance factor

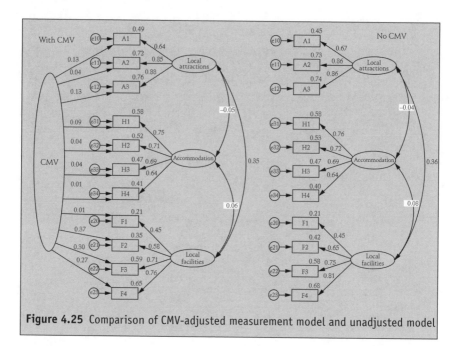

Figure 4.25 Comparison of CMV-adjusted measurement model and unadjusted model

References

Agresti, A. (2002) *Categorical Data Analysis* (2nd edn). Hoboken, NJ: John Wiley & Sons.

Ajzen, I. (1991) The theory of planned behavior. *Organizational Behavior and Human Decision Processes* 50, 179–211.

Anscombe, F.J. (1973) Graphs in statistical analysis. *American Statistician* 27, 17–21.

Arbuckle, J. (2003) *AMOS 5 User's Guide Supplement.* Spring House, PA: AMOS Development Corporation.

Asparouhov, T. (2005) Sampling weights in latent variable modeling. *Structural Equation Modeling: A Multidisciplinary Journal* 12 (3), 411–434.

Babbie, E. (2010) *The Practice of Social Research* (12th edn). Belmont, CA: Wadsworth.

Baron, R.M. and Kenny, D.A. (1986) The moderator-mediator variable distinction in social psychological research: Conceptual, strategic, and statistical considerations. *Journal of Personality and Social Psychology* 51, 1173–1182.

Bigano, A., Hamilton, J.M. and Tol, R.S. (2006) The impact of climate on holiday destination choice. *Climatic Change* 76 (3), 389–406.

Bloor, D. (1976) *Knowledge and Social Imagery.* Chicago, IL: Chicago University Press.

Brown, T.A. (2006) *Confirmatory Factor Analysis for Applied Research.* New York: The Guilford Press.

Byrne, B.M. (2009) *Structural Equation Modeling with AMOS: Basic Concepts, Applications, and Programming* (2nd rev. edn). London: Routledge.

Byrne, B.M. (2011) *Structural Equation Modeling with MPlus: Basic Concepts, Applications, and Programming.* London: Routledge.

Carr, S.C., McWha, I., MacLachlan, M. and Furnham, A. (2010) International–local remuneration differences across six countries: Do they undermine poverty reduction work? *International Journal of Psychology* 45 (5), 321–340.

Chatterjee, S. and Hadi, A.S. (2006) *Regression Analysis by Example* (4th edn). Hoboken, NJ: John Wiley & Sons.

Cole, S.T. and Illum, S.F. (2006) Examining the mediating role of festival visitors' satisfaction in the relationship between service quality and behavioral intentions. *Journal of Vacation Marketing* 12 (2), 160–173.

Curran, P.J., West, S.G. and Finch, J.F. (1996) The robustness of test statistics to nonnormality and specification error in confirmatory factor analysis. *Psychological Methods* 1 (1), 16.

Denis, D.D. and Legerski, J. (2006) Causal modeling and the origins of path analysis. *Theory and Science* 7 (1). See http://theoryandscience.icaap.org/content/vol7.1/denis. html. (accessed Feb 2017)

Fisher, K. (2008) *The Wall Street Waltz*. Hoboken, NJ: John Wiley & Sons.

Fornell, C. and Bookstein, F.L. (1982) Two structural equation models: LISREL and PLS applied to consumer exit-voice theory. *Journal of Marketing Research* 19 (4), 440–452.

Furnham, A. (1986) Response bias, social desirability and dissimulation. *Personality and Individual Differences* 7 (3), 385–400.

Gage, N.L. (1978) *The Scientific Basis of the Art of Teaching*. New York: Teachers College Press.

Hair, J.F., Babin, B.J., Money, A.H. and Samouel, P. (2005) *Essentials of Business Research Methods*. Hoboken, NJ: John Wiley & Sons.

Hair, J.F., Black, W.C., Babin, B.J. and Anderson, R.E. (2010) *Multivariate Data Analysis: A Global Perspective* (7th edn). Upper Saddle River, NJ: Pearson.

Hair, J.F., Ringle, C.M. and Sarstedt, M. (2011) PLS-SEM: Indeed a silver bullet. *Journal of Marketing Theory and Practice* 19 (2), 139–152.

Hair, J.F., Hult, G.T.M., Ringle, C. and Sarstedt, M. (2016) *A Primer on Partial Least Squares Structural Equation Modeling (PLS-SEM)*. Thousand Oaks, CA: Sage Publications.

Hayduck, L.A. (1996) *LISREL Issues, Debates and Strategies*. Baltimore, MD: Johns Hopkins University Press.

Hayes, A.F. (2013) *Introduction to Mediation, Moderation, and Conditional Process Analysis: A Regression-Based Approach*. New York: Guilford.

Henseler, J., Hubona, G., & Ray, P. A. (2016). Using PLS path modeling in new technology research: updated guidelines. *Industrial management & data systems*, 116(1), 2-20.

Holmes-Smith, P. and Rowe, K.J. (1994) The Development and Use of Congeneric Measurement Models in School Effectiveness Research: Improving the Reliability and Validity of Composite and Latent Variables for Fitting Multi-Level and Structural Equation Models. Paper presented at the International Congress for School Effectiveness and Improvement, Melbourne.

Hox, J.J. (2010) *Multilevel Analysis: Techniques and Applications* (2nd edn). Oxford: Routledge Academic.

Jöreskog, K.G. (1967) A general approach to confirmatory maximum likelihood factor analysis. *ETS Research Bulletin Series* 1967 (2), 183–202.

Jöreskog, K.G. and Sorbom, D. (1976) *LISREL III: Estimation of Linear Structural Equation Systems by Maximum Likelihood Methods*. Chicago, IL: National Educational Resources, Inc.

Jöreskog, K.G. and Sorbom, D. (1993) *LISREL 8: Structural Equation Modeling with the SIMPLIS Command Language*. Hillsdale, NJ: Lawrence Erlbaum Associates.

Jöreskog, K.G., Olsson, U.H. and Wallentin, F.Y. (2016) *Multivariate Analysis with LISREL*. Springer: Cham, CH

Kaplan, D. (2009) *Structural Equation Modeling: Foundations and Extensions* (2nd edn). Los Angeles, CA: Sage.

Kelloway, E.K. (2013) *Using MPlus for Structural Equation Modeling: A Researcher's Guide*. London: Sage.

Knapp, T.R. and Sawilowsky, S.S. (2001) Constructive criticisms of methodological and editorial practices. *The Journal of Experimental Education* 71 (1), 65–79.

Lise, W. and Tol, R.S.J. (2002) Impact of climate on tourist demand. *Climatic Change* 55, 429–449.

MacKinnon, D. (2008) *Introduction to Statistical Mediation Analysis*. New York: Taylor & Francis.

MacKinnon, D.P., Fritz, M.S., Williams, J. and Lockwood, C.M. (2007) Distribution of the product confidence limits for the indirect effect: Program PRODCLIN. *Behavior Research Methods* 39 (3), 384–389.

Matthews, R. (2000) Storks deliver babies (p=0.008). *Teaching Statistics* 22 (2), 36–38.

McGill, T., Hobbs, V. and Klobas, J. (2003) User-developed applications and information systems success: A test of DeLone and McLean's model. *Information Resources Management Journal* 16 (1), 24.

Meuleman, B. and Billiet, J. (2009) A Monte Carlo sample size study: How many countries are needed for accurate multilevel SEM? *Survey Research Methods* 3 (3), 45–58.

Mieczkowski, Z. (1985) The tourism climatic index: A method of evaluating world climates for tourism. *Canadian Geographer* 29 (3), 220–233.

Miles, J. and Shevlin, M. (2001) *Applying Regression & Correlation: A Guide for Students and Researchers*. London: Sage.

Modis, T. (2007) Sunspots, GDP and the stock market. *Technological Forecasting & Social Change* 74, 1508–1514.

Podsakoff, P.M. and Organ, D.W. (1986) Self-reports in organizational research: Problems and prospects. *Journal of Management* 12 (4), 531–544.

Podsakoff, P.M., MacKenzie, S.B., Lee, J.-Y. and Podsakoff, N.P. (2003) Common method biases in behavioral research: A critical review of the literature and recommended remedies. *Journal of Applied Psychology* 88 (5), 879–903.

Podsakoff, P.M., MacKenzie, S.B. and Podsakoff, N.P. (2012) Sources of method bias in social science research and recommendations on how to control it. *Annual Review of Psychology* 63 (1), 539–569.

Preacher, K.J. and Hayes, A.F. (2004) SPSS and SAS procedures for estimating indirect effects in simple mediation models. *Behavior Research Methods, Instruments, & Computers* 36, 717–731.

Reinartz, W., Haenlein, M. and Henseler, J. (2009) An empirical comparison of the efficacy of covariance-based and variance-based SEM. *International Journal of Research in Marketing* 26 (4), 332–344.

Ringle, C.M., Sarstedt, M. and Straub, D.W. (2012) A critical look at the use of PLS-SEM in *MIS Quarterly*. *MIS Quarterly* 36 (1), iiv–8.

Shapin, S. and Schaffer, S. (1989) *Leviathan and the Air-Pump: Hobbes, Boyle, and the Experimental Life*. Princeton, NJ: Princeton University Press.

Sharma, S., Mukherjee, S., Kumar, A. and Dillon, W.R. (2005) A simulation study to investigate the use of cutoff values for assessing model fit in covariance structure models. *Journal of Business Research* 58 (7), 935–943.

Silvert, W. (2001) Modeling as a discipline. *International Journal of General Systems* 30 (3), 261–282.

Snijders, T.A.B. and Bosker, R.J. (1999) *Multilevel Analysis: An Introduction to Basic and Advance Multilevel Modeling*. London: Sage.

Sobel, M.E. (1982) Asymptotic intervals for indirect effects in structural equations models. In S. Leinhart (ed.) *Sociological Methodology* (pp. 290–312). San Francisco, CA: Jossey-Bass.

Song, H., Witt, S.F. and Li, G. (2009) *The Advanced Econometrics of Tourism Demand*. New York: Routledge.

Thompson, B. (2001) Significance, effect sizes, stepwise methods, and other issues: Strong arguments move the field. *The Journal of Experimental Education* 70 (1), 80–93.

Thrane, C. (2004) How to present results from logistic regression analysis in hospitality and tourism research. *Tourism and Hospitality Research* 5 (4), 295–305.

Trusty, J., Thompson, B. and Petrocelli, J.V. (2004) Practical guide for reporting effect size in quantitative research in the *Journal of Counseling & Development*. *Journal of Counseling and Development* 82, 107–110.

van de Schoot, R., Hoijtink, H., Hallquist, M.N. and Boelen, P.A. (2012) Bayesian evaluation of inequality-constrained hypotheses in SEM models using Mplus. *Structural Equation Modeling: A Multidisciplinary Journal* 19 (4), 593–609.

Wheaton, B., Muthen, B., Alwin, D.F. and Summers, G.F. (1977) Assessing reliability and stability in panel models. *Sociological Methodology* 8 (1), 84–136.

Whittingham, M.J., Stephens, P.S., Bradbury, R.B. and Freckleton, R.P. (2006) Why do we still use stepwise modelling in ecology and behaviour? *Journal of Animal Ecology* 75, 1182–1189.

Williams, L.J. and Brown, B.K. (1994) Method variance in organizational behavior and human resources research: Effects on correlations, path coefficients, and hypothesis testing. *Organizational Behavior and Human Decision Processes* 57 (2), 185–209.

Wold, S., Martens, H. and Wold, H. (1983) The multivariate calibration problem in chemistry solved by the PLS method. In B. Kågström and A. Ruhe (eds) *Matrix Pencils: Proceedings of a Conference Held at Pite Havsbad, Sweden, March 22–24, 1982* (pp. 286–293). Berlin/Heidelberg: Springer Berlin Heidelberg.

Wold, S., Geladi, P., Esbensen, K. and Öhman, J. (1987) Multi-way principal components- and PLS-analysis. *Journal of Chemometrics* 1 (1), 41–56.

Wold, S., Trygg, J., Berglund, A. and Antti, H. (2001) Some recent developments in PLS modeling. *Chemometrics and Intelligent Laboratory Systems* 58 (2), 131–150.

Wooldridge, J.M. (2009) *Introductory Econometrics* (4th edn). Mason, OH: Cengage Learning.

5   Time-Dependent Phenomena and Forecasting

This chapter contains a quick overview of time series analysis methods and their use for forecasting purposes. In addition, different uses of time series are discussed, such as simple non-linear analysis techniques to provide different ways of studying the basic characteristics of the structure and the behaviour of a tourism system.

Time is an important variable in many tourism phenomena and the evolution of some observable quantity (arrivals or stays of tourists, for example, or their expenditures) is often studied. Time is also the basis for all forecasting activities, probably the trickiest and most difficult task, yet perhaps the most attempted. Forecasting is the logical conclusion of many statistical analyses. After having measured a certain quantity and having described its characteristics or having assessed the reliability of assumptions about the phenomenon it represents, we try to foresee what may happen in a future period or in a different situation.

A time series consists of a number of observations measured at (preferably) equally spaced time intervals. Typical examples used in tourism record tourist arrivals and stays. Analysis of a time series is performed with two main objectives: understanding the evolution (and sometimes the nature) of the phenomenon described by the series of observations, and predicting future values of the observed variable. The idea at the basis of all the methods developed for analysing a time series is that the time sequence possesses some kind of internal structure that represents the phenomenon. The aim of the study is to highlight the signal provided by this structure by separating it from the noise generated by random statistical fluctuations of the variable measured, or measurement errors. Once the main patterns are established, it is possible to interpret the phenomenon, to build a model and to extrapolate its behaviour. Moreover, as with any statistical procedures, it is possible to assess the significance and the reliability of the outcomes.

The study of time series is of crucial importance in many (if not all) disciplines and the techniques developed have reached quite high levels of sophistication. Hundreds of works describe techniques in depth and many software programs have been implemented for automating operations that otherwise would be long and tedious calculations. The wide availability of many techniques makes it possible to apply different methods to the same set of data. This is an important achievement. As with many other statistical methods, in fact, time series analysis is not an exact science. The experience and the interpretation of the researcher play a central role. Trying different possibilities and different models can help to highlight differences that are sometimes subtle, but can strongly affect the outcomes of the analysis, particularly if these are in the realm of prediction. For example, one of the most delicate steps in performing an autoregressive integrated moving average (ARIMA) study is identifying the most appropriate model to use. Many pages of the most renowned books on the topic (see, e.g. Chatfield, 1996; Hamilton, 1994) are devoted to this issue, which is an important one that could save a lot of time doing the long and complex calculations involved. Today, however, (purists will strongly disagree) the availability of many good computer programs has greatly diminished the value of these procedures. In a very short time, the researcher can apply a wealth of different models and choose at the end the one that is deemed to be the best one for the case under study.

As said, the literature on time series is a very extensive one and many works exist on this topic. On the other hand, the methods employed are numerous, for example Song and Li (2008) examined more than 100 papers recently published and identified about 50 different methods for analysing time series. As well as basic general-purpose textbooks (Box & Jenkins, 1976; Chatfield, 1996; Gouriéroux & Monfort, 1997; Hamilton, 1994), tourism-specific applications are described in the literature (Frechtling, 1996; Song & Witt, 2000; Witt & Witt, 1992) and their characteristics (effectiveness, accuracy, predictive power) are compared in review papers (Athiyaman & Robertson, 1992; Burger et al., 2001; Chen et al., 2008; Smeral, 2007; Song & Li, 2008; Uysal & Crompton, 1985; Witt & Witt, 1995, 2000).

Given this wide availability of works, the aim of this chapter is not to repeat well-known descriptions of methods. Rather, after a very brief review of the basic concepts, we shall concentrate on a number of collateral aspects that are often a little neglected by the relevant literature or risk escaping notice with respect to the general problem, but play an important role. Many of these techniques are quite complex and difficult, but their basic concepts can be easily understood (at least intuitively), and the availability of specific software programs makes them more than usable. Moreover, the interpretation of the results is usually relatively simple and straightforward.

Basic Concepts of Time Series

Classically, a time series is considered as a function of time composed of three main components: trend, a long-term variation of the underlying level; seasonality, systematic movements related to specific calendar periods; and an irregular component, random (or almost random) irregular fluctuations. These elements can be combined in different ways to give rise to the observed series; they can be added (additive model) or multiplied (multiplicative model) or combined in mixed ways. The (strong) underlying hypothesis is that the variable observed at time t is related in some way to the previous observations; in other words, the system measured through that variable has a linear behaviour and the fluctuations detected are due to some random effects (e.g. measurement errors).

The simplest model for analysing a time series consists of the identification of these components, and with the results obtained the researcher usually also attempts a forecast. The decomposition model most frequently used is the additive one. The choice of model is normally done by examining a plot of the original series. When the magnitude of the seasonal variations is fairly constant, no matter what the changes in the trend, additive models are suitable. When the amplitude of the seasonal variations varies, the pattern is called multiplicative seasonality and a multiplicative model will be more appropriate. Different trials with different models enable the best possible solution to be chosen depending on the specific series to be examined. It is important to note here that, as for any statistical technique, the sample size is important. If the series of observations contains too few points, the analysis and the resulting forecasts risk being seriously flawed. Obviously, the longer the series, the better; at least 40–100 points are considered necessary to ensure reasonable results.

As well as the simple decomposition method, many other models can be used to analyse a time series. The most commonly used are briefly reviewed in the following sections. These methods and the calculations involved, as for the simple decomposition, can be easily implemented using a standard spreadsheet program for a series of moderate length (a few dozen points). Common statistical software (SPSS, STATA, SAS, R, etc.) and programming environments such as Matlab or GAUSS have a number of functions suitable for this type of analysis. Dedicated software programs are also available.

Example: Simple decomposition of a time series

Figure 5.1 shows a typical example of a time series containing 60 monthly observations of tourist arrivals; in it, a trained eye can easily recognise the different components.

In some cases, the irregular fluctuations are very pronounced, so that they make it difficult to recognise the general behaviour of the series. In these cases, the random components can be *smoothed* by applying a moving average (MA) to the series. This consists of obtaining a new series whose data points are the means of a certain number of adjacent values. Figure 5.2 shows the result after having averaged six adjacent values

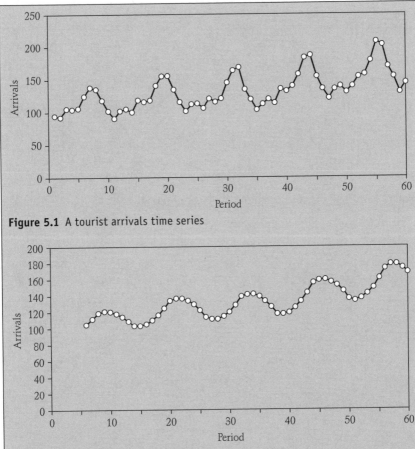

Figure 5.1 A tourist arrivals time series

Figure 5.2 Moving average of order 6

(MA of order 6). The general behaviour of the series and its variations are very clear.

The trend component can be extracted by performing an ordinary least squares (OLS) regression. The most common model is a simple linear regression, but, depending on the shape of the series, several different regression types can be used: quadratic, exponential, logistic, etc.

Once the trend component has been identified (Figure 5.3), this is subtracted from the original series giving the result shown in Figure 5.4.

The detrended series is a levelled curve in which the seasonal component is much more evident. The terms are derived by averaging out the values of similar periods and drawing a chart such as Figure 5.5 which reports the averages of the monthly values with their standard deviations. As can be seen, the deviations are relatively similar, indicating that the seasonal effect is relatively stable across the period considered.

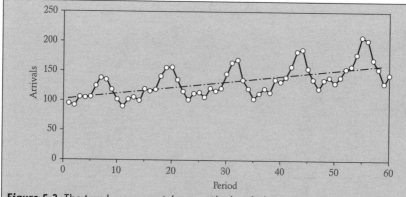

Figure 5.3 The trend component (unsmoothed series)

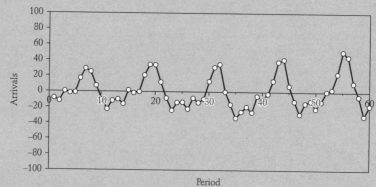

Figure 5.4 The detrended series

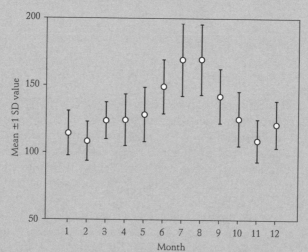

Figure 5.5 Average monthly values over the series period (bars are 1 standard deviation)

To simplify a comparison with other series, (normalised) seasonal indices can be calculated by dividing them by the grand average of the series (Figure 5.6). The situation depicted here is a typical one for a tourism destination where some months (in our example the summer months) show a much higher value than the average (strong seasonality).

When seasonal effects are also removed, the final result is a series of more or less random fluctuations (Figure 5.7). In an ideal model, these fluctuations have a normal distribution with a zero average (Figure 5.8).

Once all the components have been identified and checked, a prediction for future periods can be made by calculating some new points along the trend line and readjusting (summing) the respective seasonal indices as shown in Figure 5.9.

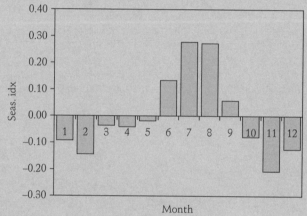

Figure 5.6 Seasonal (monthly) indices

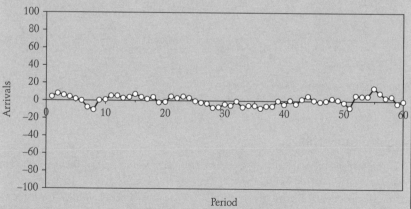

Figure 5.7 Irregular component

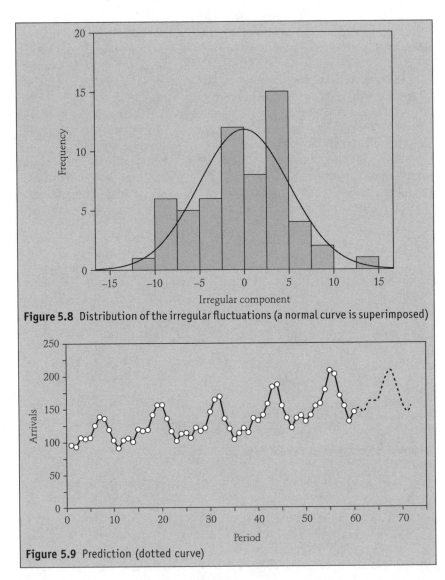

Figure 5.8 Distribution of the irregular fluctuations (a normal curve is superimposed)

Figure 5.9 Prediction (dotted curve)

Smoothing methods

The simple MA used in the example described can also be employed to forecast some future values of the time series under study. In its simplest form, all observations are given equal weight and further values are forecast by taking the mean of earlier observations. Different attempts will give the best number of values to average (order of the MA). For example, if the past three observations $(v_{t-1}, v_{t-2}, v_{t-3})$ are considered sufficient, the new forecast value V_t will be

$$V_t = \text{mean}\left(v_{t-1}, v_{t-2}, v_{t-3}\right)$$

This technique is not very effective, and, most importantly, does not take into account any trend component. More sophisticated smoothing methods have been proposed in which the previous observations are weighted with decreasing values. In other words, recent observations, closer in time to the element considered, are considered to be more influential than older values (more distant in time). A well-known scheme is exponential smoothing. Here, the smoothing weights decrease exponentially. A series value V_t is given by

$$V_t = \alpha v_t + (1-\alpha)V_{t-1}$$

where the parameter α is called the smoothing constant. Even in this case, the technique does not explicitly consider the trend component.

Exponential smoothings can be combined in different ways. An interesting case is the triple exponential smoothing method known as Holt–Winters from the names of its proponents (Holt, 1957; Winters, 1960). A little more complication allows this method to account for the most important components of a time series: seasonality and trend. The model assumes that an observation V at time t is given by

$$V_t = \left(L+T_t\right)S_t + \varepsilon_t$$

where S is the seasonal factor, T is the trend, L is an initial level value and ε is an error term.

Once the initial values for L_0, T_0 and $S_{0,1},..., S_{0,n}$ (seasonal factors) have been estimated, the values in the series are calculated as

$$L_{t+1} = \alpha(V_{t+1} / S_{t+1}) + (1-\alpha)(L_t + T_t)$$

$$T_{t+1} = \beta(L_{t+1} - L_t) + (1-\beta)T_t$$

$$S_{t+p+1} = \gamma(V_{t+1} / L_{t+1}) + (1-\gamma)S_{t+1}$$

The three parameters are $0 \le \alpha \le 1$; $0 \le \beta \le 1$; $0 \le \gamma \le 1$; (they are the smoothing weights). The forecast values (for $t=1,..., n$, these will be the recalculated values of the series) are determined by

$$F_t = (L_{t-1} + T_{t-1})S_t$$

$$...$$

$$F_{t+1} = (L_t + T_t)S_{t+1}$$
$$F_{t+n} = (L_t + nT_t)S_{t+n}$$

The Holt–Winters scheme can be easily implemented in a spreadsheet. In this case, α, β and γ can be assigned any initial values; then, by minimising the mean of the absolute differences between the original values and the calculated ones, the best values for the parameters can be determined.

Autoregressive integrated moving average models

The most sophisticated and well-known family of time series methods is the one originated from the work of Box and Jenkins (1976). It is used, along with its many variations, in studies and has an established tradition in tourism (De Gooijer & Hyndman, 2006; Sheldon & Var, 1985; Song & Li, 2008; Song & Witt, 2000; Witt & Witt, 1992).

ARIMA models, as they are commonly called, are based again on the idea that a series is composed of parts. In this case, the parts are an autoregressive (AR) one, a contribution from an MA and a factor involving derivatives of the time series (I). The autoregressive component stems from the idea that individual values, $v(t)$, of a time series at time t can be expressed as a linear function of the preceding observations. The second contribution (MA) derives from the hypothesis that time series values depend on the preceding estimation errors, ε_i, the difference between actual values and forecast or recalculated values. These past errors are taken into account in estimating the subsequent time series value. The combination of the AR and MA component gives an ARMA model expressed as

$$v(t) = \sum_{i=1}^{p} a_i v(t-i) - \sum_{i=1}^{q} b_i \varepsilon(t-i)$$

where a_i and b_i are the parameters of the model and p and q are called the order of the AR and MA models (the composite model is denoted ARMA(p,q)).

The estimation of the orders comes from analysis of the data series. The AR term is determined by drawing an autocorrelation function (ACF) chart, essentially a weighted MA over past observations. The plots (see for example Figure 5.10) show the correlations between values in a time series at time t and time $t-n$ for different lags (the difference between the times at which two observations were recorded) n. Confidence levels are customarily shown on the drawing (horizontal lines) allowing for quick identification of the significant values (the values above or below these lines). The ACF is calculated after having removed seasonal and trend components in order to ensure stationarity in the data examined.

The MA order is estimated by using a partial autocorrelation function (PACF) plot. After the correlation terms at each lag are removed, what is left is called the partial autocorrelation term. In other words, PACF gives the correlation between a value v_t and v_{t-n} not accounted for by lags 1 to $n-1$.

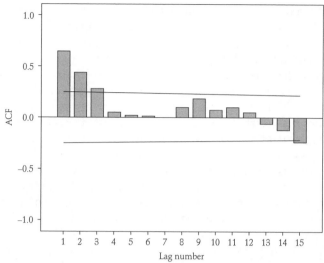

Figure 5.10 ACF plot for the series depicted in Figure 5.1 after having removed seasonal component and trend

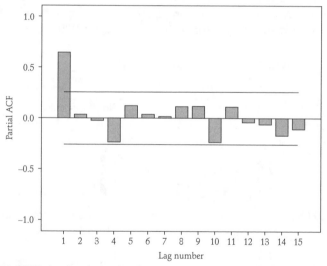

Figure 5.11 PACF plot for the series depicted in Figure 5.1 after having removed seasonal component and trend

PACF plots, like ACF plots, show horizontal confidence level lines to easily identify significant values (see Figure 5.11).

The residuals of these correlations represent the error terms which should be normally distributed around 0 and not correlated with one another. If a number of significant autocorrelations exist, the model has not been specified properly, and some alternatives should be considered. This assumption can be tested using the Ljung–Box test (Ljung & Box, 1978).

ARIMA models have as an important assumption the stationarity of the series. A stationary series is a series in which the mean and the variance of the values do not vary significantly with time (strong or first-order stationarity). If the correlation function depends only on the difference between different time periods, the series is said to be weakly (or second order) stationary. In practical terms, an effect such as a trend is a clear symptom of non-stationarity.

The most common method to obtain a stationary series is differencing. A new series is calculated whose terms are the differences between adjacent terms. Simple trend can be removed by differencing the series once, while more complex non-stationarities may require subsequent differentiations. If stationarity is obtained after d steps, the original series is said to be integrated of order d: $I(d)$; a stationary series will be $I(0)$. Before differencing, other transformations to the original series can be applied, always with the objective of achieving the best possible stationarity: taking logarithms and calculating square roots are well known and used examples. When differentiation is required before using an ARMA model (integration will be needed after application of the model), we speak of ARIMA. The parameter d of an ARIMA(p,d,q) model gives the number of differentiation steps needed.

Table 5.1 shows some ACF and PACF sample charts along with the associated ARIMA models. More complete examples can be found in standard textbooks on the subject (see for example Frechtling, 2001: 125–128).

Table 5.1 ACF and PACF plots for some ARIMA models

Model	ACF	PACF
ARIMA (0,0,0)	No significant lags	No significant lags
ARIMA (0,1,0)	Linear decline at lag 1, with many lags significant	Single significant peak at lag 1
ARIMA (1,0,0)	Exponential decline, with first two or many lags significant	Single significant positive peak at lag 1
	Alternative exponential decline with a negative peak ACF(1)	Single significant negative peak at lag 1

Table 5.1 (Continued)

Model	ACF	PACF
ARIMA (0,0,1)	Single significant negative peak at lag 1	Exponential decline of negative value, with first two or many lags significant

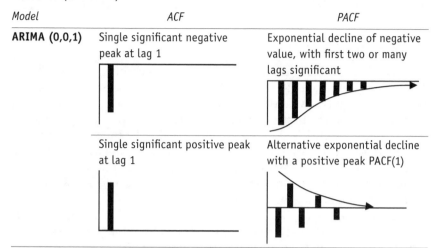

| | Single significant positive peak at lag 1 | Alternative exponential decline with a positive peak PACF(1) |

Filtering Techniques

The transformations and smoothing techniques applied to a time series are also called filters. The algorithms applied act as a sift, taking the original data as input and outputting the transformed series. The concepts of filtering derive from the engineering literature. Filtering implies generating a combination of successive elements of a series of values $v(t)$ and is usually given as a function of lag L. As well as achieving stationarity before using some of the analysis methods discussed in the previous sections, a filter can be used to extract hidden information in the data by removing the noise due to the irregular components.

As a function of time, a time series can be decomposed into a set of frequency components using the Fourier theorem. A filter is applied to some of these components thus allowing some specific behaviour such as short- or long-term cyclic components to be emphasised or removed. The most used methods are MAs, differentiations, logarithm and square root transformations. Given a series of values $x(t)$, the filter obtains a new series $y(t)$ containing the new values transformed by applying a certain function $f(L)$:

$$y(t) = f(L)x(t)$$

Most filters require iterative computation of the values involved and some can be quite heavy from a computational point of view. Scripts for many of the most popular filters can be easily found for the most used statistical or econometric software or application environments such as STATA, SAS, R, Matlab, Eviews, Gauss. Special filters have also been proposed, and are quite often used, for specific operations; one example is the Hodrick–Prescott filter.

Hodrick–Prescott filter

The Hodrick–Prescott (H-P) filter is an algorithm which allows calculating a smooth long-term trend component in a time series. The H-P algorithm is a non-parametric non-linear procedure, that is: no assumptions are needed about the type of trend as in some of the previously discussed methods. Even if criticised (Ravn & Uhlig, 2002), the filter is widely used in the economics literature where its main function is in identifying cyclic behaviours in economic and financial time series (business cycles), and it has received some attention in the tourism literature (Gouveia & Rodrigues, 2005; Guizzardi & Mazzocchi, 2009).

The H-P filter is able to remove the long-term trend in a series without affecting the short-term fluctuations too much. Essentially, a series is split into a stationary and a non-stationary component (the trend) in such a way that the squared deviation of actual values from trend is minimised subject to a smoothness constraint weighted by a parameter λ. Large values of λ make the resulting trend series smoother. Common values for λ are: 6.25 for annual data, 1,600 for quarterly data, 129,600 for monthly data and 6,250,000 for daily data (Ravn & Uhlig, 2002). A general formula to calculate λ is $\lambda=(10 \text{ FREQ})^2$; where FREQ is the frequency of observations defined as the number of observations per year. However, as usual, different tests will provide the best parameter for the case under study.

For example, Figure 5.12 shows a synthetic time series and the trend line calculated by applying the H-P filter. This trend would have been identified with difficulty with standard methods such as OLS regressions.

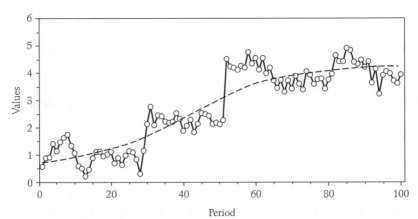

Figure 5.12 A synthetic time series and the trend identified by applying the H-P filter (dotted line)

Comparing Time Series Models

As seen in the previous sections, many different techniques and models can be used to analyse a time series. When used for forecasting, it is important to assess the capability of a specific method to provide reliable results. Obviously, the best test is to compare the predictions with the actual values once time has passed. However, it is also important to be able to assess the reliability of the method used in advance, in order to provide reasonable predictions. A procedure that can be applied is the following. The original time series is divided into two parts: an initialisation set and a test set. Usually, the test set has a length comparable to the one which will be forecast using the model built on the initialisation set. Different methods are applied to the initialisation set in order to analyse the series, build a model and predict some values. These are then compared by running the model with the values in the test set. Several measures are available to assess the goodness of the methods used; they are based on the series of differences found between the observed and the predicted forecast (called errors or deviations). Table 5.2 lists the most used measures.

The tracking signal (TRS) is the ratio of the cumulative error to the mean absolute error (MAE) and is used to highlight a method that is producing 'biased' outcomes which have consistently higher or consistently lower calculated values (ideally, the tracking signal should have values between ±6). These deviations can also be used to optimise a specific method and to better tune the parameters for that method (see, for example, the discussion of the Holt–Winters model). The most commonly used for TRS forecasting are MAE and mean absolute percentage error (MAPE); the second has the advantage of being independent from measurement scales and is considered to be the most appropriate in assessing the analysis method used (Witt & Witt, 1992). A rough scale for the accuracy of a model (or a forecast) can be based on MAPE (Table 5.3), following the suggestion of Lewis (1982: 40).

Table 5.2 Error measures for a time series ($|\bullet|$ indicates the absolute value)

ERR	Error	e_t=actual-forecast
PERR	Percentage error	$p_t=e_t/$actual
CERR	Cumulative error	$=\Sigma\, e_t$
MSE	Mean squared error	$=\text{mean}(e_t^2)$
RMSE	Root mean squared error	$=\sqrt{\text{MSE}}$
MAE or MAD	Mean absolute error (or deviation)	$=\text{mean}(|e_t|)$
MdAE	Median absolute error	$=\text{median}(|e_t|)$
MAPE	Mean absolute percentage error	$=\text{mean}(|p_t|)$
MdAPE	Median absolute percentage error	$=\text{median}(|p_t|)$
TRS	Tracking signal	CERR/MAE

Table 5.3 MAPE and forecasting accuracy

MAPE	Forecasting accuracy
Less than 10%	Highly accurate
10%–20%	Good
20%–50%	Reasonable
Greater than 50%	Inaccurate

When comparing (and choosing) time series analysis methods it is important to bear in mind that no silver bullet exists. As many scholars have pointed out, in fact, even the most sophisticated methods may fail to give really reliable results (Tideswell *et al.*, 2001). Their effective use requires experience, a sound knowledge of the mathematical techniques and, obviously, of the specific situation studied. It is difficult to choose the most suitable technique as similar methods give different results in different conditions or environments (Papatheodorou & Song, 2005), or even depend on country-specific cultural values or management practices (Wackera & Sprague, 1998). In these circumstances, the best approach is to be guided by a principle of parsimony and, as Smeral (2007) concludes, use the simplest and quickest method.

Combining Forecasts

Combining forecasts coming from different methods has been suggested several times as a way to improve the final outcome. The idea is that possible biases associated with different methods are likely to differ and the forecast errors are very probably uncorrelated, therefore (considering them as random noise) their combination will statistically average out to zero.

The result is that, when we have a very large number of different forecasts (the larger the sample, the better), the final standard error will be very small. In other words, given the universal validity of the central limit theorem, a combination of a certain number of predictions is likely to be more accurate than the forecast coming from any single source. In any case, the combined forecast is at least as reliable as those from which it has been derived.

Empirically, after the initial proposal of Bates and Granger (1969), the idea has proved to be effective in several fields (Newbold & Granger, 1974; Palm & Zellner, 1992), and it has been demonstrated that a combination of forecasts generally leads to considerable improvements in accuracy. Despite that, as Wong *et al.* (2007) note, this suggestion has not received much attention in tourism.

There are several possible ways to combine different forecasts. The most simple is to calculate a simple arithmetic mean. This average can then be weighted, and a number of weighting schemes have been devised. Normally, they calculate weights based on the past performance of each model. However, several studies have shown that the simple average can generate reliable forecasts and may be more robust than weighted average combinations (Makridakis & Winkler, 1983; Palm & Zellner, 1992; Wong et al., 2007).

These results open the way to a further important practical consideration. Forecasting has historically been approached in two ways: quantitative and qualitative. Although a quantitative time series forecast may be quite sophisticated, it still has large uncertainties. The main issue is the risk of oversimplification of the parameters defining the system and, most importantly for real systems, the lack of consideration of extraordinary events or other exogenous elements that influence the development of the time series. On the other hand, a qualitative method, typically based on experts' opinions, may be able to predict future behaviours and outcomes through the capability to read the market. Such methods rely on the subjective judgement of the interviewees, who can be strongly biased and, obviously, are able to provide only hints, without numeric indications (Uysal & Crompton, 1985). One possible solution is to combine the two approaches thus compensating for their weaknesses and reinforcing their predictive powers (Davies, 2003; Faulkner & Valerio, 1995).

Example: Mixed forecasts

An example is the following, concerning the city of Vienna and its Schönbrunn Palace (Baggio & Antonioli Corigliano, 2008). The quantitative forecast is based on a model using a time series of monthly tourism arrivals. A simple decomposition method is implemented with a spreadsheet application in order to ease the process of analysis. The forecast extends for six months. The qualitative prediction comes from a panel of tourism experts, mainly travel agents and tour operators from several countries having Vienna as a major destination. An email questionnaire asks them to evaluate, on a scale from 0 (much worse) to 200 (much better), the performance and the behaviour of their outgoing market for a six-month time span. All values are transformed as indices using the previous semester as a basis. An overall forecast is then derived by averaging the outcomes of both methods. The technique is implemented with a simple spreadsheet and has proven to be reasonably easy to use and able to provide timely evaluations. Table 5.4 shows two consecutive semesters worth of data.

As can be seen from the MAPE, the overall accuracy obtained is quite good.

Table 5.4 A combined forecast

Origin	Time series forecast	Experts panel's forecast	Combined (average) forecast	Actual	MAPE (%)
October 2005–March 2006					
Global	105	109	107	108	0.9
Germany	101	100	100	99	1.0
Italy	111	100	105	112	6.3
Spain	129	127	128	12	4.9
April–September 2006					
Global	100	125	115	109	5.5
Germany	105	115	110	100	10.0
Italy	112	120	115	104	10.6
Spain	120	130	125	109	14.7

Summarising, a practical approach to combine forecasts can be the following (Armstrong, 2001):

- use different methods and data (better if more than five of both);
- use some qualitative method to gather expert judgements and transform these into a quantitative prediction;
- combine by simply averaging the forecasts or, if well-documented differences exist, use MAPE measures as weights (in case of very large variations in the predictions a 5% trimmed mean can be effective).

Correlation between Series

When two or more time series are measured in the study of certain phenomena, it may be important to establish whether there is some kind of correlation between them or whether a causal relationship can be found. For example, we might measure economic growth indicators (e.g. gross domestic product [GDP], exports) and tourism outputs and try to assess if and how tourism influences the economy (Cortés-Jiménez et al., 2009; Kaplan & Çelik, 2008; Khan, 2005), or test whether tourist arrivals at a specific location or resort are correlated with arrivals of tourists at the geographic area in which that location sits.

A simple correlation/regression analysis may provide an answer such as in the following example.

Example: Correlation between time series

Consider the series depicted in Figure 5.13; the values have been collected by measuring tourist arrivals (the same series shown in Figure 5.1) along with the number of visits to the location's website. The two series are correlated (although in a limited way, see Figure 5.14).

However, this technique completely disregards the variable *time*, which can be quite important. In fact, looking at Figure 5.13, it is possible to see a more remarkable effect: the patterns of variation are very similar, with a phase displacement. The Arrivals series looks delayed in time (lagged) with respect to the *Web visits* one.

A popular technique to highlight this effect is cross-correlation analysis. Cross-correlation is a standard method for estimating the degree to which two series are correlated. Consider two series $x_i(t)$ and $y_i(t)$. The cross-correlation r at lag L can be calculated: $r(x(i), y(i), L)$. By repeating the calculation for a number of lags $L=0, 1, 2,\ldots n$, the result is a cross-correlation series with length $2n$. The only issue with this simple application is that, even when a relationship exists, it may fail to give a meaningful result if the series have strong predictable components (trend or seasonality) or are highly auto-correlated (or if both conditions occur). The solution is to filter each of the series in order to obtain a stationary sequence. The consequence of filtering is that the

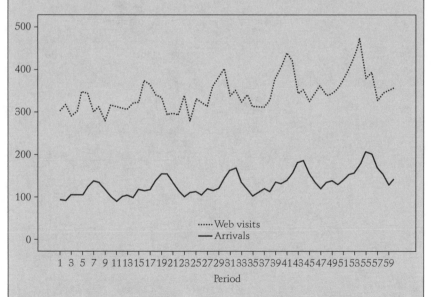

Figure 5.13 Tourist arrivals and Web visits time series

cross-correlation contains clear peaks that indicate the actual relationship between the series and the lag at which it most strongly occurs.

Figure 5.15 shows the results of the analysis (using the SPSS cross-correlation function) after having differenced the series (the simplest filter to remove trend and seasonal effects). The lag used is 12, because for a tourism series a year is the main unit of measurement. Lag 2 shows

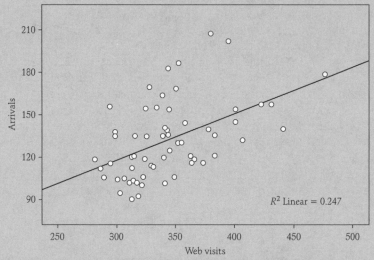

Figure 5.14 Correlation between the time series shown in Figure 5.13

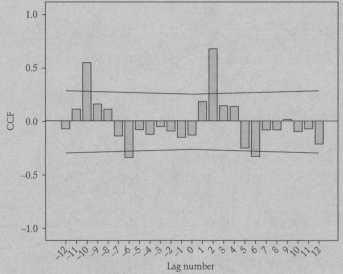

Figure 5.15 Cross-correlation between the series shown in Figure 5.13

a clear peak (the one at lag –10 is the symmetric representation of this); therefore, we conclude in favour of the existence of a positive correlation between the series. This indicates that, in this case, when Web visits reach a peak, tourist arrivals peak two months after.

Cross-correlation is symmetric and, as such, it is not suitable for assessing causality within relationships. Many approaches have been proposed to assess the directional characteristic of an interaction between time series. The most popular explores whether predicting the values of one series can be enhanced by integrating information from another. This test, proposed by Granger (1969), is based on the idea that, if the variance of the prediction error of a time series $X(t)$ at time t is decreased by including past observations from a time series $Y(t)$ in a linear regression model, then $Y(t)$ is said to have a causal effect on $X(t)$. The roles can be inverted to evaluate possible impacts in the opposite direction. The Granger test is a linear test; therefore, it may underestimate the relationships and increase the error of estimate when used with non-linear data. If non-linearity is present, it may be possible to eliminate it by filtering the data with double differencing or by applying some transformation (logarithmic, square root, etc.).

Example: Causal correlations

Let us examine again the previous example. The hypothesis tested here is that a Granger-causes is a relatively common expression. The calculations, performed with the Econometric toolbox for Matlab (LeSage & Pace, 2009), give the following results (Table 5.5).

In the two possible relationships between Web visits and Arrivals, the null hypothesis is of independence (i.e. no relationship). The results show that a significant relationship (p-value <0.05) is observed only in the second case where Arrivals is the dependent variable.

We can conclude that the number of Web visits has a causal effect on the tourists' arrivals.

Table 5.5 Granger test results

Granger causality tests		
Equation Web visits	F-value	F-probability
Web visits	18.5421	0.0000
Arrivals	0.5168	0.5994
Equation Arrivals		
Web visits	54.0556	0.0000
Arrivals	22.8299	0.0000

Stationarity, Stability and System Representations

Stationarity, as already stated, is an important concept in the analysis of a time series. Many models (ARIMA in particular) used to study a time series and to forecast future behaviours are valid only in the presence of this characteristic. A stationary time series is one whose statistical properties, such as mean, variance, autocovariance and autocorrelation, are all constant over time. A stationary process has the property that it is a mean reverting process: it will fluctuate around its mean and will cross the mean line an infinite number of ways (over very long time periods). Stationarity represents a critical assumption in the analysis of time series data. Its importance rests on the fact that its conditions are indispensable for an accurate estimation of the parameters and models that describe the data. In most conditions, at a given time only one observation is accessible, therefore stationarity guarantees that any portion of a series is similar to any other portion. If mean, variance and covariance of the series do not vary along the series (do not depend on time), but depend only on the lag between observations, it is possible to apply the statistical analyses described above and estimate the parameters.

Furthermore, we may extend this concept and give it a real-world interpretation. A tourism destination, like many other socio-economic aggregates, is a complex system. This means, essentially, that in studying a tourism system we expect to find a number of different components (the stakeholders), of different sizes and functions, interconnected in many possible ways; typically these connections are of a non-linear nature. The overall result is a system whose behaviour is somehow unpredictable. It can manifest properties that cannot be derived by simply composing (linearly) the behaviours and the characteristics of its components. In some cases, it is able to resist huge external shocks (natural disasters, for example) without altering its evolutionary path too much; in some other cases, a similar system can be completely disrupted by some seemingly insignificant event. Some stakeholder can act as a catalyst for incredible socio-economic growth in some cases, while in other situations similar behaviours do not have any recognisable effects. A complex system is self-similar, it will look like itself at different scales, if magnified or made smaller in a suitable way (Baggio, 2008; Bar-Yam, 1997; Farrell & Twining-Ward, 2004).

A time series, in this context, may be seen as the record of the system characteristics at different time steps and its long-term behaviour is closely connected with the behaviour of the system it represents (Sprott, 2003). From this point of view, stationarity can measure the capability of a system to continue its evolution absorbing possible external (or internal) shocks. This can be true for the whole series or for the parts that satisfy this requirement. In other words, if a tourism system, in its measurable expression, exhibits a consistent stationarity, at least for a reasonably long period of time, it means that, in that period of time, the system is able to recover from disturbances quickly. Possible deviations from this behaviour will be seen as structural breaks in the time series, with a clear change in the series trend and/or level. In this case, we may conclude that the system was not able to react to shocks of the magnitude experienced.

Different techniques can be used to measure stationarity and its influence on a tourism system (Aly & Strazicich, 2002; Eugenio-Martin *et al.*, 2005; Narayan, 2005). A number of proposals have been made to determine whether a time series can be considered to exhibit substantial stationarity. This set of statistical tests comprises the well-known Dickey–Fuller test (Dickey & Fuller, 1979), both in the simple (DF) and the augmented (ADF) version, and the variations proposed by Phillips and Perron (PP test: Phillips & Perron, 1988) and by Zivot and Andrews (ZA test: Zivot & Andrews, 1992) and, more recently by Lee and Strazicich, (LS test: Lee & Strazicich, 2003). Metes (2005) provides a good description of the tests and a comparison of their applicability, limitations and power.

The main idea behind these stationarity tests (called unit root tests) is that, after having allowed for a weak trend, the time series is checked against the hypothesis of modifications or breaks in the trend (or in the level) that can shock the system to prevent it from returning to the previous behaviour, permanently moving it away from its past track. All the tests have as null hypothesis the existence of a unit root: the non-stationarity of the series. They are all modifications of the first ADF test which has proved to be of very low power particularly when the series has a structural break, a sudden change in the level or the trend slope or both; the variations also give an estimate of the break position (the time interval at which the break occurs). Rejecting the null hypothesis thus means that the series (and the system), even in presence of a major change in its behaviour (a structural break), is fundamentally stable (the series is stationary) and the shock that may have a break has no long-term effects on it.

All these tests calculate a *t* statistic whose critical values, however, have been computed differently from the standard *t* distribution. The tests are one-tailed tests and the critical values depend on the number of data points and on the shape of the series (presence of break in level or trend or both). Many of these values have been published. The main reference for them is the work of MacKinnon (1996) and the works cited above. Table 5.6 gives some asymptotic values (if the series is short, the values are slightly higher) useful for a quick assessment (adapted from Lee & Strazicich, 2004; Metes, 2005).

A recognised problem with unit root tests is that they suffer from low power. This means that it is often not possible to reject the null hypothesis, wrongly concluding that the series is not stationary. Multiple tests should be run before accepting any hypothesis. When different tests provide different results (i.e. some accept the hypothesis and some reject it), a

Table 5.6 Asymptotic critical values for unit root tests

Test	Break	α 0.01	α 0.05	α 0.10
ADF	None	−2.61	−1.95	−1.61
	Level	−3.35	−2.90	−2.59
	Trend and level	−4.07	−3.47	−3.16
PP	None	−2.59	−1.95	−1.61
	Level	−3.50	−2.89	−2.58
	Trend and level	−4.03	−3.44	−3.14
ZA	None	−5.34	−4.8	−4.48
	Level	−4.93	−4.42	−4.11
	Trend and level	−5.57	−5.08	−4.82
LS	None	−4.24	−3.57	−3.21
	Trend and level	−5.15	−4.51	−4.21

further investigation is needed in order to assess how the data conform to the hypotheses and limitations of the tests and what their power is in the specific situation.

When a break is present, its significance can be assessed by using a specific test. Originally described by Chow (1960), the test verifies whether the coefficients in two linear regressions on different data sets are equal. It is used to test for the presence of a structural break which, in most cases, can be interpreted as a break in the general trend of the series. Suppose that the linear trend component can be written as: $Y=f(t)$. It is possible to split the data into two groups (at the break to be verified) and recalculate the trend components of the two subseries: $Y_1=f_1(t)$ and $Y_2=f_2(t)$. The null hypothesis of the Chow test is that the parameter sets of the two regressions are equal (i.e. $f_1=f_2$).

The test statistic can be easily calculated in the following way. Let S_C be the sum of squared residuals from the combined data (the whole series), S_1 be the one of the first group and S_2 that of the second group; N_1 and N_2 are the number of observations in each group and k is the total number of parameters used in the test (in this case, 3), $df_1=k$, $df_2=N_1+N_2-2k$.

The Chow test statistic is

$$F_{Chow} = \frac{[S_C - (S_1 + S_2)]/df_1}{(S_1 + S_2)/df_2}$$

The test statistic follows an F distribution with df_1 and df_2 degrees of freedom: $F(df_1, df_2)$. Calculations can be performed with a standard spreadsheet program.

Example: Stationarity tests

Consider the series depicted in Figure 5.16, which represents the economic contribution of the tourism industry to a destination (expressed as monthly index values). A break is clearly visible between periods 14 and 15.

The unit root analysis is conducted using the Gauss programs provided by J. Lee (available at: https://sites.google.com/site/junsoolee/codes). Choosing a trend and level model, the results are as in Table 5.7.

By comparing these values with the critical values, it is possible to conclude that the ADF test accepts the non-stationarity hypothesis, while all the others reject it at 0.01. This conclusion is quite normal in many cases like the one presented here. The ADF test is known in the literature to perform poorly in the presence of structural breaks such as the ones that can be seen in the series under study.

The break is identified by PP and ZA (correctly, judging from Figure 5.16) at time step 14. The significance of this break is assessed with the Chow test. In this case $F_{Chow}=6.169$, $df_1=3$ $df_2=22$, the resulting p-value is 0.003 (for the case examined, the critical values of F at $\alpha=0.1$; 0.05; 0.01 are: 2.3512; 3.0491; 4.8166). The break is therefore significant at the 0.05 level.

Table 5.7 Test results

Test	Test statistic	Break identified at time
ADF	−2.231	–
PP	−5.674	14
ZA	−6.205	14
LS	−6.628	13

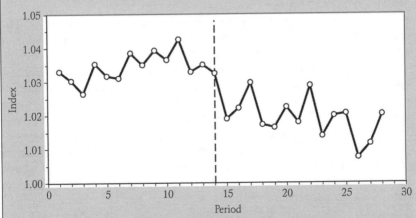

Figure 5.16 Contributions of tourism to the economy of a destination (index values)

Predictability

Other general system characteristics can be explored with the analysis of a time series. First of all, its intrinsic linearity (or non-linearity), which is a basic prerequisite for the use of standard methods to analyse a series and attempt future predictions. If we accept the general assumption that a tourism system is a complex adaptive system, the main consequence is the impossibility of formulating long-term predictions about its behaviour (Waldrop, 1992). However, it is still possible to use the methods devised so far to attempt a forecast, with the only limitation of not extending them too far in time. The underlying hypothesis, never declared but implicitly assumed in almost all of the forecasting works, is that, for limited amounts of time, a complex system, unless it experiences a very big and disruptive shock, has a kind of inertia which pushes it along a temporarily stable evolutionary path (Andersen & Sornette, 2005).

Non-linearity (BDS test)

The most known and used method to test for non-linearities in a time series is that of Brock, Dechert and Scheinkman (Brock *et al.*, 1987, 1996), and aims at detecting a form of serial dependence in a time series. The BDS test explores whether the observations are deterministic or stochastic. In other words, it tests the null hypothesis of an independent and identically distributed (iid) random variable. If the null hypothesis is rejected, the series shows a certain degree of non-linearity. If this is very high, the series represents a chaotic system. The BDS test cannot test chaos directly, but only non-linearity, provided that any linear dependence has been removed from the data (i.e. the series has been detrended and corrected for seasonality). The test is a two-tailed test and asymptotically standard normal (e.g. at $\alpha=0.05$, the critical value is ±1.96).

The test uses as a parameter the *embedding dimension* of the series. The behaviour of a complex system can be described by drawing its movement in the phase space. This is a geometrical *n*-dimensional space, in which the coordinates are the main variables of the system. At least in theory, it is possible to write a number of differential equations (equations of motion) with these variables. They are chosen in such a way that complete knowledge of all the variables determines the state of the system at one time in a unique way. The phase space is the set of all possible states of the system. The embedding dimension of the system is the dimension of this phase space. In practical terms, the embedding dimension is guessed at by using a number of different techniques based on the analysis of a time series (Kantz & Schreiber, 1997).

The BDS test can be computationally intensive and several software programs have been proposed (Belaire-Franch & Contreras, 2002); they calculate the test statistic for several embedding dimensions (to be specified) and provide an assessment of the significance of the results. Normally, the programs are run by specifying different possible embedding dimensions and choosing the one for which the BDS statistic is highest. The Matlab scripts used in the example that follows are by Kanzler (available at:http://econpapers.repec.org/software/bocbocode/t871803.htm).

Long-range dependency (Hurst exponents)

Long-range dependency in a time series means that it is possible to find a statistical dependence between an observation and its precedents which decays more slowly than exponentially.[1] Historically, this phenomenon has been related with slow decays of correlations and, more importantly, with certain self-similar processes (Mandelbrot, 1982).

The effect can be seen by examining the ACF of the series, estimating the length of its decay. The most known and used method, however, to assess a long dependency in a time series is connected to Hurst (1951). Hurst, a British hydrologist, spent a long time studying the Nile and issues related to water storage and the size of reservoirs. A perfect reservoir will store enough water during a dry season. The amount of water flowing into and out of it can be seen as a random process (the inflow is driven by rainfall, the outflow by water demand). Hurst devised an index to help determine the optimal dam size the Nile river's volatile rain and drought conditions. Its index H is estimated from a series of observations rather than calculated theoretically.

The method used is called rescaled range analysis (R/S analysis). Consider a series and split it into a number n of intervals of different length. For each interval, it is possible to calculate the range R and the standard deviation S of its values. If $E[R(n)]$ is the expected value (the mean) of $R(n)$ and $E(S(n))$ that of $S(n)$, Hurst found that their ratio scales follow a power law (C is a constant term):

$$\frac{E[R(n)]}{E[S(n)]} = Cn^{H} \ \text{ for } n \to \infty$$

The exponent H is called the Hurst exponent (or parameter) and gives a measure of the randomness of the process studied. Its value is in the range $0<H<1$. A value of 0.5 indicates the absence of long-range dependence and therefore designates a pure random process. Values between 0.5 and 1 indicate a persistent phenomenon. If there is an increase in a certain interval of times, there will probably be an increase in the subsequent intervals (the reverse for a decrease). Values between 0 and 0.5 characterise series with anti-persistent behaviour: an increase is likely to be followed by a decrease (and vice versa). Phenomena with $H \neq 0.5$ typically have a complex structure;

$H=1$ denotes an exactly self-similar process (i.e. a fully chaotic system). In addition to the original R/S method, many other techniques have been proposed to calculate H (Peng *et al.*, 1995; Taqqu *et al.*, 1995). As in other cases, its estimation is more an art than a science. Many conditions (noise, linear dependencies, cyclic behaviours, etc.) can affect the determination of H and the outcomes are usually not particularly robust. When examining real data, it is always useful to use extreme caution and avoid relying on the results of any single technique. Filtering the series is usually suggested in the literature. Several software programs and scripts are available for computing H (a simple internet search will provide updated links). Those used in the following example are Matlab scripts by Chu Chen available at: http://www.mathworks.com/matlabcentral/fileexchange/19148.

Example: Non-linear analysis

A word of caution is important before examining the following example. All the procedures used are extremely data hungry. They work well when the series examined consists of several thousand values (they are today almost common practice in the analysis of financial data such as stock quotations, exchange rates, etc.). This greatly reduces applicability in the tourism field where even a five-year monthly series is an exception. However, when it is possible to collect a reasonably sized series (500–1000 points), Hurst exponent methods are able to provide quite useful insights. The following example uses a monthly series of tourist overnight stays at Elba, a well-known Italian destination. The series cover the period 1954–2008 and contains 660 values. The series is shown in Figure 5.17, along with its smoothed trend.

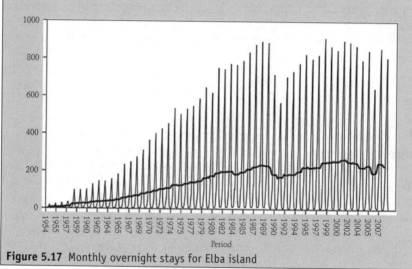

Figure 5.17 Monthly overnight stays for Elba island

As a first step, the series is filtered (log transformed and differenced) in order to remove trend and seasonality components. A BDS test is used to assess the overall linearity of the series. The results are shown in Table 5.8. The table also shows the results for the test applied to a purely random time series and to a series obtained from the Lorenz attractor, the archetypal chaotic system discovered by the American meteorologist (Lorenz, 1963). Values in parentheses are the *p*-values for the tests. The random series has very low BDS statistic values, showing a substantial suitability for the usual analysis methods, while the Lorenz one exhibits all its chaotic behaviour.

Hurst analysis conducted using several methods provides an estimation (average of the results) of $H=0.64$ for the Elba series. The random one used above has $H=0.49$, almost in line with what is expected for a random process, while the time series representation of the Lorenz attractor gives $H=0.83$, in good agreement with the estimate (0.82) obtained by De la Fuente *et al.* (1998). The values calculated for Elba reflect a certain level of persistence indicating a moderate possibility of making predictions.

The overall results of the analysis clearly show that our system, the Elba destination, cannot be considered a fully linear system, its complexity and a certain degree of tendency towards a chaotic regime are evident, even if not excessive, as already determined with different techniques (Baggio, 2008). Therefore, the researcher should be very careful in attempting a long-term forecasting exercise, and some mixed qualitative-quantitative method able to provide different scenarios seems advisable.

Table 5.8 BDS test for different time series

Embedding dimension	Elba	Random	Lorenz
2	34.52 (0.005)	1.56 (0.999)	488.40 (0.005)
3	33.48 (0.005)	1.03 (0.999)	524.26 (0.005)
4	34.46 (0.005)	0.60 (0.999)	568.99 (0.005)
5	35.86 (0.005)	0.49 (0.999)	633.14 (0.005)

Note: Significance in parentheses.

Note

(1) A quantity decays exponentially if it decreases at a rate proportional to its value. The relationship is then: $X_N = X_0 e^{-k}$.

References

Aly, H. and Strazicich, M.C. (2002) Terrorism & Tourism: Is the Impact Permanent or Transitory? Time Series Evidence from Some MENA Countries. Economic Research Forum. See https://www.trc.bus.ucf.edu/cdn/economics/workingpapers/2000-10.pdf (accessed Feb 2017).

Andersen, J.V. and Sornette, D. (2005) A mechanism for pockets of predictability in complex adaptive systems. *Europhysics Letters* 70 (5), 697–703.

Armstrong, J.S. (2001) Combining forecasts. In J.S. Armstrong (ed.) *Principles of Forecasting: A Handbook for Researchers and Practitioners* (pp. 417–439). Boston, MA: Kluwer Academic Publishing.

Athiyaman, A. and Robertson, R.W. (1992) Time series forecasting techniques: Short-term planning in tourism. *International Journal of Contemporary Hospitality Management* 4 (4), 8–11.

Baggio, R. (2008) Symptoms of complexity in a tourism system. *Tourism Analysis* 13 (1), 1–20.

Baggio, R. and Antonioli Corigliano, M. (2008) A practical forecasting method for a tourism organization. Proceedings of the International Conference: Knowledge as Value Advantage of Tourism Destinations, Malaga, 29–31 October.

Bar-Yam, Y. (1997) *Dynamics of Complex Systems*. Reading, MA: Addison-Wesley.

Bates, J.M. and Granger, C.W.J. (1969) The combination of forecasts. *Operational Research Quarterly* 20, 451–468.

Belaire-Franch, J. and Contreras, D. (2002) How to compute the BDS test: A software comparison. *Journal of Applied Econometrics* 17, 691–699.

Box, G.E.P. and Jenkins, G.M. (1976) *Time Series Analysis. Forecasting and Control* (rev. edn). San Francisco, CA: Holden-Day.

Brock, W.A., Dechert, W.D. and Scheinkman, J.A. (1987) A Test for Independence Based on the Correlation Dimension (Working paper). University of Wisconsin at Madison.

Brock, W.A., Dechert, W.D., Scheinkman, J.A. and LeBaron, B. (1996) A test for independence based on the correlation dimension. *Econometric Reviews* 15 (3), 197–235.

Burger, C.J.S.C., Dohnal, M., Kathrada, M. and Law, R. (2001) A practitioners guide to time-series methods for tourism demand forecasting: A case study of Durban, South Africa. *Tourism Management* 22, 403–409.

Chatfield, C. (1996) *The Analysis of Time Series* (5th edn). New York: Chapman & Hall.

Chen, R.J.C., Bloomfield, P. and Cubbage, F.W. (2008) Comparing forecasting models in tourism. *Journal of Hospitality and Tourism Research* 32, 3–21.

Chow, G.C. (1960) Tests of equality between sets of coefficients in two linear regressions. *Econometrica* 28 (3), 591–605.

Cortés-Jiménez, I., Pulina, M., Riera i Prunera, C. and Artis, M. (2009) Tourism and Exports as a Means of Growth (Working Paper 2009/10). Nottingham University, Research Institute of Applied Economics.

Davies, B. (2003) The role of quantitative and qualitative research in industrial studies of tourism. *International Journal of Tourism Research* 5, 97–111.

De Gooijer, J.G. and Hyndman, R.J. (2006) 25 years of time series forecasting. *International Journal of Forecasting* 22, 443–473.

De la Fuente, I.M., Martinez, L., Aguirregabiria, J.M. and Veguillas, J. (1998) R/S analysis in strange attractors. *Fractals* 6, 95–100.

Dickey, D.A. and Fuller, W.A. (1979) Distribution of the estimators for autoregressive time series with a unit root. *Journal of the American Statistical Association* 74, 427–431.

Eugenio-Martin, J., Sinclair, M.T. and Yeoman, I. (2005) Quantifying the effects of tourism crises: An application to Scotland. *Journal of Travel and Tourism Marketing* 19 (2/3), 23–36.

Farrell, B.H. and Twining-Ward, L. (2004) Reconceptualizing tourism. *Annals of Tourism Research* 31 (2), 274–295.

Faulkner, B. and Valerio, P. (1995) An integrative approach to tourism demand forecasting. *Tourism Management* 16 (1), 29–37.

Frechtling, D.C. (1996) *Practical Tourism Forecasting*. Oxford: Butterworth-Heinemann.

Frechtling, D.C. (2001) *Forecasting Tourism Demand: Methods and Strategies*. Oxford: Butterworth-Heinemann.

Gouriéroux, C. and Monfort, A. (1997) *Time Series and Dynamic Models*. Cambridge: Cambridge University Press.

Gouveia, P.M. and Rodrigues, P.M.M. (2005) Dating and synchronizing tourism growth cycles. *Tourism Economics* 11 (4), 501–515.

Granger, C.W.J. (1969) Investigating causal relations by econometric models and cross-spectral methods. *Econometrica* 37, 424–438.

Guizzardi, A. and Mazzocchi, M. (2009) Tourism demand for Italy and the business cycle. *Tourism Management* 31 (3), 367–377.

Hamilton, J.D. (1994) *Time Series Analysis*. Princeton, NJ: Princeton University Press.

Holt, C.C. (1957) Forecasting seasonals and trends by exponentially weighted averages (O.N.R. Memorandum 52/1957): Carnegie Institute of Technology. Reprinted with discussion in: *International Journal of Forecasting* (2004) 20, 5–13.

Hurst, H.E. (1951) Long-term storage of reservoirs: An experimental study. *Transactions of the American Society of Civil Engineers* 116, 770–799.

Kantz, H. and Schreiber, T. (1997) *Nonlinear Time Series Analysis*. Cambridge: Cambridge University Press.

Kaplan, M. and Çelik, T. (2008) The impact of tourism on economic performance: The case of Turkey. *International Journal of Applied Economics and Finance* 2 (1), 13–18.

Khan, H. (2005) Tourism and trade: Cointegration and Granger causality tests. *Journal of Travel Research* 44 (2), 171–176.

Lee, J. and Strazicich, M.C. (2003) Minimum Lagrange multiplier unit root test with two structural breaks. *The Review of Economics and Statistics* 85 (4), 1082–1089.

Lee, J. and Strazicich, M. (2004) Minimum LM unit root test with one structural break (Working paper). Department of Economics, Appalachian State University, Boone, NC.

LeSage, J.P. and Pace, R.K. (2009) *Introduction to Spatial Econometrics*. Boca Raton, FL: Chapman & Hall/CRC.

Lewis, C.D. (1982) *Industrial and Business Forecasting Methods*. London: Butterworths.

Ljung, G.M. and Box, G.E.P. (1978) On a measure of lack of fit in time series models. *Biometrika* 65, 297–303.

Lorenz, E.N. (1963) Deterministic nonperiodic flow. *Journal of Atmospheric Sciences* 20, 130–141.

MacKinnon, J.G. (1996) Numerical distribution functions for unit root and cointegration tests. *Journal of Applied Econometrics* 11, 601–618.

Makridakis, S. and Winkler, R.L. (1983) Averages of forecasts: Some empirical results. *Management Science* 29, 987–996.

Mandelbrot, B.B. (1982) *The Fractal Geometry of Nature*. San Francisco, CA: W.H. Freeman and Co.

Metes, D.V. (2005) Visual, Unit Root and Stationarity Tests and Their Power and Accuracy. Summer NSERC student report. See http://www.stat.ualberta.ca/~wiens/home%20page/pubs/BSc%20reports/metes.pdf (accessed Feb 2017).

Narayan, P.K. (2005) Testing the unit root hypothesis when the alternative is a trend break stationary process: An application to tourist arrivals in Fiji. *Tourism Economics* 11 (3), 351–364.

Newbold, P. and Granger, C.W.J. (1974) Experience with forecasting univariate time series and the combination of forecasts. *Journal of the Royal Statistical Society. Series A* 137 (2), 131–165.

Palm, F. and Zellner, A. (1992) To combine or not to combine? Issues of combining forecasts. *Journal of Forecasting* 11, 687–701.

Papatheodorou, A. and Song, H. (2005) International tourism forecasts: Time-series analysis of world and regional data. *Tourism Economics* 11 (1), 11–23.

Peng, C.K., Havlin, S., Stanley, H.E. and Goldberger, A.L. (1995) Quantification of scaling exponents and crossover phenomena in nonstationary heartbeat time series. *Chaos* 6, 82–87.

Phillips, P.C.B. and Perron, P. (1988) Testing for a unit root in time series regression. *Biometrika* 75, 335–346.

Ravn, M.O. and Uhlig, H. (2002) On adjusting the Hodrick–Prescott filter for the frequency of observations. *Review of Economics and Statistics* 84 (1), 371–380.

Sheldon, P.J. and Var, T. (1985) Tourism forecasting: A review of empirical research. *Journal of Forecasting* 4, 183–195.

Smeral, E. (2007) World tourism forecasting: Keep it quick, simple and dirty. *Tourism Economics* 13 (2), 309–317.

Song, H. and Li, G. (2008) Tourism demand modelling and forecasting: A review of recent research. *Tourism Management* 29, 203–220.

Song, H. and Witt, S.F. (eds) (2000) *Tourism Demand Modelling and Forecasting: Modern Econometric Approaches.* Oxford: Pergamon.

Sprott, J.C. (2003) *Chaos and Time-Series Analysis.* Oxford: Oxford University Press.

Taqqu, M., Teverovsky, V. and Willinger, W. (1995) Estimators for long-range dependence: An empirical study. *Fractals* 3, 785–798.

Tideswell, C., Mules, T. and Faulkner, B. (2001) An integrative approach to tourism forecasting: A glance in the rearview mirror. *Journal of Travel Research* 40, 162–171.

Uysal, M. and Crompton, J.L. (1985) An overview of approaches to forecast tourism demand. *Journal of Travel Research* 23 (4), 7–15.

Wackera, J.G. and Sprague, L.G. (1998) Forecasting accuracy: Comparing the relative effectiveness of practices between seven developed countries. *Journal of Operations Management* 16 (2–3), 271–290.

Waldrop, M. (1992) *Complexity: The Emerging Science and the Edge of Order and Chaos.* London: Simon and Schuster.

Winters, P.R. (1960) Forecasting sales by exponentially weighted moving averages. *Management Science* 6, 324–342.

Witt, S.F. and Witt, C.A. (1992) *Modelling and Forecasting Demand in Tourism.* London: Academic Press.

Witt, S.F. and Witt, C.A. (1995) Forecasting tourism demand: A review of empirical research. *International Journal of Forecasting* 11, 447–475.

Witt, S.F. and Witt, C.A. (2000) Forecasting tourism demand: A review of empirical research. In C.A. Tisdell (ed.) *The Economics of Tourism* (Vol. 1; pp. 141–169). Cheltenham: Edward Elgar.

Wong, K.K.F., Song, H., Witt, S.F. and Wu, D.C. (2007) Tourism forecasting: To combine or not to combine? *Tourism Management* 28, 1068–1078.

Zivot, E. and Andrews, D.W.K. (1992) Further evidence on the great crash, the oil-price shock and the unit-root hypothesis. *Journal of Business and Economic Statistics* 10 (3), 251–270.

Part 2

Numerical Methods

Introduction to Part 2

The methods and techniques presented and discussed in the previous chapters can be considered standard means for analysing and describing the data most commonly collected by academics and practitioners in tourism and hospitality studies. Part 2 presents a few methods that, although used by some, can be seen as more advanced additions to the tourism researcher's toolbox.

The methods are quite common in other disciplines and have a solid foundation both from a theoretical and a 'practical' point of view. Maximum likelihood estimates, Monte Carlo methods and agent-based models are described and discussed with examples of their application to tourism-related problems.

In addition, a chapter is devoted to a brief account of the recent and rapidly evolving world of Big Data, one of the most important by-products of the extremely diffused use of the modern online environments.

These chapters are grouped together as they share an important common feature: the necessity of a computer. For the methods discussed so far, a computer is a useful tool and today no one would venture starting a factor analysis or the computation of regression coefficients without some calculating machinery. However, the techniques discussed in this part are absolutely not usable without the power and ease of use of modern personal computers. The alternative would be to replicate efforts such as the one described by W.S. Gosset (better known by his pen name Student) in his milestone paper 'The probable error of a mean':

Before I had succeeded in solving my problem analytically, I had endeavoured to do so empirically. The material used was a correlation table containing the height and left middle finger measurements of 3000 criminals, from a paper by W. R. Macdonell (Biometrika, Vol. I, p. 219). The measurements were written out on 3000 pieces of cardboard, which were then very thoroughly shuffled and drawn at random. As each card was drawn its numbers were written down in a book, which thus contains the measurements of 3000 criminals in a random order.

Finally, each consecutive set of 4 was taken as a sample – 750 in all – and the mean, standard deviation, and correlation of each sample determined. The difference between the mean of each sample and the mean of the population was then divided by the standard deviation of the sample, giving us the z of Section III. This provides us with two sets of 750 standard deviations and two sets of 750 z's on which to test the theoretical results arrived at. (Student, 1908: 13)

Definitely not practical, also when considering that the typical number of replications in a Monte Carlo simulation, for example, is 100 or 1000 times higher, or that we can collect millions of records from online sources.

The content of this part is organised as follows.

Maximum Likelihood Estimation

The idea behind maximum likelihood estimation is to employ a generalised procedure able to find the value of one or more parameters for a given statistic which makes its likelihood distribution a maximum. These provide efficient methods for quantifying uncertainty and to assess confidence limits. As for the other methods described in this part, the estimation methodology is simple, but the calculations involved can be quite intense. Modern computer power is therefore the only practical way of using these methods.

Monte Carlo Methods

Monte Carlo methods are a class of computational algorithms that provide approximate solutions to a variety of mathematical problems. They depend on repeated random sampling to perform statistical experiments and can be loosely defined as statistical simulation methods. Monte Carlo simulation methods are especially useful in studying systems with a large number of interdependent degrees of freedom.

Big Data

This chapter contains a brief description of the much discussed topic of Big Data. A characterisation and definition is followed by a brief description of the technological architecture used and consideration of some of the statistical issues surrounding Big Data. A discussion of machine learning techniques, along with an example, closes the chapter.

Simulations and Agent-Based Modelling

Agent-based modelling and numerical simulations are means that facilitate exploring the structural and dynamic characteristics of systems that may prove intractable with analytical methods. This chapter examines what are complex adaptive systems, when are agent-based models a useful methodology to analyse systems, what are issues that relate to them and where they have been applied successfully. As an application example, a simple model is built to analyse the movements of tourists and the relationship between these and the attractiveness of a tourism destination.

References

Student (1908) The probable error of a mean. *Biometrika* 6 (1), 1–25.

6 Maximum Likelihood Estimation

This chapter discusses maximum likelihood (ML) estimations and the numerical methods to evaluate them. A brief account is given of likelihood ratio tests as well. Some typical examples show possible applications.

Estimating Statistical Parameters

When studying a certain phenomenon, in tourism and in many other disciplines, the researcher attempts to find some general laws or principles that rule the phenomenon in order to understand its behaviour and to make predictions for the future. Usually, it is not possible to observe (and measure) all the effects and the causes directly, so some hypotheses are formulated. These are stated in terms of probability distributions (often families of distributions). The form of the relationships ruling the phenomenon is then derived by testing the validity and reliability of the assumptions made and finding the best possible fit between hypotheses and empirical data.

An ML procedure consists of finding a statistical estimator (a measurable function of the data) that can be used to estimate unknown parameter values. The method is considered to be quite robust (although exceptions exist) and able to provide estimators with good statistical properties (consistent, unbiased and efficient). Maximum likelihood estimates (MLEs) are flexible and can be applied to many different models and types of data, even in situations in which these cannot be easily classified within known distributions. In other words, for simple cases, such as normally distributed data, it is possible to calculate the distribution parameters (mean and variance) with a formula that is valid for the whole population and (hopefully) also for a sample drawn from that population. In some cases, however, distributions are much more complicated or no population formulas exist (e.g. exponential, power law, Beta, Weibull, etc., distributions). In these situations, an MLE procedure allows a candidate estimator to be found, and offers an efficient tool for determining uncertainties and confidence bounds of parameters (Eliason, 1993; Le Cam, 1990). The idea is very general and applies to non-linear as well as linear models.

Essentially, the value sought is determined by maximising the likelihood distribution function of some global parameter. Although *likelihood* and *probability* are almost synonymous in common language, technically (in statistical parlance) *probability* allows the prediction of unknown outcomes based on known parameters, while *likelihood* provides an estimate of unknown parameters based on known data.

Consider, for example, the case shown in Figure 6.1. A number of observations, x_i, have been made. We have two possible probability distributions $f(x)$, A and B, which can be candidates for having generated the observed sample. Rather obviously, curve A looks the best solution. Curve B would imply too small probabilities for the observed x_i. The problem solved by MLE procedures is to formally justify this intuitive conclusion.

The idea and the methods were first proposed by Fisher, building on the work of 18th-century mathematicians (Aldrich, 1997; Stigler, 2007), and originates essentially from his criticisms of the arbitrariness in the techniques commonly used for fitting empirical data (ordinary least squares [OLS] above all).

As stated, MLE is intuitively simple. Assume that there is a sample x_i with an associated probability distribution varying with a certain parameter θ (the mean or the standard deviation, for example): $f(x_i, \theta)$. In other words, given the sample data, we are interested in the probabilities associated with different values of θ. The *likelihood* of this distribution is the product of these values (here, obviously, we assume independence of the probabilities):

$$L(\theta) = \prod_i f(x_i, \theta)$$

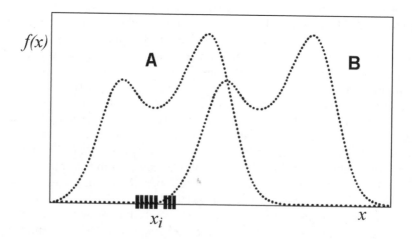

Figure 6.1 Empirical observations $f(x)$ along with two probability distributions

The MLE procedure consists of maximising $L(\theta)$. It is common practice to consider the logarithm of these expressions, called *log-likelihood*:

$$l(\theta) = \sum_i \log(f(x_i, \theta))$$

In regions where $f(x,\theta)$ is not very small, $L(\theta)$ can be very large, and maximising a sum is much easier than working with products. It is worth remembering here that any function transformed by applying a monotonously increasing function (the logarithm) reaches extreme values for the same argument. That is: $L(\theta)$ and $l(\theta)$ will reach their maximum values for the same value of θ:

$$\hat{\theta} = \text{argmax}(L(\theta)) = \text{argmax}\,\log(L(\theta)) = \text{argmax}(l(\theta))$$

Now, remembering a little calculus, the task is relatively straightforward. The maximum of a well-behaved (continuous and differentiable) function is obtained by finding the value for which the first derivative equals zero and the second derivative is negative:

$$\frac{\partial l(\theta)}{\partial \theta} = 0; \quad \frac{\partial^2 l(\theta)}{\partial \theta^2} < 0$$

These conditions will provide the desired value $\hat{\theta}$ (roots of the equations). The variance (for large samples) equals approximately the negative of the reciprocal of the second derivative of the log-likelihood function evaluated at $\hat{\theta}$:

$$\sigma^2(\hat{\theta}) \cong 1 \Big/ \left(\frac{\partial^2 l(\theta)}{\partial \theta^2} \Big|_{\theta=\hat{\theta}} \right)$$

A simple example may help to clarify the whole procedure. Consider a Poisson distribution which is commonly used in modelling count data such as the arrivals at an information desk, or the visitors to a museum or attraction. The formula is

$$p(x_i; \lambda) = \frac{\lambda^{x_i} e^{-\lambda}}{x_i!}$$

This gives the probability of x_i occurrences when the expected value (i.e. the mean time between arrivals) is λ.

The log-likelihood function can be written as

$$l(\lambda) \propto -N\lambda + \ln \lambda \sum x_i$$

The derivatives of this expression are

$$\frac{\partial l(\lambda)}{\partial \lambda} = -N\lambda + \frac{1}{\lambda}\sum x_i \quad \text{and} \quad \frac{\partial^2 l(\lambda)}{\partial \lambda^2} = -\sum -\lambda^2 x_i$$

Solving the first expression, we find:

$$\lambda_{\text{MLE}} = \frac{1}{N}\sum x_i$$

which, as well, always makes the second derivative negative; it is therefore the maximising value for the log-likelihood function. In this way, we have found the MLE for the Poisson distribution and, essentially, have justified the use of the sample mean as the best choice for estimating the distribution.

More generally, and when more parameters are involved, the MLE procedure can be summarised as follows:

- write a likelihood function for the data;
- take the logarithms to obtain a log-likelihood function;
- derive the log-likelihood function with respect to all the parameters and find the roots;
- calculate the second partial derivatives with respect to the parameters;
- build a matrix of these second partial derivatives and calculate the negative inverse (in other words, we solve the resulting system of equations);
- the diagonal elements of the resulting matrix are the variances of the MLE for the parameters.

Unfortunately, simple analytical solutions such as the one found for the Poisson distribution are obtainable only in few cases, and for the most known and used distributions. Often, the form of the distribution is unknown or the number of parameters is high. In these situations, an analytic solution is not possible and numerical methods must be used instead.

Many algorithms exist for maximising a function, even when an analytic expression does not exist. The most used, even if it has some limitations, is the Newton–Raphson method (Press *et al.*, 1992; Ypma, 1995). All of these algorithms are iterative techniques which start from some initial guess of the value sought after, and then incrementally update that guess. The iteration is continued until a (local) maximum of the function is achieved. In some cases, some of these methods may not guarantee a convergence.

Practically all the modern statistical software packages (SPSS, Stata) or development environments (R, Python, Matlab) offer some form of procedure or collections of scripts for ML computations. Factor analysis, correlation and regression studies, goodness-of-fit tests and analysis of variance (ANOVA) are only some examples of statistical functions that can be approached in this way.

Although appealing for their conceptual simplicity, MLE methods can be quite difficult when a mathematically rigorous approach is needed or desired. The properties (continuity, differentiability, etc.) of a likelihood function may turn out to be hard to assess and to interpret, mainly when real empirical data are involved. Numerical and computational methods may help, but caution is needed in their application in order to preserve the meaning of the solutions that may be found. The suggestions made by Le Cam (1990) with a bit of humour should be carefully considered before and during the use of an ML procedure (and not only for MLEs):

Basic Principle 0. Do not trust any principle. [...]

Principle 1. Have clear in your mind what it is that you want to estimate.

Principle 2. Try to ascertain in some way what precision you need (or can get) and what you are going to do with the estimate when you get it.

Principle 3. Before venturing an estimate, check that the rationale which led you to it is compatible with the data you have.

Principle 4. If satisfied that everything is in order, try first a crude but reliable procedure to locate the general area in which your parameters lie.

Principle 5. Having localized yourself by (4), refine the estimate using some of your theoretical assumptions, being careful all the while not to undo what you did in (4).

Principle 6. Never trust an estimate which is thrown out of whack if you suppress a single observation.

Principle 7. If you need to use asymptotic arguments, don't forget to let your number of observations tend to infinity.

Principle 8. J. Bertrand said it this way: 'Give me four parameters and I shall describe an elephant; with five, it will wave its trunk'. (Le Cam, 1990: 165)

Example: Fitting a probability distribution from empirical data

Finding the correct probability distribution of a series of empirical observations can be extremely important for understanding the phenomenon under study and for reliable statistical analysis, particularly when inferences are to be made. ML methods can help provide an answer.

Consider for example the data depicted in Figure 6.2. The histogram represents 500 measurements of the inter-arrival times (in minutes) of tourists at a certain site.

As Figure 6.2 shows, a fit using a normal distribution (dotted curve superimposed) could be considered reasonable. In such a case, however, a gamma distribution could also be used. The gamma distribution is defined in terms of a shape parameter θ and a scale parameter k (Everitt, 2006). It can be derived as the sum of n exponentially distributed random variables and is typically used in queuing models or flows of data in telecommunication equipment.

ML analysis will provide us with the best choice between the two distributions. The analysis can be performed using standard Matlab functions. The only warning is that Matlab has a function (*fminsearch*) to minimise a given function, therefore the log-likelihood used must be inverted (a negative log-likelihood must be used). The functions *gamlike* and *normlike* provide the required values, and the likelihood surfaces thus calculated are shown in Figure 6.3.

As can be seen from Figure 6.3, the gamma distribution likelihoods are definitely lower than those calculated in the normal hypothesis (remembering that, due to the particular software employed [Matlab] we have transformed a maximisation problem into a minimisation one); therefore, the best choice for this case is a gamma distribution. Figure 6.4 better shows the difference between the two possible fits of the data under analysis.

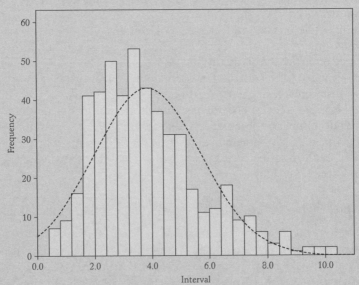

Figure 6.2 Histogram of 500 observations of inter-arrival times (in minutes) of tourists at a site. A normal curve (dotted curve) is superimposed

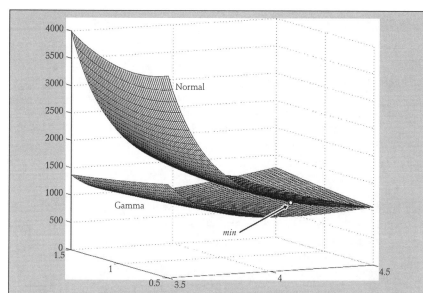

Figure 6.3 (Negative) likelihood surfaces for the data in Figure 6.2

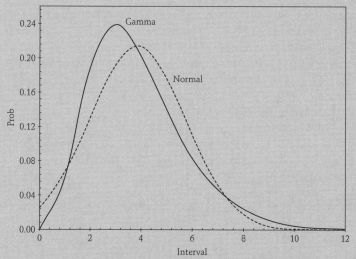

Figure 6.4 The two possible fits (gamma and normal) for the data in Figure 6.2

The two parameters calculated are: $\theta=4.2786$ and $k=0.9002$. From these, according to the definition of the gamma distribution, it is possible to derive:

- mean$=\theta k=3.85$;
- mode$=\theta(k-1)=2.95$;
- variance$=\theta^2 k=3.47$.

Example: Incomplete data

An interesting application of MLE concerns the estimation of parameters when data present some incompleteness. Consider, for example, the case of a survey questionnaire in which not all the answers have been given or the collection of multivariate observations where some condition prevents (randomly) the measurement of all the variables for some cases.

An ML parameter estimation allows researchers to derive appropriate parameter estimates and draw inference from incomplete data when data are missing at random (MAR).

The technique is described by Dempster *et al.* (1977) and, more recently by Schneider (2001) who also provides a set of Matlab scripts to perform the analysis (available at: http://climate-dynamics.org/software/#regem) and in Truxillo (2005), which contains a set of STATA programs.

The algorithm employed is called expectation-maximisation (EM) and iterates through two steps to obtain the estimates. The basic assumption is that data are multivariate and normally distributed, and missing observations are MAR (i.e. the probability that a value is missing does not depend on the missing value). The parameters of a probability distribution are estimated from the incomplete set of data by iteratively maximising the likelihood of the available data. This likelihood function depends on these parameters (Dempster *et al.* 1977). As a result, the researcher obtains an estimate of the mean vector and covariance matrix. These can then be used in subsequent analyses to obtain estimates of model parameters and standard errors, to perform hypothesis tests or to make predictions.

The first step of the algorithm is an expectation (E) step. In this step, missing values are imputed according to an initial guess. In the second step, a maximisation (M) step, the completed data are processed using an ML estimation considering the data as though they were complete and mean and covariance estimates are updated. These updated values are then used in a new E step in order to find new estimates of the missing values. The two steps (E and M) are repeated until the maximum change in the estimates from one iteration to the next does not exceed a convergence criterion. The result of this process is a mean vector and a covariance matrix that use all available information.

Example: Fitting a power–law distribution

MLE is a powerful method for estimating the values of the parameters of a statistical model obtained by fitting empirical data. The most widely used technique in these cases is an OLS linear regression and, when all the assumptions are satisfied (uncorrelated normal errors with identical variances), OLS regression is fully equivalent to MLE; they lead to identical results. In many cases, however, this is not true and an MLE procedure must be used in order to obtain meaningful results.

One case in which this situation arises is when empirical data are recognised as obeying a power–law distribution. This happens when the number or frequency of an observed quantity varies as a power of some of its attribute, the mathematical relation has the form: $p(x) \sim kx^{-\gamma}$ ($\gamma > 1$).

This distribution can be found in a large number of natural and artificial phenomena. Well-known laws such as those due to Pareto (1896) or Zipf (1949) follow this behaviour. It has been found to rule income and wealth distributions, the size of cities and firms, political expenditures or stock market returns (Gabaix, 2009). In statistical physics, a power–law relationship in some parameter is one of the common signatures of a non-linear dynamic process, which is, at a point, self-organised, thus signifying the complexity of the system under study (Komulainen, 2004). Tourism is no exception and a number of investigations have uncovered powerlaw behaviours (Baggio, 2008; Lew, 2008; Ulubaşoğlu & Hazari, 2004).

The curve appears as an exponential with a very long tail (Figure 6.5, left) and, for better visualising its properties, is usually drawn on a log-log chart (Figure 6.5, right).

When considering a power–law relationship, we are interested in calculating the exponent γ, called the scaling exponent or parameter. In theory, a logarithmic transformation, leading to $\log p(x) \sim \log k - \gamma \log x$ would allow use of a linear regression for this calculation (Figure 6.5, right). However, when real empirical data are involved, this estimate can be highly problematic and lead to inconsistent answers as pointed out by many scholars (Clauset *et al.*, 2009; Goldstein *et al.*, 2004; Newman, 2005). The suggestions for finding a working solution are many, such as making a linear regression on the log-log cumulative distribution function, or on log-binned data. For example, it is possible to calculate a cumulative distribution $N(>k) \propto k^{a}$ (Figure 6.6, panel B, axes are logarithmic), conduct a logarithmic transformation, then fit it with a software package,

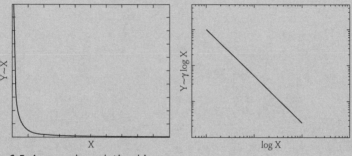

Figure 6.5 A power–law relationship

estimating the exponent, α. The correct exponent for the distribution will then be $|\gamma|=|\alpha|+1$.

However, the best possible solution is to use an MLE procedure to calculate the scaling exponent and its standard error. Clauset, as a companion to his paper (Clauset *et al.*, 2009), provides a series of Matlab, R and Python scripts for performing these calculations (available at: http://tuvalu.santafe.edu/~aaronc/powerlaws/).

The following example uses these scripts. Suppose you have collected the data shown in Figure 6.7, which are the distribution of the connections

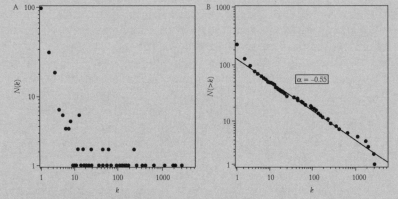

Figure 6.6 Power–law distribution (A) and cumulative power–law distribution (B) with a (log) linear fit

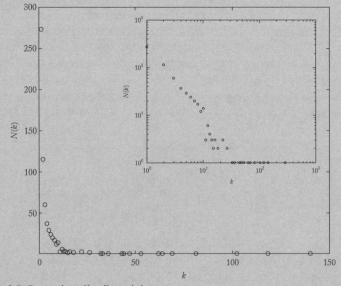

Figure 6.7 Power–law distributed data

existing in a network formed by tourism operators (Baggio *et al.*, 2010). The power–law behaviour is evident, and better rendered in the inset drawn on log-log axes.

A linear regression on the logarithmic transform of these data will be highly biased by the numerous points having different high values for k. This will result in an incorrectly low value (g=1.16) for the scaling exponent, although with a good coefficient of determination (R^2=0.85). The MLE procedure, instead, provides a value of g=2.32±0.27, which better represents the slope of the log-curve in the central region, the most interesting one. Figure 6.8 shows both fits and visually justifies the choice of an MLE approach.

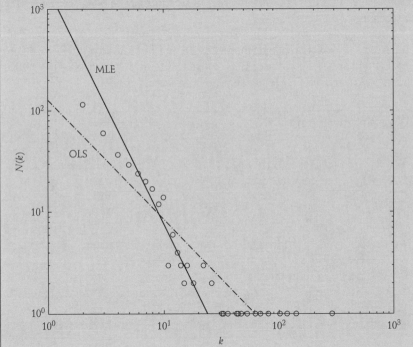

Figure 6.8 OLS (dashed line) and MLE (solid line) fit for the data shown in Figure 6.7

Likelihood Ratio Test

After having collected empirical observations, a probabilistic model is sought by trying to fit the data to a certain distribution. It may happen that more solutions, normally with different characteristics in terms of parameters, are found. We are interested in assessing whether it is possible to restrict the number of parameters (for example by imposing a set of linear constraints on the parameters) in order to have a *simpler* solution. The likelihood ratio test can be used to perform this comparison.

Let us assume that we have two models and we have calculated their likelihoods L_1, L_2 (as discussed in the previous section, these will be log-likelihoods) and that the one with more parameters fits at least as well as the second ($\log L_1 > \log L_2$), the test compares the null hypothesis L_1 against the alternative L_2. The test statistic is

$$D = -2(\log L_1 - \log L_2) = -2\log\left(\frac{L_1}{L_2}\right)$$

Asymptotically (i.e. for large samples), D can be approximated by a χ^2 distribution with $df = (df_1 - df_2)$ degrees of freedom (df_1 and df_2 are the degrees of freedom of Models 1 and 2).

For example, if Model 1 has five parameters with log-likelihood$=-2100$ and Model 2 has three parameters with log-likelihood$=-2091$, we have $D=18$, $df=2$ and the p-value of the corresponding χ^2 distribution is $p=0.0001$, thus allowing us to decide in favour of the second model.

Example: Choice of regression models

An example of the use of a likelihood ratio test for choosing between models is presented by Huybers (2003). The paper discusses the determinants of destination choice by domestic tourists.

Perceptions and feelings of tourists visiting a destination were measured in order to develop a preference ordering. Primary data were collected through a survey which assessed the relative importance of a number of destination and trip attributes, and gathered respondent characteristics.

The analysis estimated a good fit with both a nested logit and a multinomial logit model (these are two possible logistic regression models, see Hilbe [2009]). A likelihood ratio test was performed in order to choose between the two and, in this case, the nested logit was preferred.

References

Aldrich, J. (1997) R.A. Fisher and the making of maximum likelihood 1912–1922. *Statistical Science* 12 (3), 162–176.

Baggio, R. (2008) Symptoms of complexity in a tourism system. *Tourism Analysis* 13 (1), 1–20.

Baggio, R., Scott, N. and Cooper, C. (2010) Network science: A review with a focus on tourism. *Annals of Tourism Research* 37 (3), 802–827.

Clauset, A., Shalizi, C.R. and Newman, M.E.J. (2009) Power-law distributions in empirical data. *SIAM Review* 51 (4), 661–703.

Dempster, A.P., Laird, N.M. and Rubin, D.B. (1977) Maximum likelihood from incomplete data via the EM algorithm. *Journal of the Royal Statistical Society B* 39 (1), 1–38.

Eliason, S.R. (1993) *Maximum Likelihood Estimation: Logic and Practice.* London: Sage.

Everitt, B.S. (2006) *The Cambridge Dictionary of Statistics* (3rd edn). Cambridge: Cambridge University Press.

Gabaix, X. (2009) Power laws in economics and finance. *Annual Review of Economics* 1, 255–293.

Goldstein, M.L., Morris, S.A. and Yen, G.G. (2004) Problems with fitting to the power-law distribution. *The European Physical Journal B*, 41, 255–258.

Hilbe, J.M. (2009) *Logistic Regression Models.* Boca Raton, FL: Chapman & Hall/CRC.

Huybers, T. (2003) Domestic tourism destination choices: A choice modelling analysis. *International Journal of Tourism Research* 5 (6), 445–459.

Komulainen, T. (2004) Self-similarity and power laws. In H. Hyötyniemi (ed.) *Complex Systems: Science on the Edge of Chaos (Report 145, October 2004).* Helsinki: Helsinki University of Technology, Control Engineering Laboratory.

Le Cam, L. (1990) Maximum likelihood: An introduction. *International Statistical Review* 58 (2), 153–171.

Lew, A.A. (2008) Long tail tourism: New geographies for marketing niche tourism products. *Journal of Travel and Tourism Marketing* 25 (3), 409–419.

Newman, M.E.J. (2005) Power laws, Pareto distributions and Zipf's law. *Contemporary Physics* 46 (5), 323–351.

Pareto, V. (1896) *Cours d'Economie Politique.* Geneva: Droz.

Press, W.H., Teukolsky, S.A., Vetterling, W.T. and Flannery, B.P. (1992) *Numerical Recipes in C: The Art of Scientific Computing* (2nd edn). Cambridge: Cambridge University Press.

Schneider, T. (2001) Analysis of incomplete climate data: Estimation of mean values and covariance matrices and imputation of missing values. *Journal of Climate* 14, 853–871.

Stigler, S.M. (2007) The epic story of maximum likelihood. *Statistical Science* 22 (4), 598–620.

Truxillo, C. (2005) Maximum likelihood parameter estimation with incomplete data. *Proceedings of the 30th SAS Users Group International Conference, Philadelphia, 10–13 April.* See http://www2.sas.com/proceedings/sugi30/111-30.pdf. (accessed Feb 2017)

Ulubaşoğlu, M.H. and Hazari, B.R. (2004) Zipf's law strikes again: The case of tourism. *Journal of Economic Geography* 4, 459–472.

Ypma, T.J. (1995) Historical development of the Newton–Raphson method. *SIAM Review* 37 (4), 531–551.

Zipf, G.K. (1949) *Human Behavior and the Principle of Least Effort: An Introduction to Human Ecology.* Cambridge: Addison-Wesley.

7 Monte Carlo Methods

Monte Carlo methods are well known in many fields, and prove crucial in cases in which analytical estimates are impossible or very complicated. They are based on the multiple replication of a single calculation by varying the parameters taken from a randomly generated distribution. This chapter discusses the methods and provides some typical application examples.

Numerical Experiments

The calculation of some quantities of interest may depend on a fairly large number of parameters and variables. Normally, all these are known 'statistically'. This means that it is possible to have available a value, an average or typical value and some interval in which this value varies (standard deviation, standard error, interquartile range or other dispersion measure). Then, usually, the quantity of interest is calculated using these average values (provided a reliable model is available, i.e. a mathematical expression binding parameters and variables). The final outcome will thus be our best estimate, based on the best estimates of all the parameters involved.

Oftentimes, however, this first approximation is not fully satisfactory and we would like to be able to obtain some further information regarding our quantity, typically its variation interval or, better, its probability distribution. For example, we may want to estimate the different risk probabilities associated with a certain investment or with the sales of a new service, or the possible confidence limits of a forecast.

In theory, the variations can be calculated on the basis of the variations associated with the parameters used in the calculation. The method is well known and widely used in experimental disciplines (Barford, 1967; Taylor, 1982). However, both in theory and in practice, when the distributions involved are less common or do not exist because we only have an empirical distribution, the applicability is limited. For example, when non-linear functions are involved, the error estimates can be biased due to the approximations used in the series expansions: the bias in the error calculated for a logarithmic function, $\log x$, increases with x since the expansion to $1+x$ is a good approximation only for small x. Regression techniques usually assume that errors are uncorrelated, but the errors of the parameters derived do not always follow this assumption (e.g. slope and intercept in linear regression are correlated with the correlation coefficient). Another case is in regard to some distributions, such as the Cauchy distribution, for which it is not possible to define a variance.

In such cases, a technique known as Monte Carlo is extremely useful and powerful. Monte Carlo methods (also termed *experiments* or *simulations*) are a class of numerical algorithms based on repeated random sampling. In the treatment of an analytic model, single-point estimates are typically used. For any uncertain variable, a best estimate is available and different combinations are chosen to provide (typically) best, worst and most likely cases. The outcomes are recorded, resulting in a series of what-if scenarios. A Monte Carlo simulation performs a random sampling from the probability distribution functions of the required inputs and generates a large number (hundreds or thousands) of possible results. These can then be analysed with standard statistical methods to derive averages and probability distributions. In this sense, Monte Carlo methods can be loosely defined as statistical simulation methods.

The idea of, and the need for, this type of calculation is very clearly expressed by one of its original proponents, Stanislaw Ulam, who recalls the birth of the method:

> The first thoughts and attempts I made to practice [the Monte Carlo Method] were suggested by a question which occurred to me in 1946 as I was convalescing from an illness and playing solitaires. The question was what are the chances that a Canfield solitaire laid out with 52 cards will come out successfully? After spending a lot of time trying to estimate them by pure combinatorial calculations, I wondered whether a more practical method than 'abstract thinking' might not be to lay it out say one hundred times and simply observe and count the number of successful plays. This was already possible to envisage with the beginning of the new era of fast computers, and I immediately thought of problems of neutron diffusion and other questions of mathematical physics, and more generally how to change processes described by certain differential equations into an equivalent form interpretable as a succession of random operations. Later ... [in 1946, I] described the idea to John von Neumann, and we began to plan actual calculations. (Eckhardt, 1987: 131)

The idea, published by Metropolis and Ulam (1949), was successfully used to ease the complicated calculations made by the scientists involved in the now infamous Manhattan Project during which researchers at the US Los Alamos National Laboratory developed nuclear weapons for the Second World War (Metropolis, 1987). The method's name refers to the casino-city of Monaco, Monte Carlo, because of the central role that probability plays in both Monte Carlo methods and games of chance.

Monte Carlo simulation methods are especially useful in studying systems with a large number of coupled degrees of freedom, such as fluids, disordered materials or cellular structures. More broadly, they are useful for modelling phenomena with significant uncertainty in inputs, a common situation when dealing with social and economic systems.

The essence of a probability experiment is to deal with the possible outcomes of an event or phenomenon and the frequency of its occurrence. This relationship between events and their likelihood is the probability distribution for the experiment. It is possible to assign random variables to the outcomes. This associates a measurable value with each event that, ideally, is significant to the subject of the experiment. The expected value of a random variable is the mean of its value across all possible events, weighted against their probability of happening. By sampling a large number of experiment outcomes, it is possible to obtain a good estimate of the random variable's expected value.

There is no single Monte Carlo method, rather the term describes a large class of approaches that follow a common pattern (Robert & Casella, 2004; Sobol, 1994):

- a model (meaning a mathematical expression) exists for the phenomenon under study;
- a domain of possible input parameters is defined;
- the inputs are generated randomly from the domain using a certain probability distribution;
- the computation is performed for each of the input parameters;
- the results of the individual computations are aggregated to derive the final result.

The canonical example when discussing Monte Carlo methods is that concerning the calculation of an approximate value for π. Suppose π is unknown and no other knowledge exists for a way of guessing it. It is possible to derive its value by using a simple geometrical approach. It is known that π is the ratio between the area of a circle and its radius squared. It is possible to draw a quarter of a circle inscribed in a square, and, for simplicity, let us assume that the square side has a unit length.

In this situation, the ratio between the area of the circle, A_C, and the area of the square, A_S, is

$$\frac{A_C}{A_S} = \frac{\frac{1}{4}\pi R^2}{R^2} = \frac{1}{4}\pi$$

Now, let us think of uniformly dropping some objects (of the same size) on this figure (see left panel in Figure 7.1). Since the ratio between the two

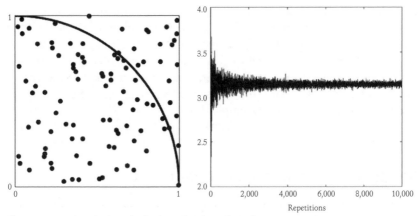

Figure 7.1 Monte Carlo calculations for the value of π

areas is $\pi/4$, the objects will fall on the figure in approximately the same ratio. In other words, if we drop a reasonably large number of objects, count how many fall inside the circle, and divide this by the total number of objects, we obtain an estimate for $\pi/4$.

The drop can be simulated numerically by generating a series of random numbers uniformly distributed between 0 and 1. Considering these in pairs, they can be thought of as the coordinates (x, y) of a point whose distance from the origin is $d = \sqrt{x^2 + y^2}$. All pairs for which $d \leq 1$ will belong to the circle. Four times the ratio between the number of pairs inside the circle and the total number of pairs is our estimate for π. The right panel in Figure 7.1 shows the calculated value with respect to the number of random units generated. The approach to the correct value as the number of samples increases is evident. With 10^4 replications the error made is of order 10^2, relatively good for such a simple method.

Another application of Monte Carlo is the evaluation of definite integrals, a task that is often quite difficult to perform with standard analytical methods. The idea is to consider a definite integral such as the following: $I = \int_a^b f(x)dx$. This integral, applying the mean value theorem of calculus, can be approximated by

$$I_{\text{APPROX}} = (b-a)\overline{f} \approx (b-a)\frac{1}{N}\sum_{i=1}^{N} f(x_i)$$

where the points x_i cover the range of integration.

When there is a large number of points N, I_{APPROX} tends to the exact value I. It is possible to select the points x_i randomly from a given probability distribution and use a Monte Carlo simulation to calculate the final value. If the points are selected at random over the interval $[a, b]$, the central limit theorem says that the set of all possible sums over different $\{x_i\}$ will have a Gaussian (normal) distribution. The standard deviation σ_N of the different values of I_{APPROX} is a measure of the uncertainty in the integral's value. This error decays as $1/\sqrt{N}$ independently of the dimensionality of the integral.

It must be noted here that these methods provide only an approximation to the value sought after. Analysis of the approximation error is thus a major factor to consider when employing these methods, and the attempt to minimise it is one of the reasons why many different Monte Carlo methods exist.

Random and Pseudorandom Numbers

Monte Carlo methods require large volumes of random numbers. This necessity has stimulated the development of numerical algorithms to generate them, a practice far quicker and easier to employ than the perusing of tables as previously used for statistical sampling. The main issue in this area is that a computer is not a probabilistic machine, but a rigidly deterministic one. Generation of a series of random numbers must therefore be performed using some special 'trick'. One option would be (and has been used on some occasions) to connect a computer to a real system and draw upon the randomness existing in nature. Fluctuations in the temperature of a processor, length and time between telephone calls, emission of radiation by radioactive materials have been proposed and used. However, in addition to the obvious difficulty and impracticality, these techniques still suffer from the problem of providing irregular and poorly distributed samples.

The method used today consists of generating what are called pseudorandom numbers. Through a suitable and sufficiently sophisticated algorithm, it is possible to create a series of numbers that is barely distinguishable from a random sequence. Writing such algorithms is not an easy task, but today many good examples exist such as the well-known and widely used 'Mersenne Twister' of Matsumoto and Nishimura (1998).

A pseudorandom sequence, being generated by a deterministic process, can be sufficiently long to allow practical use in statistical analyses, but it eventually repeats itself. The longer the sequence the better, obviously, but the repetition can also be helpful. The basis for these algorithms is a number used as the starting point, a *seed*. Starting with the same seed will generate the same sequence and this characteristic is used to reproduce the same situation, which is good, for example, when testing new models. Normally, the pseudorandom generators used by the most common software packages produce (pseudo) random numbers uniformly distributed in the interval [0,1]. This standard uniform distribution, denoted $U(0,1)$ can then be used to obtain random numbers distributed in any other interval, say between *min* and *max*, by calculating $U(\text{min},\text{max})=\text{min}+U(0,1)\times(\text{max}-\text{min})$.

$U(0,1)$ is also the starting point for obtaining a sample which follows an arbitrary distribution (Collins, 2008; Devroye, 1986; Hull & Dobell, 1962). There are several methods to obtain such a sample. A general procedure is the inverse transform sampling method. This uses the cumulative distribution function of the target random variable and can be sketched as follows (valid for univariate distributions, those needed in a Monte Carlo simulation):

(1) Generate n pseudorandom numbers in $[0,1]$: $u_1, u_2, \ldots, u_n$.
(2) Consider an arbitrary probability distribution $f(x)$ and calculate its cumulative function $F(x)$.
(3) Calculate the inverse $F^{-1}(x)$, the desired values will be calculated as $x_i = F^{-1}(u_i)$. If the probability distribution is a discrete one (for example in the case of an empirical distribution), the values will be given by $x_i = \inf\{x_i; F(x_i) \le u_i\}$ (inf stands for the minimum value of the function).

In practice, all the best known and used software applications (SPSS, STATA, SAS, etc., see the Appendix Software programs for references) provide ready-to-use functions for obtaining the needed values sampled from the best-known distributions. The above description is useful for cases in which the distribution is not included in the software used or one has to deal with an empirical probability distribution calculated from observed quantities.

Example: Profit of an investment

Let us assume a tour operator wishes to guess the risk associated with the introduction of a new product. To do that, we need to calculate the probability distribution for the possible profits (or losses) coming from the sales of the product (for the more economically inclined, for the sake of simplicity we assume that the market is a perfect competition market, i.e. there is no influence on the price of the product).

Now, a simple equation (model) for the profit is: Profit$=(Q^*P)-(Q^*C_V+C_F)$; where Q is the quantity demanded, P is the market price, C_V the variable costs and C_F the fixed costs.

The following assumptions are made:

- Q varies uniformly between 500 and 1000;
- P is normally distributed with mean=€400.00 and standard deviation=€100.00, truncated so that the minimum is €300.00;
- C_V is normally distributed with mean=€200.00 and standard deviation=€50.00, truncated so that the minimum=€70.00 and the maximum=€300.00;
- C_F=€50,000.

Figure 7.2 shows the resulting profit distributions for 1,000 and 10,000 iterations. The latter is, rather obviously, the most well 'defined' outcome. The calculations provide a value of about 815 'pieces' sold at an average price of €452.89 (SD=€264.88) yielding a margin of about 28.0%. What is more, it is possible to deduce that there is a probability of 7.1% of losing money (profit ≤0) which represents the risk for the whole operation.

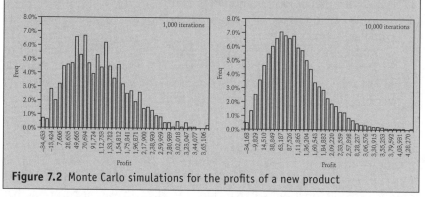

Figure 7.2 Monte Carlo simulations for the profits of a new product

Example: Solar panel output power

As a further example, let us consider the situation in which a hotel manager wants to evaluate the installation of a series of solar panels on the roof of his hotel in order to produce as much electric power as possible. The main issue is calculating the effective electric power delivered by a photovoltaic panel for the geographic area in which the hotel is located.

A quick back-of-the-envelope calculation can be performed as follows. The sun emits a certain amount of electromagnetic radiation. This amount is well known (astronomers call it solar constant) and, on average, measured at the top of the atmosphere is worth 1367 W/m² (for this example, Watts have been chosen as units because they are more commonly used for practical purposes). This value is an annual average and takes into account the radiation received by the whole earth. Now, approximating our planet to a sphere, the quantity of radiation received by the part facing the sun (approximated as a circle) is ¼ of that value (the ratio between the area of a circle and of a sphere with the same radius R: $\pi R^2/4\pi R^2$).

The atmosphere selectively controls the passage towards the earth's surface of the various components of solar radiation. A portion of radiation is reflected back by the uppermost layers of the atmosphere; some is either absorbed or scattered in all directions by atmospheric gases, vapours and dust particles. On average, roughly 30% of the solar radiation arriving on top of the earth's atmosphere reaches ground level. Finally, all these quantities refer to a surface facing the sun. For a place at a certain latitude λ (for simplicity we consider a flat, grounded surface), we need to multiply them by cos(λ). Once the amount of solar radiation arriving on a square metre of ground-level surface is known, it is possible to calculate how much of it is converted into electricity by considering the efficiency of a photovoltaic cell. Commercially available industrial equipment have an average efficiency of 10–15%.

Our hotel manager can easily calculate an average yield, but if some more precise figure, and particularly if the possible variations of this output are needed, the calculation becomes much more complex. All the quantities mentioned above have variations due to a number of different factors, many not easily measurable. To cite only some of the most important: solar radiation depends on the time of the year and on solar activity; atmosphere absorption depends on solar radiation, weather conditions, pollution; solar panel installation efficiency depends on the actual characteristics of the installation, panel temperature, dust deposits.

All these variations are known in the technical and scientific literature only as experimental quantities (i.e. we can find standard deviations and distribution shapes) and no simple set of equations can be written to take all of them into account. Finally, even when they are known, it can be quite difficult to combine different experimental errors and variations coming from different distributions. Therefore, a Monte Carlo simulation is one of the few possible approaches to the problem.

In our case, it is possible to assume the following values for the quantities needed:

- solar radiation (top of atmosphere): 1367 W/m^2;
- atmospheric absorption: 27%;
- variation in solar radiation at ground level: 65 W/m^2;
- solar panel efficiency: 12%;
- variation in panel efficiency: 5%.

Finally, we perform the calculation for a location at latitude 51.5°N (the latitude of London). We further assume that the distribution of solar radiation is normal and that of the panel efficiency is log-normal (which shows up as a skewed Gaussian distribution).

With these input values and assumptions, a Monte Carlo simulation is run. The results are shown in Table 7.1 and Figure 7.3.

As Figure 7.3 shows, there are some differences between the distribution of values calculated depending on the number of repetitions, but for 10^4 and 10^5 repetitions the curves are quite similar and we can deduce that this is a satisfactory number for obtaining a meaningful result. Averaging the results, we obtain a final value of 18.6 ± 6.1 W/m^2 which is in good agreement with what the literature reports for a similar case (MacKay, 2009).

Table 7.1 Monte Carlo simulation for the yield of a solar panel

Number of repetitions	Average (W/m²)	Standard deviation (W/m²)
10^2	18.88	6.27
10^3	18.46	5.99
10^4	18.55	5.98
10^5	18.65	6.01

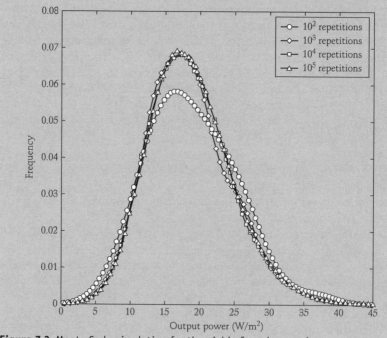

Figure 7.3 Monte Carlo simulation for the yield of a solar panel

References

Barford, N.C. (1967) *Experimental Measurements: Precision, Error and Truth*. New York: John Wiley and Sons.

Collins, J.C. (2008) Testing, Selection, and Implementation of Random Number Generators (Report: ARL-TR-4498). MD Army Research Laboratory, Aberdeen. See http://www.arl.army.mil/arlreports/2008/ARL-TR-4498.pdf (accessed March 2010).

Devroye, L. (1986) *Nonuniform Variate Generation*. New York: Springer-Verlag.

Eckhardt, R. (1987) Stan Ulam, John von Neumann, and the Monte Carlo method. *Los Alamos Science, Special Issue* (15), 131–137.

Hull, T.E. and Dobell, A.R. (1962) Random number generators. *SIAM Review* 4 (3), 230–254.

MacKay, D.J.C. (2009) *Sustainable Energy: Without the Hot Air*. Cambridge: UIT Cambridge Ltd.

Matsumoto, M. and Nishimura, T. (1998) Mersenne Twister: A 623-dimensionally equidistributed uniform pseudorandom number generator. *ACM Transactions on Modeling and Computer Simulation* 8 (1), 3–30.

Metropolis, N. (1987) The beginning of the Monte Carlo method. *Los Alamos Science, Special Issue* (15), 125–130.

Metropolis, N. and Ulam, S. (1949) The Monte Carlo method. *Journal of the American Statistical Association* 44 (247), 335–341.

Robert, C.P. and Casella, G. (2004) *Monte Carlo Statistical Methods*. New York: Springer-Verlag.

Sobol, I.M. (1994) *A Primer for the Monte Carlo Method*. Boca Raton, FL: CRC Press.

Taylor, J.R. (1982) *An Introduction to Error Analysis*. Oxford: Oxford University Press.

8 Big Data

This chapter contains a brief description of the much discussed topic of Big Data. A characterisation and definition is followed by a brief description of the technological architecture used and consideration of some of the statistical issues surrounding Big Data. A discussion of machine learning techniques, along with an example, closes the chapter.

In recent years, information and communication technologies (ICTs) have seen an incredible series of developments that have made data collection and analytical tools and applications available to individuals and organisations. One consequence of this expansion is that a vast number of digital records are transferred over a wide range of channels, and much of these data can be collected, stored and studied. Moreover, the relatively recent addition of sensor data (data derived from devices that sense their environment) has further widened this possibility.

The term commonly used to refer to this phenomenon is *Big Data*. This expression is, however, somewhat misleading because it focuses on only one aspect of the phenomenon, the large quantities of data involved. Although large quantity is the most visible feature, other characteristics are worthy of attention because they drive the issues and the opportunities associated with this development.

The main attributes of Big Data, much referred to in both popular media and the scientific and scholarly literature are (Chen *et al.*, 2014; Laney, 2001):

- *Volume*: Whence the name. The billions of gigabytes collected, available for analysis and analysed to discover unknown patterns or answer questions.
- *Velocity*: Signals the rate with which data are created and modified.
- *Variety*: Coming from very diverse environments, data assume a wide range of forms and shapes; the largest part is of a highly unstructured nature such as descriptive texts, pictures, videos or sounds. Moreover, the data often refer to specific times or places.

These characteristics, however, do not tell the whole story, and some more 'Vs' can be added:

- *Value*: Recognises both the need for a Big Data study project to generate value for the individual or the organisation that runs it and the increasing economic importance of the market which is growing around this theme.
- *Variability*: Intrinsic feature of most unstructured records that can assume quite different *meanings* in different contexts, even if they have similar forms, and the variance in these meanings that can occur over time.
- *Veracity*: Questions that arise about the reliability, the validity and the completeness of the data collected. Veracity can determine the outcomes of a Big Data project. This is especially true when automated decision-making is incorporated in the project: given the difficulty of dealing with high volumes of data, the variability at stake and questions of meaning and interpretation posed by ambiguities, inconsistencies or approximations in the models used.
- *Visualisation*: The need for presenting complex stories in comprehensible ways, rendering them graphically, in order to clarify key decisions and outcomes and convey limitations clearly. This issue is relevant when selecting analyses to be undertaken as well as when presenting results which are, by necessity, derived from selected, and sometimes complex, analyses conducted with a subset of the many variables that could be included.

Many more features could be added, such as the completeness of the data used, which are often regarded as whole populations instead of just samples; the resolution (i.e. the amount of detail) that target individual elements; the relational nature of variables that might be common to different sources; and the flexibility needed when analysing data collections to allow scaling or extension to additional variables and cases (Mayer-Schönberger & Cukier, 2013).

With this scenario it is difficult to reach a simple (and even univocal) characterisation or description of Big Data. Here, we adopt the view of Boyd and Crawford (2012) who define Big Data as:

... a cultural, technological, and scholarly phenomenon that rests on the interplay of:

1. Technology: maximizing computation power and algorithmic accuracy to gather, analyze, link, and compare large data sets.
2. Analysis: drawing on large data sets to identify patterns in order to make economic, social, technical, and legal claims.
3. Mythology: the widespread belief that large data sets offer a higher form of intelligence and knowledge that can generate insights that were previously impossible, with the aura of truth, objectivity, and accuracy. (Boyd & Crawford, 2012: 663)

Example: Analysing travellers' digital trails

Big Data can be a very useful source of information for the tourism sector. Two works are worth mentioning here. Both base their analysis and considerations on large volumes of data. Telefónica and RocaSalvatella (Sust *et al.*, 2014) collected one month of mobile phone traffic and credit card transaction data in Madrid and Barcelona (about 700,000 phones and 170,000 cards), and used it to uncover detailed activities and expenditures of international visitors to the two cities. In particular, analysis of real movements and spending allowed the firms to obtain information about:

- visitors' main country of origin;
- country of origin of tourists who choose Madrid and those who choose Barcelona;
- length of stay by country of origin;
- trips between the two destinations, Barcelona and Madrid;
- days and areas where foreign visitors prefer to stay;
- average daily spending and cumulative spending throughout the entire stay, and distribution of expenses among different activities.

Although some of these indicators could have been collected with traditional surveys, it must be recognised that the reliability attained by looking at *actual* movements, instead of *reported* declarations is quite high, and could not be quantified without Big Data analysis.

A second example is the study of the global mobility of people conducted by Hawelka *et al.* (2014) who geotagged one year's worth of tweets (almost 1 billion) and derived patterns and characteristics of the movements of international travellers (Figure 8.1).

The authors estimate the volume of international travellers by country of residence, together with the mobility profiles and temporal patterns. The analysis of the community structure of the Twitter

Figure 8.1 The network of movements of people for the top 30 countries and the mobility areas of international travellers (adapted from Hawelka *et al.*, 2014)

mobility network reveals spatially cohesive regions that follow the world's regional divisions. The temporal patterns reveal the seasonal distribution of the travels for the different countries. Moreover, the outcomes are validated by comparing them with global tourism statistics and mobility models. The results show also that the distribution of travels is slightly different from the one that is usually reported (e.g. by international organisations such as the United Nations World Tourism Organisation [UNWTO]), putting in the top positions as for arrivals: USA, UK, Spain, France, Germany and Italy. These results show that geolocated tweets can be a good proxy of global mobility behaviour, but indicate also that some work is needed for merging the two views (new Big Data and old traditional accounts) in order to increase the capacity to study the tourism phenomenon.

Technology

The most known and used framework for operating with Big Data is Hadoop (White, 2015). Hadoop is a Java open source project of the Apache Software Foundation for storage and large-scale distributed processing of data sets on clusters of *commodity* hardware.[1] It supports an unlimited number of nodes (computers) that can hold and process vast quantities of data (of the order of petabytes: 10^{15} bytes).

The architecture is designed to be highly modular. The basic scheme of a possible implementation is shown in Figure 8.2.

The main elements are:

- *Hadoop Distributed File System (HDFS)*: A highly fault-tolerant distributed file system, commonly used as the source and output location of data in Hadoop jobs. Originally developed by Google, HDFS is designed to store large data sets reliably, and to stream them at high speed to user applications. In a large cluster, thousands of

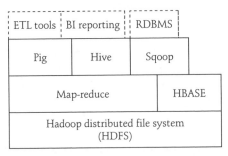

Figure 8.2 A schematic representation of Hadoop architecture

servers can both host directly attached storage devices and execute user applications. By distributing storage and computation across many servers, it is possible to satisfy growing user requests while ensuring high performance and low costs.

- *Map-Reduce*: A software framework that permits parallel processing of large data sets. Map-Reduce jobs are divided into two parts and are executed using a large number of nodes connected in a cluster. The *Map* function splits a query into various parts, and processes data at the single node level (worker nodes). The *Reduce* function combines the different results, in the master node, to form the final outcome.
- *HBASE*: A NoSQL (Not Only SQL) database system that provides random real-time (read/write) access to data. NoSQL database management systems (DBMS) differ from those most commonly used in that they are non-relational, i.e. they do not follow the tabular scheme of relational DBMS, nor do they use traditional structured query language (SQL) to access data. They are used in very large databases that may suffer from performance problems caused by the limitations of SQL and the relational model. NoSQL databases can better and more efficiently accommodate different classes of objects such as documents, images, sounds, videos.
- *Pig*: A high-level platform for creating Map-Reduce programs, especially suited to handling very long data pipelines (data processing elements connected in series), which is a limitation of SQL.
- *Apache HIVE*: Data warehouse software that facilitates reading, writing and managing large data sets residing in distributed storage using different databases (also SQL).
- *Sqoop*: A connectivity tool for moving data between non-Hadoop data stores (such as relational databases or data warehouses) into Hadoop.

As illustrated in Figure 8.2, many user applications can be built on top of these layers, such as:

- *ETL tools*: To extract, transform and load (ETL) data from and to heterogeneous sources. Tasks are typically executed in parallel: while data are being transferred, some transformation steps run, processing the data that have already been received to prepare them for loading into the final target (a database, an operational data store or a data warehouse).
- *BI reporting*: Various reporting tools that process data for business intelligence (BI) tasks.
- *RDBMS*: The usual and still widely used relational database systems.

Big Data architectures like Hadoop find a natural environment in cloud services, the internet-based computing facilities that many organisations offer and that provide shared processing resources (hardware and software) on demand.

Data collection tools

Many applications exist to provide, and in some ways control, access to the wealth of data that online social networks (OSNs) collect. When a specific investigation is required, the main question is how to gather records that will underpin meaningful results. Collecting tweets, Facebook posts, reviews or similar items can be a rather complicated task.

One possibility is to resort to a data provider (see for example www. bigdatavendors.com). However, this can be a rather expensive solution, at least for a small company or destination, as prices can be quite high. The second possibility is to use some applications developed for other purposes, but which also provide a plug-in for downloading data for analysis. Examples are NodeXL (nodexl.codeplex.com), a free network analysis add-in for Excel, or Gephi (gephi.org), an open source platform for visualisation and analysis of complex networks. However, these solutions are not fully satisfactory because of their intrinsic limitations in the amount of data they can handle, or the type of information they can collect; the plug-ins are designed to supplement the products' main scope, and not necessarily totally in line with what might be needed for collection and analysis of Big Data.

When a personalised approach is required, the skills and the resources needed (in terms of hardware and software) are relatively moderate. A normal PC (or a cluster of low-cost machines) can be equipped with a number of open source libraries that, with limited intervention, allow data collection to be customised (one example is the system presented in d'Amore *et al.* [2015]).

Some Statistical Remarks

Collecting, processing, analysing and interpreting data have been for centuries the task of statistics. All the methods we know and use, however, have been designed to treat moderate quantities of structured data. Big Data thus poses a number of issues which undermine, in many cases, the validity of the standard statistical methods. Some authors have even suggested that Big Data mean the end of statistical methods (Anderson, 2008), maintaining that hypothesis testing, the basic tenet of many statistical procedures, is no longer needed and that the petabytes of data available online can provide, simply by looking for patterns, all the answers required.

However, the large data sets from online sources are often unreliable, and their dynamic nature frequently prevents any attempt to replicate a study for confirmatory purposes. Errors and gaps can be magnified when multiple data sets are used together. The large quantities of data suffer from a well- and long-known *curse of dimensionality* (Keogh & Mueen, 2011), that puts conventional analytical methods under stress (Fan *et al.*, 2014). In the absence of a very clear research objective and an associated rigorous data collection plan, the risk of discovering meaningless outcomes or reaching deceptive conclusions is quite high. One example is the recent revision to the Google Flu Trends indicator which was contaminated by a number of unrelated factors (Lazer *et al.*, 2014).

Here, we mention some of the most important issues in this regard. The first one concerns statistical significance, at least as it is commonly understood. Most investigations performed on Big Data lead to *precisely inaccurate* results that may hide biases in the sources. Such biases are easily overlooked due to inflated significance generated by the size used (McFarland & McFarland, 2015). This raises questions about the common notion underlying much statistical analysis that 'more data is better'. When millions of records are examined, the usual *statistical significance* can lose its meaning and give a false impression of precision. Many statistical tests use the idea of measuring the distance between an observation and an expected value, divided by a measurement of the variability of the data (variance), where the variance is calculated as the average distance from a central point (e.g. the mean) divided by the number of data points:

$$\text{test}_{\text{value}} = \frac{\left|\text{observed} - \text{expected}\right|}{\sqrt{\text{variance}}} \quad \text{and variance} = \frac{\left|\text{observed} - \text{central\_point}\right|}{N}$$

As these equations indicate, incredibly significant values can come from the simple size effect, without the calculated level of significance indicating a 'real' effect of theoretical or practical significance.

One more problem comes when looking for *patterns*. These can be expressed in terms of correlations found between a variety of records. However, it is known that samples in poor agreement may have high correlation (Bland & Altman, 1986), since correlations can be present even when completely random sequences are considered, or when some strong effect, such as a trend over time, exists.

For example, in a large set of series of observations (time series), there are a great number of pairwise combinations. Since $C(n,2) = n!/(2! \, (n-2)!)$, for 1000 series the result is 499,500, and the probability of finding a very large correlation (e.g. with a correlation coefficient $r \geq 0.8$) by chance exceeds 90% (Granville, 2013).

Finally, when there are too many variables in a regression model (i.e. the number of parameters to be estimated is larger than the number of observations), the risk of *overfitting* is very high. In other words, there is a very high risk of the statistical model describing random error or noise instead of the underlying relationship.

Big Data studies often have an exploratory objective. In such cases, many of the issues and the concerns about possible errors may be mitigated by using a Bayesian approach (for a simple introduction see Zyphur & Oswald [2015]). Bayesian methods are based on an interpretation of probability as a measure of uncertainty which can be modified according to established rules when more information related to an initial position can be gained. In particular, they allow the incorporation of hypotheses in the analysis (by means of the initial probability distributions), and may be more easily used in solving problems and hypotheses whose structure is too complex for conventional methods. Also, Bayesian methods can better accommodate situations in which phenomena continue to develop as data are collected. By their nature, Bayesian methods are computationally heavy. They definitely require good software tools. Good introductions, with examples and computer codes are in books by Kruschke (2015, based on R) and Downey (2013, freely available, based on Python), among others.

Artificial Intelligence and Machine Learning

The very characteristics of Big Data call for extensive use of hardware and software. The main architecture has been described above. Here, we briefly describe the most common approach to the analysis of Big Data, the use of *artificial intelligence* and *machine learning*. The terms, which come from different disciplines, have almost become synonyms, but machine learning is the faster growing field and has produced the most widely used techniques for automatically treating data.

Machine learning is 'programming of a digital computer to behave in a way which, if done by human beings or animals, would be described as involving the process of learning' (Samuel, 1959: 211). Thus, machine learning involves giving a software program the ability to modify its behaviour according to events and outcomes, without being explicitly programmed to cope with each specific type of event or outcome. The learning is formally defined by Mitchell (1997: 2) as 'a computer program is said to learn from experience E with respect to some task T and some performance measure P, if its performance on T, as measured by P, improves with experience E'. Applications range from data mining programs that discover general rules or patterns in large data sets, to information filtering systems that automatically identify users based on interests or preferences, to clustering a large collection of objects into a small number of classes, to recognising shapes or sounds and so on.

The different algorithms used for machine learning are classified into two main groups: supervised and unsupervised.

Supervised learning

The algorithm is *trained* on a predefined and classified set of data. A model is prepared through this training process and validated. The processing continues until the model achieves a desired level of accuracy on

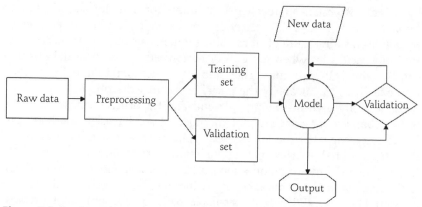

Figure 8.3 A schematic representation of supervised learning

the training data. Then, new data can be added and results obtained (see a schematic representation in Figure 8.3).

Examples of supervised machine learning algorithms are regression models, classification algorithms (e.g. k-Nearest Neighbours), support vector machines, neural networks and Bayesian networks.

Unsupervised learning

The model is prepared by inferring structures from the input data. Unsupervised learning processes are typically recursive, with successive refinements that are run until validation shows that a specified level of accuracy[2] is reached (Figure 8.4).

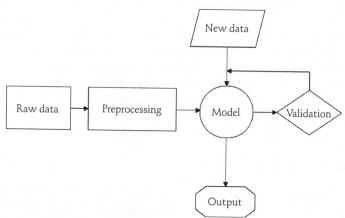

Figure 8.4 A schematic representation of unsupervised learning

Clustering algorithms (e.g. hierarchical or *k*-means) and dimensionality reductions (e.g. principal component analysis or factor analysis) are examples of unsupervised learning algorithms.

Example: Topic detection

Different types of machine learning algorithms can be used to investigate different problems. Menner *et al.* (2016) used the two classes of machine learning techniques (supervised and unsupervised) to identify topics or product features (such as room, service, food and drink) in a collection of hotel reviews. They collected 1200 user reviews from the TripAdvisor website. The documents were cleaned and preprocessed to split them into different sentences.

The first phase of the analysis consisted of a series of unsupervised learning algorithms that aimed to create a list of items (concepts) to be further classified. First of all, the most frequent words and verbs were identified through a frequency analysis. The identified terms were then weighted in terms of their frequency and of the number of documents or sentences in which they occurred. This formed the basis for a *k*-means clustering procedure. A third algorithm was used for latent semantic indexing (LSI), a technique used to reduce the number of dimensions in a vector space with minimal loss of information. Menner *et al.*'s goal was to reduce the variety of words within each text segment, given the existence of several words to describe the same object (e.g. a hotel room). LSI was used to summarise all the words with similar contextual meaning into *concepts*. A concept thus represents the (latent) semantic of all those words, and is the topic examined.

The second step was performed using supervised learning algorithms. The authors chose a named entity recognition (NER) from a number of possible algorithms. NER aims to help the user structure text so that relevant information can be extracted more easily. The entities considered can be words that represent persons, organisations, features or locations, depending on the objectives of the specific study. Here, the algorithm was modified in order to recognise topics of interest (separating them from non-topics). A step of pre-classification for every single word was performed manually. Then pre-classified records were enriched with linguistic or grammatical content (surrounding words within a sentence, part of speech, etc.).

The results were then examined and the accuracy (number of correct classifications), precision (fraction of items that were relevant) and recall (fraction of relevant items detected) of the algorithm were measured against the known qualities of the data set. Results are shown in Table 8.1.

Table 8.1 Evaluation of different steps in topic learning

Step	Accuracy (%)	Recall (%)	Precision (%)
Identification of frequent words	82.9	94.2	53.2
Keyword clustering	88.5	62.8	73.6
LSI	85.5	48.9	66.9
NER	75.2	77.9	73.8

Source: Menner et al. (2016).

As can be seen, the overall outcomes are quite good. As the authors state, their approach only detects the topics mentioned. It can be complemented by a sentiment analysis that aims to determine users' attitudes to a specific topic (see e.g. Schmunk et al., 2014). The combination of the two approaches could provide a hotelier with a way to recognise customers' opinions and to identify positive and negative trends. Once programmed, this approach should be faster and less biased than other investigation methods, including traditional questionnaire-based surveys.

Concluding Remarks

In this chapter, we have only scratched the surface of a relatively recent phenomenon that is growing at a fast pace and is becoming more important every day as the availability and sophistication of tools and methods increase. For tourism scholars and practitioners, Big Data offer an unprecedented opportunity for understanding the complex patterns of a contemporary globally interconnected society and better exploration of tourism, which is highly dynamic.

By accessing the huge number of trails left behind by the online activities of billions of individuals, it is possible to distil valuable information on practically countless aspects of interest for researchers, practitioners and managers, at the same time removing many of the biases that characterise traditional investigation techniques. That is not to say that traditional techniques lose their validity, but they can be greatly enriched, so that the combined information provides more valid and reliable insights and informs more effective choices. Nonetheless, despite the apparent universal availability of Big Data, actually collecting the data needed to meet a specific objective can be, from a practical point of view, a tricky task. Issues of time, cost and competence may be difficult at the moment for small companies and organisations to overcome, but the rapid development of the area is already offering practical solutions to these issues.

Notes

(1) That is, relatively inexpensive, widely available and more or less interchangeable or compatible with other hardware. In popular terms: some standard *off-the-shelf* hardware (PC).

(2) Technically, as defined by the International Organisation for Standardisation (ISO), the accuracy of a measurement system is the degree of closeness of the measurements of a quantity to that quantity's true value.

References

Anderson, C.K. (2008) The End of Theory: The Data Deluge Makes the Scientific Method Obsolete. *Wired Magazine*. See http://www.wired.com/science/discoveries/magazine/16-07/pb_theory (accessed December 2015).

Bland, J.M. and Altman, D. (1986) Statistical methods for assessing agreement between two methods of clinical measurement. *The Lancet* 327 (8476), 307–310.

Boyd, D. and Crawford, K. (2012) Critical questions for big data: Provocations for a cultural, technological, and scholarly phenomenon. *Information, Communication & Society* 15 (5), 662–679.

Chen, M., Mao, S. and Liu, Y. (2014) Big data: A survey. *Mobile Networks and Applications* 19 (2), 171–209.

d'Amore, M., Baggio, R. and Valdani, E. (2015) A practical approach to big data in tourism: A low cost Raspberry Pi cluster. In I. Tussyadiah and A. Inversini (eds) *Information and Communication Technologies in Tourism 2015 (Proceedings of the International Conference in Lugano, Switzerland, February 3–6)* (pp. 169–181). Berlin/Heidelberg: Springer.

Downey, A. (2013) *Think Bayes*. Needham, MA: Green Tea Press/O'Reilly Media.

Fan, J., Han, F. and Liu, H. (2014) Challenges of Big Data analysis. *National Science Review* 1 (2), 293–314.

Granville, V. (2013) The curse of big data. See http://www.analyticbridge.com/profiles/blogs/the-curse-of-big-data (accessed June 2014).

Hawelka, B., Sitko, I., Beinat, E., Sobolevsky, S., Kazakopoulos, P. and Ratti, C. (2014) Geo-located Twitter as proxy for global mobility patterns. *Cartography and Geographic Information Science* 41 (3), 260–271.

Keogh, E. and Mueen, A. (2011) Curse of dimensionality. In C. Sammut and G.I. Webb (eds) *Encyclopedia of Machine Learning* (pp. 257–258). New York: Springer.

Kruschke, J.K. (2015) *Doing Bayesian Data Analysis, Second Edition: A Tutorial with R, JAGS, and Stan* (2nd edn). London: Academic Press.

Laney, D. (2001) 3D Data Management: Controlling Data Volume, Velocity and Variety. 6 February (Research Note 949). See http://blogs.gartner.com/doug-laney/files/2012/01/ad949-3D-Data-Management-Controlling-Data-Volume-Velocity-and-Variety.pdf (accessed October 2015).

Lazer, D., Kennedy, R., King, G., & Vespignani, A. (2014). The parable of Google Flu: traps in big data analysis. *Science*, 343(6176), 1203–1205.

Mayer-Schönberger, V. and Cukier, K. (2013) *Big Data: A Revolution that will Transform How We Live, Work, and Think*. New York: Houghton Mifflin Harcourt.

McFarland, D.A. and McFarland, H.R. (2015) Big Data and the danger of being precisely inaccurate. *Big Data & Society* 2 (2), 1–4.

Menner, T., Höpken, W., Fuchs, M. and Lexhagen, M. (2016) Topic detection: Identifying relevant topics within touristic UGC. In A. Inversini and R. Schegg (eds) *Information and Communication Technologies in Tourism 2016* (pp. 411–423). Heidelberg: Springer.

Mitchell, T.M. (1997) *Machine Learning*. New York: McGraw Hill.

Samuel, A. (1959) Some studies in machine learning using the game of checkers. *IBM Journal* 3, 211–229.

Schmunk, S., Höpken, W., Fuchs, M. and Lexhagen, M. (2014) Sentiment analysis: Implementation and evaluation of methods for sentiment analysis with Rapid-Miner®. In Z. Xiang and I. Tussyadiah (eds) *Information and Communication Technologies in Tourism 2014* (pp. 253–265). Heidelberg: Springer.

Sust, V.O., Illera, E.G., Solana Berengué, A., González García, R., Peláez Alonso, M.V., Tomé Torres, M.J., Roca Verard, G., Lloret Albert, O., Capellades Ramos, X. and Rodríguez Rodríguez, P. (2014) *Big Data and Tourism: New Indicators for Tourism Management*. Barcelona: Telefónica I+D and RocaSalvatella. See http://www.rocasalvatella.com/sites/default/files/big_data_y_turismo-eng-interactivo.pdf (accessed September 2015).

White, T. (2015) *Hadoop: The Definitive Guide, 4th Edition – Storage and Analysis at Internet Scale*. Sebastopol, CA: O'Reilly Media.

Zyphur, M.J. and Oswald, F.L. (2015) Bayesian estimation and inference: A user's guide. *Journal of Management* 41 (2), 390–420.

9 Simulations and Agent-Based Modelling

Jacopo A. Baggio

Agent-based modelling and numerical simulations are means that facilitate exploring the structural and dynamic characteristics of systems that may prove intractable with analytical methods. This chapter examines what are complex adaptive systems (CAS), when are agent-based models (ABMs) a useful methodology to analyse systems, what are issues that relate to them and where they have been applied successfully. As an application example, a simple model is built to analyse the movements of tourists and the relationship between these and the attractiveness of a tourism destination.

Complex Adaptive Systems and Simulations

Social and ecological systems might be inherently impossible to predict (Bernstein *et al.*, 2000) and can be defined as CAS. It is not easy to define CAS in an unambiguous way. However, following Levin (2002), a system can be called complex when a certain number of elements interact in interdependent ways. These interactions are typically non-linear and, although 'simple' at a local level, build up in a non-predictable way, generating behaviours and structures not understandable as a straightforward composition of the local characteristics: the sum is 'greater' than the sum of its parts.

CAS can be thought of as a system with specific characterising features (Levin, 2002; Waldrop, 1992):

- *Non-determinism.* It is impossible to precisely determine the behaviour of CAS; the only predictions that can be made are probabilistic.
- *Presence of feedback.* Whether positive or negative, loops are present in such systems and the relationships that form between the components become more important than the components themselves.
- *Distributed nature.* It becomes very difficult to precisely locate functions and properties.

- *Qualitative difference between larger and slower functions* (or cycles) and smaller and faster ones (Holling, 2001, 2004; Levin, 2002; Waldrop, 1992).
- *Limited decomposability.* The structure of such systems is studied as a whole. The interactions between the components are fundamental variables, thus it is very difficult, if not impossible, to analyse CAS by decomposing them.
- *Self-similarity.* A system will have similar structures at different scales.
- *Emergence and self-organisation.* Global structures might emerge in a CAS, although it is not possible to foresee these by looking at its components.

Examples of CAS are interactions between species in an ecosystem, the behaviour of consumers and/or people and groups in a community, the stock market, the immune systems, river networks and patterns of birds' flight. These systems represent emergent configurations that are not possible to understand via an approach that reduces a complex system into sub-components, assuming that relations between these sub-components are stable and static (i.e. a reductionist approach).

The study of CAS calls for a new strategy, where cross-disciplinary comparisons are carried out in order to identify features that are common to different systems in different domains (Lansing, 2003). CAS differ from systems studied in other disciplines such as classical physics. In classical physics, success is achieved thanks to the high power of theoretical predictions, and to the accurate representation of that part of reality that the researcher wants to represent (Henrickson & McKelvey, 2002). Such theoretical models do not have the same predictive power when dealing with CAS. When dealing with CAS, models help the understanding of fundamental processes, and may be able to assess regularities between different systems; however, such results are always probabilistic.

It is worth mentioning, here, that formal models are a representation of reality, not reality itself, and modelling the activity of a system consist in abstracting what we think are the fundamental features of a real system for a specific purpose. Models used to represent reality can be a result of different techniques: statistical, physical, mathematical (e.g. differential equations) or simulations. Statistical models are constructed from existing data, thus they might be inherently flawed if we are to model complex systems that display non-linearities, critical thresholds or sensitive dependence from initial conditions. Statistical models are able to forecast only if the system (or features of the system) that we want to represent is fairly stable (Farmer & Foley, 2009). Unfortunately, models that assume a perfect world and that rely on stable conditions surrounding the system of interest, are not able to display patterns such as those observed in the recent financial crisis (Farmer & Foley, 2009), or in the flight patterns of birds, or the Arab Spring.

Models that are based on stable environmental conditions might be appropriate to explain the desired outcomes only under a predetermined set of conditions, and thus are inherently incapable of explaining the causal relationship, hence the outcomes of CAS. Mathematical models can be more complex, but the complexities that exist in CAS often do not allow for differential equation-based models to have exact analytical results, unless we are to greatly simplify and make strong assumptions (e.g. homogeneous individuals or species, etc.) about the system. Such strong assumptions are necessary to obtain tractable representations (e.g. the impossibility of finding an analytical solution to the three-body problem, as pointed out by Poincaré, 1892–1899). Following Galán et al. (2009) and define as mathematically intractable a formalised model that, given today's state of mathematics, cannot provide solutions or understandable insights into the model's behaviour. For example, currently, the required assumptions and simplifications needed for tractable mathematical models do not permit a correct representation of the unique features of human behaviour (e.g. reflexivity, learning and heterogeneity of agents) (Henrickson & McKelvey, 2002).

Simulations (or computational modelling) on the other hand, can be used to build formal representations of reality (thus a model) without the need for oversimplification or overly strong assumptions. They seem a natural candidate for representing CAS. However, other modelling techniques might be more appropriate for explaining the behaviour of systems that are fairly stable and in which the outcomes are a result of linear combinations of the internal relationships, rely on equilibrium and focus on universality. The laws that govern human behaviour are a result of a chain of path selections and do not passively respond to external forces: they inherently differ from certain laws of physics, such as $F=ma$.

Simulations imitate processes (Hartmann, 1996) and can be thought of as representations of reality in which it is possible to explore different hypotheses, assumptions and parameters. They provide insights into the world represented through the use of analogy (Peck, 2008). They may be helpful for descriptions, building scenarios or devising new theoretical developments (Garson, 2009; Hartmann, 1996). Simulations enable us to explore the dynamics of a real process, where it is often not possible to proceed by empirical experiments because of scale, cost, ethical considerations or theoretical impossibility and so on (Hartmann, 1996). For example, through simulations we can assess how different policies may affect the coexistence of species (Schoon et al., 2014), how well-being changes depending on different types of economic growth (Baggio & Papyrakis, 2014), how collective action is enhanced or reduced in relation to natural resource management (Baggio & Janssen, 2013) or how asymmetric information may influence tourism destination success (Baggio & Baggio, 2013).

Simulations are a powerful tool if used correctly, and more effort should be directed towards assessing the correct relationship between a system of analysis and assumptions, and understanding the behaviour of the model we want to implement to analyse the system of analysis (Silvert, 2001). Assumptions have a key and crucial role in the model-building process. Good practice requires that every equation, parameter, rule, inclusion or exclusion of variables is based on the published literature, empirical data or specific hypothesis. We need to remember that a model is only as good as its assumptions (Silvert, 2001). In this context, the primary role of a researcher is to identify and understand the implications of model assumptions. Every theoretical model, especially when seeking to represent a CAS, needs to be built through a process of continuous interaction between modellers and researchers or practitioners who deal with empirical issues. It is vital to understand what is happening in the field and how case studies, experiments and other techniques are used (Peck, 2008; Silvert, 2001).

Agent-Based Models

ABMs (or individual-based models [IBMs] as they are often called in ecology) allow the simulation of a system from the bottom-up, that is, through an ensemble of individual entities called agents. These behave according to a predetermined set of rules and are subject to defined initial parameter configurations (Bonabeau, 2002; DeAngelis & Mooij, 2005; Macy & Willer, 2002). Agents in the model can represent any scale of social or ecological organisation, from single individuals to institutions, from single organisms to species (Bonabeau, 2002; DeAngelis & Mooij, 2005; Macy & Willer, 2002; Peck, 2008; Srbljinovic & Skunca, 2003).

The use of ABM has grown consistently in the last 15 years in ecology as well as in the social sciences (Breckling et al., 2006; DeAngelis & Mooij, 2005; Macy & Willer, 2002). Human beings, as well as the environment in which they live, are definitely complex, non-linear, path-dependent and self-organising (Bonabeau, 2002; DeAngelis & Mooij, 2005; Macy & Willer, 2002). Understanding such CAS requires the use of simulations and computational models among other techniques such as in-depth case studies and experiments. Further, understanding the dynamics that govern such CAS may provide a description of a system not at a global level (i.e. using standard analytical techniques), but as an emergent configuration of the interactions between individual agents (Baggio & Papyrakis, 2013; Baggio et al., 2011; Macy & Willer, 2002; Salau et al., 2012). Even simple ABMs can display complex and surprising behaviour patterns, such as Schelling's (1969, 1971) segregation models, which provide interesting and novel information about the mechanisms of social groupings (Bonabeau, 2002).

ABMs look to be a promising technique for the study of emergent phenomena and CAS. They do not assume that a system will move towards equilibrium, although the system modelled might reach equilibrium (e.g. segregation in the Shelling model). In ABMs, at every simulation time step, agents act according to the surrounding environment and take action following the rules defined, thereby allowing for the discovery of critical thresholds and emergent behaviours not easily observable or not inferable when considering single agents. This happens, for example, when interactions between agents are characterised by non-linearities, thresholds, agent memory, path dependence and time-based correlations, such as with learning and adaptation, when space is explicit and fundamental and agents' positions are not fixed, or when populations are heterogeneous (Bonabeau, 2002; Breckling et al., 2006; DeAngelis & Mooij, 2005; Macy & Willer, 2002). This is because the description of a single agent's characteristics with reference to the whole system can be very difficult to model in an analytical way (Srbljinovic & Skunca, 2003). As agent behaviour becomes more complex, the complexity of equations increases easily beyond tractability. Moreover, in ABMs, stochasticity (i.e. probabilistic behaviour) is not 'noise', but is applied with consciousness to agents (Bonabeau, 2002).

Thus, in an ABM, agents are programmed to obey predetermined rules, reacting to certain environmental conditions, interacting between themselves and able to learn and adapt (Bonabeau, 2002; Gilbert & Terna, 2000). The modeller needs to define the agents by programming their cognitive abilities and the interactions between themselves and with the environment. More precisely, a researcher who uses computer-simulated ABM to represent a real system needs to complete a model-building process that can be delineated in three stages (Galán et al., 2009). First, the modeller needs to conceptualise the system that will be represented, thus defining the purpose, the 'research question(s)' and identifying the critical variables of the system and their interrelationships. Subsequently, it is necessary to find a set of formal specifications that is able to fully characterise the conceptual model. Finally, the model needs to be coded and implemented. As noted by Gilbert and Terna (2000), the model is iterative, every agent receives input from the environment, processes it and acts, generating a new environmental input until a predetermined condition is met (e.g. time limit or all agents find themselves in a given condition). Figure 9.1 graphically represents this process.

ABMs can generate a series (time series in most cases) of state variables at different scales. The results should be analysed using advanced statistical techniques and tools (e.g. network theoretical tools or time-series analysis), since a single simulation run is just a particular case in the infinite parameter space.

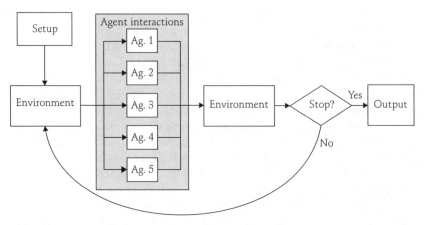

Figure 9.1 Graphical representation of the simulation process

Example: ABM applications

Numerous applications of ABMs exist, especially in the social sciences and ecology (Baggio & Baggio, 2013; Baggio & Janssen, 2013; Baggio & Papyrakis, 2014; Bernardes *et al.*, 2002; Bodin & Norberg, 2005; Cuddington & Yodzis, 2000; Hovel & Regan, 2008; Nonaka & Holme, 2007; Schelling, 1971; Schoon *et al.* 2014; Sznajd-Weron & Sznajd, 2000; Sznajd-Weron & Weron, 2002; Weins, 1997; Wilson, 1998). As an example, let us consider a model in which a number of agents are spread over a two-dimensional lattice. Each of them has an opinion that, for the sake of simplicity, can only assume two values. An agent can change his/her opinion conforming to that of his/her four immediate neighbours if they have equal opinions. Let us also assume that these changes happen with a certain probability distribution influenced by an external factor. This is the simple scheme proposed by Sznajd-Weron and Sznajd (2000), based on the well-known model for the magnetisation of a material proposed by Ising (1925), which has become probably the most famous model in the recent history of physics. This simple ABM has attracted much attention and many applications have demonstrated its validity. For example, it has been used to reproduce distributions of votes in political elections (Bernardes *et al.*, 2002); to guess how strong an advertising campaign has to be in order to help one of two products to win a whole market, even if initially it had the minority market share (Schulze, 2003); or to simulate price formation in a financial market (Sznajd-Weron & Weron, 2002).

The Schelling (1971) model of segregation re-implemented in the NetLogo environment, an agent-based modelling software, can be taken as an example (Iozzi, 2008; Wilensky, 1997). Schelling (1969, 1971) developed two different ABMs in order to explain self-segregation. The simplest uses a one-dimensional space (a line) in which two type of agents (blue and red, circle and crosses) are randomly placed. Each agent knows his/her neighbours in a specific region (number of agents left and right from a determined agent). Each agent can be in two different states: happy or unhappy, depending on how many neighbours of the same type he/she has and an internal parameter that defines a 'happiness threshold' (i.e. the percentage of similar agents wanted in the neighbourhood to be happy). If the agent is unhappy, he/she will move to another empty space (or patch). At every time step, happiness is computed and the simulation stops when no more unhappy agents exist. Even with this simple rule, it is possible to discover an interesting emergent behaviour as the population converges and self-segregates, producing regions populated by one type of agent and regions populated by the other.

The other model of segregation proposed by Schelling uses a two-dimensional space. Here, the neighbourhood is defined as the von Neumann neighbourhood (i.e. the four cells orthogonally surrounding the cell where the agent is placed). This second model resembles the first in terms of agents' attributes (happiness thresholds and movement). Again, after a certain number of time steps the model converges to a state where no unhappy agents exist, and regions of different types of agents are created (thus, again, there exists self-segregation and regions of only circles or only crosses appear). The 'strength' of self-segregation depends critically on the 'happiness threshold' of each agent, as shown in Figure 9.2.

It is possible to develop a pseudo-code that permits a better understanding of the mechanisms involved in the model. In the NetLogo environment (Wilensky, 1999), it is necessary to first set global variables and variables that will determine the properties of each single agent.

In the above example, global variables are average similarity and the percentage of unhappy agents. Average similarity is computed by looking at what percentage of agents are of the same type (the same colour in our example). Four agent-specific variables exist:

(1) *happy?* reports whether an agent is happy, thus if the threshold condition is met assumes values true or false;
(2) *similar-nearby* reports how many neighbouring patches are occupied by an agent with the same colour;
(3) *other-nearby* reports how many neighbouring patches are occupied by an agent with a different colour;
(4) *total-nearby* is the sum of the previous two variables.

Once the main variables that are used or computed by the model are defined, one has to initialise the model (thus performing a set-up procedure). It is good practice to reset all variables to zero before the set-up.

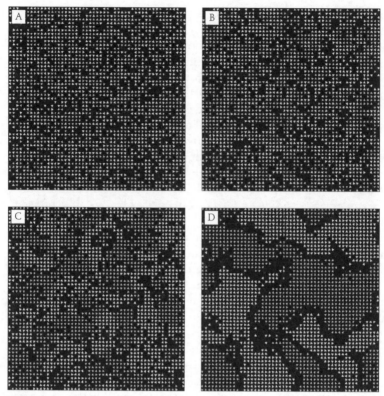

Figure 9.2 Self-segregation in the NetLogo simulation for three different values of the 'happiness threshold' for two types of agent (dark, light). Figures were generated using the same random seed (90) to ensure that the differences in the results reported graphically are only an effect of the happiness threshold parameter. A represents the initial state, B represents a world in which happiness threshold=25%, C happiness threshold=50% and D happiness threshold=75%

In the set-up of the Schelling model, it is necessary to input the number of agents that will populate our world. Once the agents are created, we need to assign them a specific colour (in the example used, agents are equally split between dark and light) and assign them to a location (agents in this case are randomly assigned). If an agent is assigned to a cell where another agent already exists, the agent will try to find another location and will move until he/she finds an empty cell. Once the agents have their own colour and are placed on the two-dimensional space, it is possible to set the 'happiness threshold' variable. In the example proposed, this threshold is equal for all the agents in the model, but it is also possible to assign different happiness thresholds to every agent (this may be an interesting extension in order to look for possible differences between the original model and the 'personalised happiness threshold model').

Once the model is set, it is possible to start the simulation, thus looking for patterns to emerge during the time development of the model. In order to run the simulation, at every time step, agents need to perform predetermined tasks. In our example, the simulation stops when all agents are happy (i.e. *happy?*=True ∀ *agent*). If there are unhappy agents, these will move, looking randomly for a new empty cell (they keep moving randomly until they find an empty cell[1]). Once all the agents have checked if they are happy or not (and in the latter case they have moved), global variables and agent-specific variables are computed, and the simulation is ready to enter a new time step. As noted earlier, the simulation will run until all the agents are happy, thus until for every agent the variable *happy?* is set to true.

Issues with Agent-Based Models

ABMs are often very complicated, both conceptually and mathematically. Assessing and evaluating ABMs can be a difficult exercise (Galán *et al.*, 2009). Scepticism exists around computational models, because the results might be counterintuitive (although counterintuitive does not necessarily mean incorrect) and often they are poorly communicated. Here, it is worth remembering that the main purpose of simulations and ABMs is to allow for new theoretical developments and advances. If the model is considered plausible (within reason) and coded correctly, even if its results might be counterintuitive, we can look towards a possible theoretical advance or the development of a new theoretical understanding of the system under study. However, there is always the risk that the results observed are a consequence of an unknown process inside the 'black box' (the computer) used to perform the simulation (Macy & Willer, 2002). The latter can be and has to be tackled by publicising the models and by exposing the models' code to the scientific community so that it will be possible to validate and to replicate the results. This is becoming more common also thanks to websites such as openabm.org (www.openabm.org): a repository where individuals can archive their computational model and accompany them with specific documentation. Another advancement in communicating models is the slow, but increased, standardisation of model documentation as put forth by Grimm *et al.* (2006, 2010). Moreover, the value of ABMs for theoretical development could be dismissed as 'muddying the water', as the number of variables, parameters and their relationships may approach the complexity seen in the real world (Peck, 2008). It is important to take into account that ABMs are not a universal solution.

Currently, there is no formal methodological procedure for ABM building, although certain similarities with all model-building methods exist.

The first step that needs to be considered is that there are no discrepancies between what we think we are representing and what the coded model is actually doing (Galán *et al.*, 2009). One needs to be careful when planning and structuring the model. In particular, it is always worth taking into account that a model has to serve a purpose, and hence, has to contain the right level of detail. As already noted, a model cannot retain all the real-world's details and it should be a simplified, although meaningful, part of reality (Axelrod, 1997; Bonabeau, 2002). When constructing a model, we need to abstract from the real world, thus in ABMs more than in other modelling techniques, it is necessary to refer to practitioners or to draw on empirical research or carefully review the existing literature in order to gain insights into processes and fundamental behaviours that characterise single agents and their relationships with these or the environment. It is important to look for implications, and evaluate that very same model.

Without a clear research question to answer, a model will not be useful in understanding the part of reality under investigation. Thus, we need to thoroughly identify assumptions and 'measure' the impact of each one of them on the results produced by the model (Galán *et al.*, 2009). ABMs should be treated carefully when looking at the quantitative aspects of the results (Bonabeau, 2002), because the importance and the validity of ABMs rely on their ability to explain different configurations arising from the set of parameters used, and in allowing a (mainly) qualitative understanding of the system studied.

ABMs and simulations need to be treated and approached differently from traditional analytical models (Peck, 2008). The most challenging aspect of ABMs resides in careful understanding and planning of how single agents will behave. The choice of rules that will allow them to interact with the environment and between themselves is a central issue. There is a need for a systematic procedure and it is necessary to avoid assumptions that are not confirmed by 'general wisdom' (existing literature, experts assessments, etc.). For example, Salau *et al.* (2015) base their model and thus assumption on exiting literature and experts' assessment in order to assess the best landscape configuration for the coexistence of prairie dogs and ferrets. As already stressed, continuous interaction and feedback between researchers and experts are necessary to shed light on the appropriate parameter space to explore and the interactions that exist between agents, and to assess the appropriateness of the model at its different stages (initiation, running, validation) (Farmer & Foley, 2009; Galán *et al.*, 2009; Peck, 2008).

Even when we engage continuously with experts and we carefully plan our simulation following all the good practices defined for the model-building process, there is still room for error and artefacts of methodology to distort the results (Galán *et al.*, 2009). More precisely, errors refer to a disparity between the coded model and the model that the modeller intended to code (e.g. the modeller wants the model to call for TaskA before TaskB, but the model runs TaskB before TaskA). It is important to highlight the fact that this type of error does not exist if there is no disparity between the actual model and what was meant by the researcher, thus it is not possible to assert that an error exists if we do not know the modeller's objectives. Obviously, the modeller's intentions should always be clearly stated. Artefacts, on the other hand, are disparities between the assumptions made by the researcher and thought to be the cause of specific results and what is actually causing them. This might happen because sometimes it is necessary to formulate hypotheses that are not critical for the representation of the system, but are required in order to run the simulation code (e.g. the size of a grid might influence the results although the very same size is not a critical assumption of the system we are modelling). It is important to point out that an artefact ceases to be an artefact as soon as it is discovered, and the cause of the results becomes known. Both errors and artefacts can be avoided. In order to avoid errors, one needs to meticulously check the coding procedure and all its parts in order to make sure that the coded model is performing exactly as it was intended to. Artefacts can be avoided by implementing a model with the same critical hypotheses but with different assumptions, in order to check how results are affected. This is a common procedure to assess the validity of the outcomes.

Evaluation of an Agent-Based Model

Validating, verifying and evaluating ABMs can be a tough task. Simulation behaviours are usually not understandable at first glance (Srbljinovic & Skunca, 2003). Nonetheless, it is possible to evaluate an ABM or a simulation. The first criterion is reliability, which can be assessed by producing different separate implementations and comparing the results. This is not, however, sufficient by itself to evaluate an ABM. Taber and Timpone (1996) propose three more methods for validating a simulation model. They ask:

(1) Do the results of a simulation correspond to those of the real world (if data are available)?
(2) Does the process by which agents and the environment interact correspond to the one that occurs in the real world (if the processes in the real world are known)?
(3) Is the model coded correctly so that it is possible to state that the outcomes are a result solely of the model's assumptions?

Answering the first two questions allows us to assess the validity of the representation (model), thereby gauging how well the real system we want to describe is captured and explained by its representation. A research example on model validation and comparison can be found in Baggio and Janssen (2013) where they assess the validity of different behavioural models on actual data stemming from an experiment relating to irrigation systems (see Baggio *et al.*, 2015). Answering the third question guarantees that the model's behaviour is what the modeller really intended it to be (Galán *et al.*, 2009). Evaluating an ABM requires data from the real world and the involvement of knowledgeable experts who might be able to give insights into the 'real' processes and dynamics to evaluate its plausibility as a representation of reality.

Moreover, it is worth stressing the importance of the conceptual accuracy that is needed in order to build ABMs that are able to advance our theoretical understanding of a system. Every part of the code in a model should be grounded in the literature or informed by experts (i.e. empirical researcher and practitioners), and the final test of any ABM is its importance in advancing understanding and the development of new formal theories.

ABM and Tourism

Tourism is a complex system as is the object named tourism destination, considered today to be a crucial unit of analysis for the understanding of the whole sector. Its behaviour can be considered that of a CAS (Baggio, 2008; Farrell & Twining-Ward, 2004; Faulkner & Russell, 1997; McKercher, 1999). A growing strand of literature has maintained that a linear deterministic description is not sufficient to explain the behaviour of a system whose components may have many different relationships among them. This problem is even more evident when considering the dynamic behaviour of a destination. As discussed in the previous sections, the most important result of an agent-based approach to modelling complexity is the realisation that it is not possible to fully predict the dynamic evolution of a complex system (Doran, 1999). It is well known that tourism forecasting is a complicated and difficult activity. It is, though, an important venture that has attracted a myriad of studies.

Usually, the quantity measured is the number of tourist arrivals, predicted by analysing an historical time series and using mathematical and statistical procedures (Song & Li, 2008; Song & Witt, 2000). However, even the most sophisticated methods seem unable to provide reliable results (Tideswell *et al.*, 2001). It is also difficult to choose the most appropriate one, as similar techniques give different results in different conditions or environments (Papatheodorou & Song, 2005), or can even be influenced by country-specific characteristics (Wackera & Sprague, 1998). What would be valuable is some method to predict, for a reasonable time span, the quantities of interest (tourist arrivals) or, given certain variations in some of the destination parameters, how these quantities may change with an accuracy sufficient to draw scenarios that can help in the decision-making or planning process.

The attractiveness of the destination is a major determinant of the arrivals of visitors to a place. Several attempts have been made to define this concept and to find measurable elements to assess it (Mazanec *et al.*, 2007; Pike, 2002). Moreover, a large number of studies have been devoted to investigating the elements that contribute to the attractiveness of a destination and how to exploit them in order to improve the destination's ranking in the international arena. The level of achieved attractiveness is known to be related to destination outcomes, such as tourist arrivals, stays or expenditures. Also, as expected, increases in destination attractiveness are reputed to be good determinants of the increase in both arrivals and stays in a location.

One interesting problem, rarely discussed, is the relationship that could exist between the effort made to improve attractiveness and the returns this improvement might provide. Moreover, while most papers describe single destination cases, the influence of other systems pursuing the same objectives and implementing similar plans is an important factor that could result in outcomes different from those expected. This is the typical problem that is almost impossible to study with analytic methods, but is a good candidate for ABM.

Example: Attractiveness of a destination and tourist arrivals

A simple model was designed to investigate the relationship between attractiveness and tourist arrivals and was implemented in the NetLogo environment (Wilensky, 1999). The model is illustrated in Figure 9.3.

There is a certain number of destinations (25), all inter-connected. An *attractiveness* attribute is assigned to each link (the route between two destinations); attractiveness assumes values (0–1) with 0 being the most attractive destination. Agents, representing travellers, are assigned to each destination at the beginning of the simulation (100 agents per destination). Each agent has a personal threshold (*change*) indicating a willingness to travel, and a memory, so that agents remember the last visited destination. Willingness to travel is randomly assigned to agents and assumes values in the interval (0–1). As a global parameter for the model, a probability to return to the previously visited destination is defined.

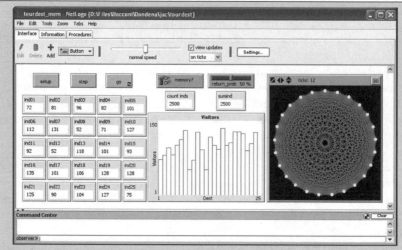

Figure 9.3 The NetLogo model of tourist arrivals

The model runs for a defined number of time steps (100). At the first time step, the agents randomly choose, with a probability dependent on the difference between their personal threshold and the attractiveness of the destinations, a place to go. All travels are single trips; agents return to their original location after visiting a new place. At each subsequent time step, agents choose the next destination following the same rule. If the probability to return is greater than zero, agents return to the last visited destination with that probability (otherwise, choice is random as for the first trip).

Results

Different simulation runs were performed. First of all, the attractiveness values were assigned according to two different distributions: random (uniform) and exponential. The latter is obviously more realistic and it mimics the real distribution of tourist arrivals to destinations (Baggio, 2008; Ulubaşoğlu & Hazari, 2004; UNWTO, 2009). The following figures report the results of the model. In all the figures, *mean arrivals* is the number of tourist arrivals per destination averaged over 100 runs and *frequency* is the number of destinations receiving that number of tourists.

When memory effects are disregarded (agents choose randomly at each time step), the distribution of arrivals resembles the attractiveness distributions (Figures 9.4 and 9.5). A second series of runs was performed with different probabilities to return to the last visited destination (run 1=0; run 2=0.25; run 3=0.5; run 4=0.75; run 5=1). Memory effects seem not to be significant in affecting the distribution of destination arrivals.

That is, the attractiveness of a destination and the willingness to travel of a single agent seem to be more important than memory effects, at least in our simplified model (Figures 9.6 and 9.7).

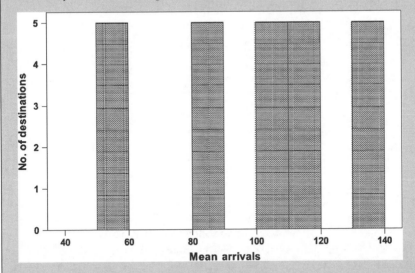

Figure 9.4 Distribution of mean arrivals when attractiveness is uniformly distributed

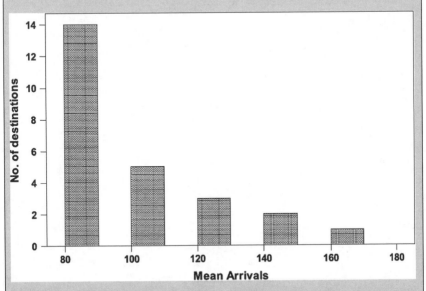

Figure 9.5 Distribution of mean arrivals when attractiveness is exponentially distributed

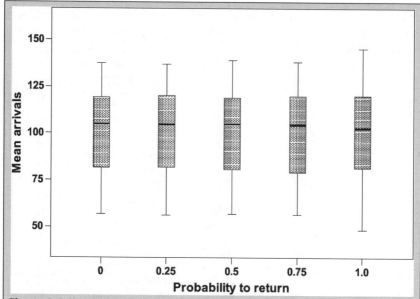

Figure 9.6 Mean arrivals for randomly distributed attractiveness and different probabilities to return

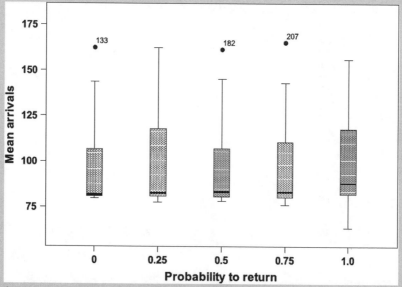

Figure 9.7 Mean arrivals for exponentially distributed attractiveness and different probabilities to return

Example: Increasing the attractiveness of a tourism destination

Let us now assume that a number of destinations put in place some actions to improve their attractiveness. How will this improvement be related to the number of visitors arriving? Will the increase radically change the final distribution of arrivals?

Three destinations with the lowest value of attractiveness were randomly selected and the simulation was run (in the same cases as above) with a 200% and a 400% increase in the attractiveness parameter (a threefold and a fivefold increase). The total number of travellers is constant (it is a fixed model parameter), but the distribution changes slightly. The three destinations experience an obvious increase in arrivals to the detriment of the others. The distributions are thus differently skewed, but, in essence, the way in which the 'world' is behaving does not seem to change significantly (Figures 9.8 and 9.9).

When we analyse the relationship between improvement in attractiveness and arrivals for the destinations considered, however, we find some important differences. Table 9.1 summarises the results. A rise in the attractiveness of a destination results in an increase in arrivals, as expected. However, the outcomes are significantly lower than the effort spent in improving the destination's image. This effect is more pronounced when the attractiveness values are exponentially distributed.

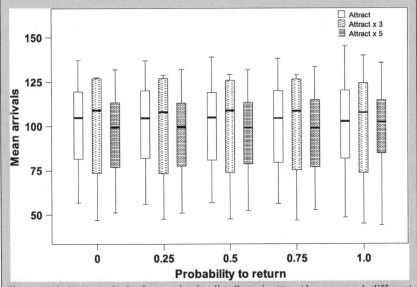

Figure 9.8 Mean arrivals for randomly distributed attractiveness and different probabilities to return, with different attractiveness for three destinations

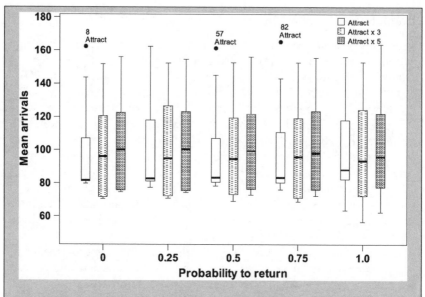

Figure 9.9 Mean arrivals for exponentially distributed attractiveness and different probabilities to return, with different attractiveness for three destinations

With a very simple ABM, it has been possible to replicate, at least at a very general level, the behaviour of travellers, and to perform a series of experiments by changing the model parameters. Different scenarios have been built and these, combined with other investigations on the subject, could be the basis for more considered decisions by a destination manager.

The model presented here is a very basic view of the phenomenon. Many assumptions made are strongly simplified, and some can also be considered not very close to a real situation. Our objective here was only to exemplify the process of ABM building. In our case, for example, it can be determined that, even with all the simplifications introduced, the model is able to render results that are reasonable and reproduce, at least at a general level, what happens in the real world. To expand the model, it is possible to increase the level of sophistication by specifying better and more realistic parameters and rules. The knowledge of a specific situation derived from other studies can give guidance in implementing more complete agent

Table 9.1 Relationship between increase in attractiveness and arrivals

| Attractiveness increase (%) | Arrivals increase | |
	Random distribution (%)	Exponential distribution (%)
200	75	53
400	124	87

behaviours (e.g. dynamic thresholds, imitation effects and cost effects), and better and more complete characterisations of the destination attractiveness qualities can be devised.

Concluding Remarks

Computational models (i.e. ABMs) and numerical simulations have recently confirmed their importance as tools to study a wide class of natural and artificial systems. Especially when dealing with CAS, computational models are fundamental to increasing our understanding of the processes and functions of such systems. Further, ABMs have proven very useful to build different scenarios and assess different policy implications on human behaviour. Obviously, many limitations relating to validity, reliability and transparency still need to be overcome. However, in the last five years there have been incredible improvements on documentation, transparency and the availability of actual large data sets to assess model validity.

This chapter has introduced CAS, and briefly discussed simulations and ABMs. The chapter has discussed issues and evaluation problems of such complex models. The use of ABMs has been demonstrated via an example relating to the interaction between the attractiveness of a tourism destination and the movement of tourists. Even a very simplified model is able to provide interesting results; however, there is also a need to continuously refine model assumptions and parameter values via a continuous interaction between models and other traditional techniques of inquiry such as well-structured case studies and experiments. In this context, ABMs can be an important generator of future scenarios to be analysed and discussed to gain better knowledge of the mechanisms governing a system's evolution.

Note

(1) For more detailed discussion of the problems of random movement and differences between the NetLogo implementation and the original movement described by Schelling, see Iozzi (2008).

References

Axelrod, R. (1997) Advancing the art of simulation in the social sciences. *Complexity* 3 (2), 16–22.

Baggio, R. (2008) Symptoms of complexity in a tourism system. *Tourism Analysis* 13 (1), 1–20.

Baggio, R. and Baggio, J.A. (2013). Modeling information asymmetries in tourism. In M. Kozak, L. Andreu, J. Gnoth, S.S. Lebe and A. Fyall (eds) *In Tourism Marketing: On Both Sides of the Country* (pp. 156–174). Newcastle: Cambridge Scholars Publishing.

Baggio, J.A. and Janssen M.A. (2013) Comparing agent-based models on experimental data of irrigation games. In R. Pasupathy, S.-H. Kim, A. Tolk, R. Hill and M.E. Kuhl (eds) *Proceedings of the 2013 Winter Simulation Conference* (pp. 1742–1753). Piscataway, NJ: IEEE Press.

Baggio, J.A. and Papyrakis, E. (2014) Agent-based simulations of subjective well-being. *Social Indicators Research* 115 (2), 623–635.

Baggio, J.A., Salau, K., Janssen, M.A., Schoon, M.L. and Bodin, Ö. (2011) Landscape connectivity and predator–prey population dynamics. *Landscape Ecology* 26 (1), 33–45.

Baggio, J.A., Rollins, N.D., Pérez, I. and Janssen, M.A. (2015) Irrigation experiments in the lab: Trust, environmental variability, and collective action. *Ecology and Society* 20 (4), 12.

Bernardes, A.T., Stauffer, D. and Kertész, J. (2002) Election results and the Sznajd model on Barabasi network. *The European Physical Journal B* 25, 123–127.

Bernstein, S., Lebow, R.N., Stein, J.G. and Weber, S. (2000) God gave physics the easy problems: Adapting social science to an unpredictable world. *European Journal of International Relations* 7 (1), 43–76.

Bodin, Ö. and Norberg, J. (2005) Information network topologies for enhanced local adaptive management. *Environmental Management* 35 (2), 175–193.

Bonabeau, E. (2002) Agent-based modeling: Methods and techniques for simulating human systems. *PNAS* 99 (Suppl. 3), 7280–7287.

Breckling, B., Middelhoff, U. and Reutera, H. (2006) Individual-based models as tools for ecological theory and application: Understanding the emergence of organisational properties in ecological systems. *Ecological Modelling* 194 (1–3), 102–113.

Cuddington, K.M. and Yodzis, P. (2000) Diffusion-limited predator- prey dynamics in Euclidean environments: An allometric individual-based model. *Theoretical Population Biology* 58 (4), 259–278.

DeAngelis, D.L. and Mooij, W.M. (2005) Individual-based modeling of ecological and evolutionary processes. *Annual Review of Ecology, Evolution and Systematics* 36, 147–168.

Doran, C.F. (1999) Why forecasts fail: The limits and potential of forecasting in international relations and economics. *International Studies Review* 1 (2), 11–41.

Farmer, J.D. and Foley, D. (2009) The economy needs agent-based modelling. *Nature* 460, 685–686.

Farrell, B.H. and Twining-Ward, L. (2004) Reconceptualizing tourism. *Annals of Tourism Research* 31 (2), 274–295.

Faulkner, B. and Russell, R. (1997) Chaos and complexity in tourism: In search of a new perspective. *Pacific Tourism Review* 1, 93–102.

Galán, J.M., Izquierdo, L.R., Izquierdo, S.S., Santos, J.I., del Olmo, R., López-Paredes, A. and Edmonds, B. (2009) Errors and artefacts in agent-based modelling. *Journal of Artificial Societies and Social Simulation* 12 (1), art. 1.

Garson, G.D. (2009) Computerized simulation in the social sciences: A survey and evaluation. *Simulation and Gaming* 40 (2), 267–279.

Gilbert, N. and Terna, P. (2000) How to build and use agent-based models in social science. *Mind & Society* 1 (1), 52–72.

Grimm, V., Berger, U., Bastiansen, F., Eliassen, S., Ginot, V., Giske, J. and DeAngelis, D.L. (2006) A standard protocol for describing individual-based and agent-based models. *Ecological Modelling* 198 (1), 115–126.

Grimm, V., Berger, U., DeAngelis, D.L., Polhill, J.G., Giske, J. and Railsback, S.F. (2010) The ODD protocol: A review and first update. *Ecological Modelling* 221 (23), 2760–2768.

Hartmann, S. (1996) The world as a process: Simulations in the natural and social sciences. In R. Hegselmann, U. Mueller and K.G. Troitzsch (eds) *Modelling and Simulation in the Social Sciences: From the Philosophy of Science Point of View* (pp. 77–100). Dordrecht: Kluwer.

Henrickson, L. and McKelvey, B. (2002) Foundations of 'new' social science: Institutional legitimacy from philosophy, complexity science, postmodernism, and agent-based modeling. *PNAS* 99 (Suppl 3), 7288–7295.

Holling, C.S. (2001) Understanding the complexity of economic, ecological, and social systems. *Ecosystems* 4 (5), 390–405.

Holling, C.S. (2004) From complex regions to complex worlds. *Ecology and Society* 9 (1), 11.

Hovel, K.A. and Regan, H.M. (2008) Using an individual-based model to examine the roles of habitat fragmentation and behavior on predator–prey relationships in seagrass landscapes. *Landscape Ecology* 23 (Suppl. 1), 75–89.

Iozzi, F. (2008) A Simple Implementation of Schelling's Segregation Model in NetLogo (Dondena Working Paper No. 15): 'Carlo F. Dondena' Centre for Research on Social Dynamics, Bocconi University. See http://www.dondena.unibocconi.it/wp15 (accessed September 2009).

Ising, E. (1925) Beitrag zur Theorie des Ferromagnetismus. *Zeitschrift für Physik* 31, 253–258.

Lansing, J.S. (2003) Complex adaptive systems. *Annual Review of Anthropology* 32, 183–204.

Levin, S.A. (2002) Complex adaptive systems: Exploring the known, the unknown and the unknowable. *Bulletin of the American Mathematical Society* 40 (1), 3–19.

Macy, M.W. and Willer, R. (2002) From factors to actors: Computational sociology and agent-based modeling. *Annual Review of Sociology* 28, 143–166.

Mazanec, J.A., Wöber, K. and Zins, A.H. (2007) Tourism destination competitiveness: From definition to explanation? *Journal of Travel Research* 46, 86–95.

McKercher, B. (1999) A chaos approach to tourism. *Tourism Management* 20, 425–434.

Nonaka, E. and Holme, P. (2007) Agent-based model approach to optimal foraging in heterogeneous landscapes: Effects of patch clumpiness. *Ecography* 30 (6), 777–788.

Papatheodorou, A. and Song, H. (2005) International tourism forecasts: Time-series analysis of world and regional data. *Tourism Economics* 11 (1), 11–23.

Peck, S.L. (2008) The hermeneutics of ecological simulation. *Biology and Philosophy* 23 (3), 383–402.

Pike, S. (2002) Destination image analysis: A review of 142 papers from 1973 to 2000. *Tourism Management* 23, 541–549.

Poincaré, H. (1892–1899) *Les Méthodes nouvelles de la mécanique céleste.* Paris: Gauthier-Villars.

Salau, K., Schoon, M.L., Baggio, J.A. and Janssen, M.A. (2012) Varying effects of connectivity and dispersal on interacting species dynamics. *Ecological Modelling* 242, 81–91.

Salau, K.R., Baggio, J.A., Janssen, M.A., Abbott, J.K. and Fenichel, E.P. (2015) Taking a moment to measure Networks-A hierarchical approach. arXiv preprint arXiv:1509.07813.

Schelling, T.C. (1969) Models of segregation. *The American Economic Review* 59 (2), 488–493.

Schelling, T.C. (1971) Dynamic models of segregation. *Journal of Mathematical Sociology* 1, 143–186.

Schoon, M.L., Baggio, J.A., Salau, K. and Janssen, M. (2014) Insights for managers from modeling species interactions across multiple scales in an idealized landscape. *Environmental Modelling and Software* 55, 53–59.

Schulze, C. (2003) Advertising effects in Sznajd marketing model. *International Journal of Modern Physics C* 14 (1), 95–98.

Silvert, W. (2001) Modelling as a discipline. *International Journal of General Systems* 30 (3), 261–282.

Song, H. and Witt, S.F. (eds) (2000) *Tourism Demand Modelling and Forecasting: Modern Econometric Approaches*. Oxford: Pergamon.

Song, H. and Li, G. (2008) Tourism demand modelling and forecasting: A review of recent research. *Tourism Management* 29, 203–220.

Srbljinovic, A. and Skunca, O. (2003) An introduction to agent based modelling and simulation of social processes. *Interdisciplinary Description of Complex Systems* 1 (1–2), 1–8.

Sznajd-Weron, K. and Sznajd, J. (2000) Opinion evolution in closed community. *International Journal of Modern Physics C* 11 (6), 1157–1165.

Sznajd-Weron, K. and Weron, R. (2002) A simple model of price formation. *International Journal of Modern Physics C* 13 (1), 115–123.

Taber, C.S. and Timpone, R.J. (1996) *Computational Modeling* (Vol. 113). Thousand Oaks, CA: Sage.

Tideswell, C., Mules, T. and Faulkner, B. (2001) An integrative approach to tourism forecasting: A glance in the rearview mirror. *Journal of Travel Research* 40, 162–171.

Ulubaşoğlu, M.H. and Hazari, B.R. (2004) Zipf's law strikes again: The case of tourism. *Journal of Economic Geography* 4, 459–472.

UNWTO (2009) *Compendium of Tourism Statistics*. Madrid: World Tourism Organization.

Wackera, J.G. and Sprague, L.G. (1998) Forecasting accuracy: Comparing the relative effectiveness of practices between seven developed countries. *Journal of Operations Management* 16 (2–3), 271–290.

Waldrop, M. (1992) *Complexity: The Emerging Science and the Edge of Order and Chaos*. New York: Simon and Schuster.

Weins, J.A. (1997) Metapopulation dynamics and landscape ecology. In I.A. Hanski and M.E. Gilpin (eds) *Metapopulation Biology, Ecology, Genetics, and Evolution* (pp. 43–62). New York: Academic Press.

Wilensky, U. (1997) NetLogo Segregation Model. Evanston, IL: Center for Connected Learning and Computer-Based Modeling, Northwestern University. See http://ccl. northwestern.edu/netlogo/models/Segregation. (accessed Feb 2017).

Wilensky, U. (1999) NetLogo. Evanston, IL: Center for Connected Learning and Computer-Based Modeling, Northwestern University. See http://ccl.northwestern. edu/netlogo. (accessed Feb 2017)

Wilson, W.G. (1998) Resolving discrepancies between deterministic population models and individual-based simulations. *The American Naturalist* 151 (2), 116–134.

Appendix: Software Programs

For more than 2000 years, calculating quantities of any kind, whether for academic and research or practical purposes, has been a long, troublesome and exhausting task. At most, with a very welcome and important advancement that appeared in the second half of the 18th century, one could think of employing sophisticated algorithms in order to split these tedious endeavours into smaller and simpler chunks so that the work could be divided, assigned to a group of people and done in parallel, increasing the speed and reliability of the results (Grier, 2005).

Today, the general availability of powerful desktop computers has made computing a relatively simple and fast activity. Statistical software applications abound. Many of them are commercial packages (and usually quite expensive, although in some cases a limited but discounted version is available for educational purposes), but the number of high-quality free (or very low-cost shareware) programs is continuously increasing and many of them are now a standard addition to the toolset of researchers and practitioners.

Moreover, even for commercial packages, the community of users has generated (and continues to generate) an incredible wealth of examples, scripts, tutorials and so on, that make the life of a newcomer (and of many experts) much easier. A simple web query containing a few keywords and the name of the package will provide almost all the sought after information and advice.

The basic use of many of these packages is relatively simple, but they typically contain dozens of functions and options and mastering one of them is not a completely painless or easy task. Moreover, they use many different conventions, definitions and algorithms so that their results may be difficult to compare. The choice is difficult as there is no single option able to satisfy all needs and habits. It is therefore advisable, before adopting one or more of these packages, to collect information and details on the candidate programs and, possibly, download a trial version (normally also available for commercial packages) and do a field test. Other factors to take into account are the existence of institutional subscriptions to commercial packages; the availability of colleagues and experts who can advise on selection and use, provide tips and indicate pitfalls; and common practice in the field and any journal(s) that are targeted for publication.

It is worth mentioning here that several online applications exist for performing statistical calculations. They are generally 'single purpose' applications and are normally well described as most of the time they are provided for educational purposes. The downside is that they cannot be used for large quantities of data. One source of information containing an extensive categorised selection of both stand-alone and online programs for statistical analyses is available at http://statpages.info/.

Often, a spreadsheet program (e.g. Microsoft Excel, http://office. microsoft.com/excel/ or the free OpenOffice, http://www.openoffice.org/) can be a useful tool. The limitations of these generic software programs is that they generally have difficulty in accommodating large sets of data and, apart from some elementary statistical functions, more complex procedures may require long preparation and a good knowledge of the software's functions. Moreover, their validity for statistical analysis has been questioned several times and algorithms and procedures are reputed by some authors to be not quite reliable (see for example McCullough & Wilson, 2002). Nonetheless, their diffusion suggests them when simple tasks are involved (Triola, 2006), and a number of additional specialised functionalities have been made available as add-ins. A list for Excel can be found at http://www.mathtools.net/Excel/Statistics/.

Software List

The following pages contain a list, by no means exhaustive, of the most important and diffused tools. A reference to other recent introductory books is also shown. The list is roughly divided into two categories: statistical packages and development environments.

The first group contains programs that are normally executed by using a graphical user interface that allows access to all statistical functions, utilities for data handling and other tools. These applications commonly offer functions and procedures accessible from menus and dialogs, facilities to import and export data in different formats, commands for manipulating data and interactive components for the generation of graphical representations. Some also offer an internal programming language with which the user can automate procedures, modify or extend the defined options available from the pull-down menus or create new types of calculations and analyses. The programs are generally available for all operating systems – Windows, Mac and Linux – and are able to run on available computer hardware configurations; just note that some may be memory hungry, particularly when large data sets are involved. In any case, the reader is advised to check the installation prerequisites.

Programming languages and development environments will require some more effort if writing computer code is not a familiar task, but they offer the greatest flexibility for analysts to design their own algorithms and procedures. Any programming language, obviously, is suitable, but those cited here are either explicitly designed for statistical computations or provide good statistically oriented toolboxes (collections of ready scripts) and are generally considered to be more user-friendly than common programming languages such as C++, Java or Fortran. Some of them are commercial products and can be quite expensive. In many cases, however, free clones exist. These show relatively good compatibility with the original language and the web provides good information about how to translate the scripts between them. Obviously, in many cases and for special functions, a direct translation is not possible and the programs must be completely rewritten. Finally, clones can be a little less stable and reliable than their original counterparts.

All the websites cited here contain documentation, reference books, examples and tutorials.

All addresses cited here were verified at the date of publication. However, the web is a dynamic environment and some links may change or become invalid. An online search using the title of the resource as keyword will allow to locate the materials desired or similar resources with relative ease.

Statistical Packages

Generic packages

Program	URL	Reference
SPSS	http://www.spss.com/	Field, 2005
A good collection of scripts provided by Raynald Levesque is available at the SPSS tools archive:http://www.spsstools.net		
MINITAB	http://www.minitab.com/	Ryan *et al.*, 2005
SAS	http://www.sas.com/	Elliott, 2000
STATA	http://www.stata.com/	Hamilton, 2008
WinIDAMS (free, Windows only)	www.unesco.org/idams/	UNESCO, 2008

Specialised programs cited in this book

Program	URL	Reference
G*Power 3 (free, Windows only) Power calculations for statistical tests	http:// www.gpower.hhu.de/	Faul *et al.*, 2007
Resampling Stats (Windows only) Bootstrap methods	http://www.statistics101.net/	Simon, 1997
TISEAN (free, Windows only) Non-linear time series analysis methods	http://www.mpipks-dresden .mpg.de/~tisean	Hegger *et al.*, 1999

AMOS (Windows only) Structural equation modelling	http://www.spss.com/amos/	Arbuckle, 2008
LISREL (Windows only) Structural equation modelling	http://www.ssicentral.com/ lisrel/	Jöreskog *et al.*, 2016
MPlus (Windows only) Latent variable modelling	http://www.statmodel.com/	Muthén and Muthén, 2006
OpenMx (free, open source) Structural equation modelling	http://openmx.psyc.virginia .edu/	OpenMx, 2010

Development environments and programming languages

Program	URL	Reference
EVIEWS	http://www.eviews.com/	Vogelvang, 2005
R (free)	http://www.r-project.org/	Braun, 2008; Crawley, 2007
Specifically developed for statistical analyses, the R environment is rich with libraries for many other tasks. Most of them can be located at the Comprehensive R Archive Network (CRAN) https://cran.r-project.org/ and its mirrors		
Python (free)	http://www.python.org/	Lutz & Ascher, 2003
Python libraries cover many different tasks. The main repository is the Python Package Index (PyPI) at https://pypi.python.org/pypi		
GAUSS	http://www.aptech.com/	Lin, 2001
Ox/OxEdit (free Gauss clone)	http://www.doornik.com/	Doornik & Ooms, 2006
A series of programs for unit root tests by J. Lee is available at https://sites. google.com/site/junsoolee/codes		
Matlab	http://www.mathworks.com/	Hanselman & Littlefield, 2004
The Matlab user community is very active and numerous applications can be found at http://www.mathworks.com/matlabcentral/fileexchange/. A useful specialised toolbox is the Econometrics Toolbox for Matlab, available at http://www.spatial-econometrics.com/ (LeSage & Pace, 2009).		

Scilab (free Matlab clone)	http://www.scilab.org/	Annigeri, 2009
Octave (free Matlab clone)	http://www.gnu.org/ software/octave/	Eaton *et al.*, 2008
FreeMat (free Matlab clone)	http://freemat.sourceforge. net/	
NetLogo	http://ccl.northwestern.edu/ netlogo/	Railsback & Grimm, 2009
A relatively easy-to-use agent-based modelling environment with a rich library of example models		

References

Annigeri, S. (2009) *Scilab – A Hands On Introduction* (3rd edn). Free ebook. See http://mars.uta.edu/mae3183/simulation/scilab_Introduction_annigeri.pdf. (accessed Feb 2017)

Arbuckle, J. (2008) *AMOS 17.0 User's Guide*. Chicago, IL: SPSS Inc.

Braun, W.J. (2008) *A First Course in Statistical Programming with R*. Cambridge: Cambridge University Press.

Crawley, M.J. (2007) *The R Book*. New York: John Wiley & Sons.

Doornik, J.A. and Ooms, M. (2006) *Introduction to Ox*. Free ebook. See http://www.doornik.com/ox/OxIntro.pdf. (accessed Feb 2017)

Eaton, J. W., Bateman, D. and Hauberg, S. (2008) *GNU Octave Manual – Version 3*. Bristol: Network Theory Ltd.

Elliott, R.J. (2000) *Learning SAS in the Computer Lab* (2nd edn). Pacific Grove, CA: Duxbury Press.

Faul, F., Erdfelder, E., Lang, A.-G. and Buchner, A. (2007) G*Power 3: A flexible statistical power analysis program for the social, behavioral, and biomedical sciences. *Behavior Research Methods* 39, 175–191.

Field, A. (2005) *Discovering Statistics Using SPSS* (2nd edn). London: Sage Publications.

Grier, D.A. (2005) *When Computers Were Human*. Princeton, NJ: Princeton University Press.

Hamilton, L.C. (2008) *Statistics with STATA* (6th edn). Pacific Grove, CA: Duxbury Press.

Hanselman, D.C. and Littlefield, B.L. (2004) *Mastering Matlab 7*. Upper Saddle River, NJ: Prentice-Hall.

Hegger, R., Kantz, H. and Schreiber, T. (1999) Practical implementation of nonlinear time series methods: The TISEAN package. *CHAOS* 9, 413.

Jöreskog, K.G., Olsson, U.H., and Wallentin, F.Y. (2016). *Multivariate Analysis with LISREL*. Switzerland: Springer.

LeSage, J.P. and Pace, R.K. (2009) *Introduction to Spatial Econometrics*. Boca Raton, FL: Chapman & Hall/CRC.

Lin, K.-P. (2001) *Computational Econometrics: GAUSS Programming for Econometricians and Financial Analysts*. Carson, CA: ETEXT Publishing.

Lutz, M. and Ascher, D. (2003) *Learning Python, Second Edition*. Sebastopol, CA: O'Reilly Media.

McCullough, B.D. and Wilson, B. (2002) On the accuracy of statistical procedures in Microsoft Excel 2000 and Excel XP. *Computational Statistics & Data Analysis* 40, 713–721.

Muthén, L.K., and Muthén, B.O. (2006) Mplus Version 7 User's Guide. Los Angeles, CA: Muthén & Muthén.

OpenMx (2010) OpenMx User Guide. See http://openmx.ssri.psu.edu/. (accessed Feb 2017)

Railsback, S.F. and Grimm, V. (2009) *A Course in Individual- and Agent-Based Modeling: Scientific Modeling with NetLogo*. In preparation, preliminary version at: http://www.railsback-grimm-abm-book.com/. (accessed Feb 2017)

Ryan, B.F., Joiner, B.L. and Cryer, J.D. (2005) *MINITAB Handbook* (5th edn). Pacific Grove, CA: Brooks/Cole–Thomson Learning Inc.

Simon, J.L. (1997) *Resampling: The New Statistics*. See http://www.resample.com/. (accessed Feb 2017)

Triola, M.F. (2006) *Elementary Statistics Using Excel* (3rd edn). Boston, MA: Addison Wesley.

UNESCO (2008) 'Documents/Publications', IDAMS Statistical Software: UNESCO and information processing tools. See www.unesco.org/idams/ (accessed 24 July 2016).

Vogelvang, B. (2005) *Econometrics: Theory & Applications With Eviews*. Edinburgh: Pearson Education–Prentice-Hall.

Subject Index

agent-based models (ABM) 226
    ABM and tourism 234
    evaluation of a model 233
    simulations 223
artificial intelligence 217

big data 210
    hadoop 213
    issues 216
    map-reduce 214
    technology 213
bootstrap 27

common method variance 143
complex adaptive systems 223
correspondence analysis 83
cosine similarity 40
cluster analysis 74
    distance measures 76
    hierarchical cluster analysis 79

data 3
    categorical data 9
    cleaning 13
    clustering see cluster analysis
    combining data 6
    harmonisation 7
    primary data 4
    quality 10
    quantitative data 9
    reduction see factor analysis
    screening 13
    secondary data 5
    standards 7
    taxonomy 3
dissimilarity measures 36
    single sample 37
    two or more samples 39

Euclidean distance 40
entropy 38

factor analysis 47
    interpretation 56
    issues in factor analysis 72

number of factors 51
rotation 56
selecting variables 54

Gini coefficient 37

Herfindahl–Hirschman index 37
Hodrick–Prescott filter 164
Hurst exponents 177

Jaccard index 40

likelihood ratio 197

machine learning 217
    supervised learning 217
    unsupervised learning 218
Mahalanobis distance 41
maximum likelihood estimation
    (MLE) 187
    fit of empirical probability distribution
      191
    likelihood ratio test 197
    MLE procedure 190
mediation and moderation in model
    building 128
meta-analysis 30
    funnel plot 32
Monte Carlo methods 200
    numerical experiments 200
    random numbers 204
multidimensional scaling 83
multilevel modelling 134
multivariate outlier detection 41

numerical simulations 223

path modelling 110

regression (logistic) 105
    quality of the model 109
regression (multiple) 99
    multicollinearity 101
    quality of the model 100
    stepwise regression 103

regression (simple) 88
    non-linearity transformations 89
    quality of the model 90
    significance 91
    validity of assumptions 93

Shannon index 38
Simpson's paradox 6
similarity measures 36
    single sample 37
    two or more samples 39
statistical tests 19
    effect size 24
    errors 20
    hypothesis testing 19
    non-parametric tests 22
    parametric tests 22
    p-values 21
    sample size and significance 26
    statistical power 24
    summary of statistical tests 34

sources of secondary tourism data 15
software list 245
    programming languages 248
    statistical packages 247
standards for data 7
structural equation modelling 114
    assumptions 118
    fit 116
    specifying model 115

time series 152
    autoregressive integrated moving
        average models (ARIMA) 160
    comparing models 165
    correlations 168
    filtering 163
    forecasting 166
    non-linear analysis 176
    predictability 176
    smoothing methods 158
    stationarity 172